W9-DCN-829

W. CAMERON FORBES AND THE HOOVER COMMISSIONS TO HAITI (1930)

Robert M. Spector

UNIVERSITY
PRESS OF
AMERICA

LANHAM • NEW YORK • LONDON

Copyright © 1985 by

University Press of America,™ Inc.

4720 Boston Way
Lanham, MD 20706

3 Henrietta Street
London WC2E 8LU England

Library of Congress Cataloging in Publication Data

Spector, Robert M. (Robert Melvin), 1926–
    W. Cameron Forbes and the Hoover commissions to
Haiti, 1930.

        Bibliography: p.
        Includes index.
        1. United States–Foreign relations–Haiti. 2. Haiti–
Foreign relations–United States. 3. Forbes, W. Cameron
(William Cameron), 1870–1959. 4. Haiti–History–
American occupation, 1915–1934. 5. United States –
Foreign relations–1929–1933. I. Title. II. Title : Hoover
commissions to Haiti, 1930.
E183.8.H2S64   1984   327.7307294   84–7245
ISBN 0–8191–3974–2 (alk. paper)
ISBN 0–8191–3975–0 (pbk. : alk. paper)

All University Press of America books are produced on acid-free
paper which exceeds the minimum standards set by the National
Historical Publications and Records Commission.

DEDICATED TO
MY DEAR WIFE CHARLOTTE W. SPECTOR
AND THE MEMORY OF
DR. VICTOR G. HEISER

CONTENTS

v

INTRODUCTION

In the fourth decade of the 20th century, the United States assumed a new attitude toward the countries of Latin-America. For approximately 150 years, the United States followed a policy that in one way or another had antagonized the nations south of the Rio Grande. From 1776 to 1902 we either ignored the Latin-American states, took advantage of their weaknesses, or assumed an attitude of condescension toward them. Our refusal to recognize the rebellious Spanish colonies until after we had safely purchased the Floridas from Spain so enraged Simon Bolivar that he refused the United States an invitation to the Panama Conference of 1826. The Monroe Doctrine appeared to many Latin-Americans to be just another method of maintaining Yankee domination of the Western Hemisphere. The annexation of Texas, Polk's corollary to the Monroe Doctrine, the War with Mexico, and our acquisition of the Panama Canal zone gave little assurance to Latin-Americans of Yankee good-will. Even the Washington Conference of 1889, which ultimately led to the formation of the Pan-American Union, seemed to our southern neighbors to be an attempt to form an alliance dominated by the United States rather than a genuine desire on our part to form a league of equal states.

The Spanish-American War led the United States from an attitude of relative abstinence in Latin-American affairs to one of active intervention. The Roosevelt Corollary together with the concept of "the white man's burden" were our justifications for repeated interferences in the internal affairs of the Caribbean nations. Through the device of the Platt amendment to the Cuban Constitution, we intervened in Cuban politics. In 1905 Theodore Roosevelt appointed an American receiver of customs for the Dominican Republic, and in 1916 the United States Navy began an occupation of that country that lasted for eight years. The year 1909 began our intervention in Nicaragua; 1915, our Occupation of Haiti; 1916, the Pershing expedition into northern Mexico for the purpose of catching the elusive Pancho Villa; while until the end of the First World War Panama was the scene of frequent interventions by United States troops for one purpose or another.

The intervention in Haiti, however, differed somewhat from those of the others. The United States went into Haiti not only to stabilize the country's politics, protect American investments and prevent European interference, but also to tutor Haiti in Anglo-Saxon democracy. It was the Philippines experiment applied to the Caribbean.

Needless to say, the United States did not win friends by her action. She did not win them in Haiti, nor in the other countries of Latin-America, nor in Europe, nor among liberals at home. Indeed, the liberal American press showed little more than contempt for the experiment in tutelage. Oswald Garrison Villard's *Nation* actually pictured the Occupation as a barbaric aggression marked by individual acts of great cruelty.

When riots in protest against the Occupation broke out in Haiti at the close of 1929, President Hoover took the occasion to determine whether or not the thirty-year policy of intervention in the Caribbean had really served valid purposes both for the United States and for the countries concerned. He sent the Forbes Commission to Haiti to do a number of things: to settle the disturbances first of all, then to assess the Occupation of the country, and finally, if that Occupation were found wanting, to determine the steps by which it might be rapidly liquidated.

Formally, there were two commissions, that of Forbes and that of the eminent Negro educator Robert Russa Moton of Tuskegee. Hoover originally had planned to send one commission composed of both distinguished white and black Americans, but Haitians themselves objected to the presence of Afro-Americans on the commission. Accordingly, the Forbes Commission consisted of white men who went to Haiti at the end of February, 1930, and remained the first two weeks in March, for the purposes mentioned above, while the Moton Commission consisted of black educators, who arrived and left Haiti in June of that same year, and whose task was solely to assess Haitian education after fifteen years of the American Occupation.

In a larger sense, the Moton Commission was only an extension of the group led by Forbes. Moton's more elaborate report on Education confirmed the findings of the first group, while Moton's consultations with Forbes through private conversations and correspondence leaves little doubt that Forbes was the dominating figure in the whole investigation.

In the end, Forbes recommended that the United States pull out of Haiti. As he wrote to Dr. Moton, it was a tragedy for us to remain there, and it was a tragedy to leave. He saw no good end to either course. The report indicates that the United States in the preceding fifteen years had gone a long way toward helping Haiti move into modern times. We were dredging her harbors, building good roads and highways, promiting order and the equality of justice for all classes, weakening the power of the élite over the black masses, establishing stable government, promoting a good public school system that would eventually eliminate the curse of general illiteracy, and creating an efficient health service available to both urban and rural communities. But it would take time to accomplish the ultimate purposes that Wilson had in mind when he ordered Admiral Caperton to occupy the country. Pulling Haiti up from early colonial times into the 20th century and beyond could demand an American presence for several generations.

On the other hand, there were forces both in the United States and in Haiti that urged early and swift withdrawal regardless of the consequences. The Depression resulting from the crash of 1929 placed a financial burden on the United States that the American people did not want to see increased by overseas ventures. The Liberal press in the United States and other countries saw the Occupation not as a means of improving the standard of living in Haiti but rather as another example of power. That same press also saw the United States as hindering by its Occupation the right of Haitians to self-determination, even if that self-determination meant a fast return to the old poverty and despair. (For Forbes, self-determination was desirable for the Haitian people, but only after they had been brought to the point where self-determination meant progress rather than retrogression.) And, to add to it all, the old rulers of the country, the so-called élite, saw themselves replaced by white Americans as the privileged class in Haiti, and the Occupation not in the light of aiding their country but rather in the light of their own disadvantage. The Occupation had a levelling effect, it appears, not entirely to the taste of the cultivated and oftentimes French-educated élite.

Forbes undoubtedly knew that to withdraw from Haiti meant a return to the corruption and evils of the pre-Occupation period. He knew that democracy is not natural to human beings, and that a lengthy period of training is essential to the democratic process. The American people won their independence from Great Britain and were able to establish imme-diately stable, democratic processes because by the year 1776 they had had one hundred and fifty years of colonial self-government and a thousand years of English constitutionalism behind them. But this was not true of Haiti, just as today it is not true of most of the newly independent countries of the world. If Haiti were to have permanent stable democracy with a high standard of living, it would need a lengthy period of schooling--and certainly enough time to eliminate illiteracy among a majority of the people. Self-determination had to come, but at the proper time. It is one thing to be independent; yet another to be independent and self-sufficient. The present troubles in the Philippines (where Forbes, 1909-13, had worked so hard to train the people in democracy) are indicative of this principle. Indepen-dence by itself is not enough; there must be more if a people is to survive in the pursuit of happiness.

But Forbes knew that to recommend the continuance of the Occupation, regardless of the good that he knew it had achieved, would be in the short run political-ly unwise. We withdrew from Haiti to stem the tide of adverse criticism, whether that criticism was grounded in logic or solid economic, social, and po-litical principles or not. It was easier for Hoover to end the criticism than to remain because of prin-ciple and continue to battle that criticism regard-less of its sources or weaknesses. Weak or strong, such criticism made considerable noise, which was something in a Depression economy that the Hoover ad-ministration could do without, especially in view of

the forthcoming 1932 presidential elections. So
Forbes recommended that we pull out and return Haiti
to whoever could catch the sceptre. After all, if we
had no program of value that the American people were
willing to support in Haiti, what else could we do
but withdraw?

Today, in Cuba, Nicaragua, El Salvador, and the
Philippines, we decry the growth of Communism. We de-
plore the spread of a system that weakens civil
liberties, freedom of religion, and freedom of
conscience. But we also fail to realize that for the
hungry masses bread for the belly is significantly
more immediately needed than civil liberties, or
freedoms of religion and conscience. Unless we have
a program—and support it—that is equal to that of
the Communists in terms of supplying the palpable
needs of the masses, Communism will be the inevitable
result. Communism does not come to a nation because
it offers a way of life superior to that of the
western democracies, but because it is the only ladder available by which under-developed peoples climb
out of the sludge of their poverty and hunger. And
Communism will come to Haiti for the same reason.
It is a catch-22 sort of situation: We fail to provide a practical alternative of workable reform to
the peoples of under-developed countries, and then
bitterly complain when they turn in desperation to
the Soviet Union. Instead of actively insisting on
reforms in El Salvador, Haiti, or the Philippines,
for example, we support fascist-type governments with
military aid so that the people are literally forced
in their effort for relief to turn elsewhere. The
American people perhaps have forgotten that their own
nation was born in revolution. Revolution is not an
unnatural process; when needed to overthrow oppressive regimes, as Jefferson reminded us, it is the
most natural of processes. Instead of sending aid to
oppressive governments because they claim to be anti-
Communist, we ourselves should be marching with the
guerrillas to overthrow them.

We could have succeeded in Haiti had we braced
ourselves against the adverse criticism and remained
to do the job that had to be done, and by so doing,
we could have shown the under-developed peoples of
the world that there is indeed an American alternative to Soviet-style Marxism. But we pulled out of
Haiti before the job was done and failed in our

responsibilities. And today Haiti is the poorest of Western Hemispheric nations, beset by a brutal dictatorship, and bathed in the darkness of ugliness and despair. Her symbol has become the poor woman who sits on a street corner night and day because she has no home and allows herself to be raped so that she can have a few pennies to buy milk for the child that clings to her body. Or the Catholic church that remains virtually empty even on Christmas Eve.

This work is primarily based upon unpublished materials--the Forbes Journals, Forbes' Personal Copy of the Report of the Commission for the Study and Review of Conditions in Haiti, his autobiographical "In Retrospect," correspondence to and from Forbes, material prepared by the State Department for the use of the commissions, and the mass of documents held by the National Archives at Washington. When Forbes died he left a ten-year restriction on the use of his Journals; for permission to use the materials prior to the expiration date, the author is indebted to the executors of the Forbes estate, particularly Mr. David Forbes of the J. Murray Forbes Company, nephew of W. Cameron Forbes.

The author is also indebted to the late Dr. E. T. Parks, Historical Division of the State Department, for permission to use the National Archives Collection of the Forbes Commission papers; the late Mr. Edward Forbes, whose personal reminiscences of his brother were very valuable; the late Mr. Robert C. Redmayne, who was a member of W. Cameron Forbes' staff from 1914 to the latter's death; and the late Dr. Victor G. Heiser, whose personal knowledge of the Haiti experience together with his permission to use the Diary he kept at the time of the Commission's visit to Haiti were enormously useful.

Extremely helpful were the late Mr. William A. Jackson, Director of the Houghton Library, Harvard University, for making the wealth of materials relating to Forbes readily accessible; Ms. Carolyn E. Jakeman, Librarian-in-Charge at Houghton, for her patient assistance; Dr. William Norton, Professor Emeritus of History, Boston University, for his thoughtful suggestions over the years of writing; Dr. Francis G. Walett, Professor Emeritus of History, Worcester State College, for his judicious comments; and Janet LeFort for the excellence with which she has prepared the manuscript for publication.

January 1984

Robert M. Spector
Worcester State College

The problem that Forbes and Moton faced in 1930 was very much the same that the United States is facing now. How do we help a nation to build a high standard of living without incurring the stigma of imperialism? If we remained in Haiti to try to do something for the people, we were either economic or military imperialists. If we withdrew and left the country to itself, we endangered the material advancements that had been made during the occupation. Forbes finally decided to advise Hoover to withdraw American forces, although he felt such a withdrawal to be a tragedy for the Haitian people. And perhaps it was. Yet to continue the occupation was to continue a comic opera in black and white. It was going to be difficult and the climb would be perilous, but the only way the black masses of Haiti could achieve their destiny was to make the ascent themselves.

Dr. Victor G. Heiser
Interview, New York City, December 1960

Chapter 1

The Forces at Work

Understanding the problems faced by the Presidential Commissions of 1930 requires a knowledge of the forces that made Haitian life what it was at that time. To restate Haiti's failures in public education, the poverty of her people, her corruption in government, the turmoil of revolution and the violence that have characterized her politics, the ruin of her commerce and her agriculture, would be only to describe surface effects. To determine and analyze the underlying forces responsible for these conditions is rather the task of this first chapter.

Nations have tried, but no nation has succeeded, in making a break with its past which is at the same time complete and permanent. As France tried and failed in her own great revolution, so also did Haiti try and fail. As the former reverted to absolutism, so did the latter. Haiti abolished the old labels and substituted new ones, but she still became once again what she had been in French colonial days. The leather whip, hated symbol of slavery, had vanished, but in its place lay a whip-like native *liane* which produced the same results. Few nations have experienced more revolutions than Haiti and had fewer benefits from them. Surely, to a large extent, the tragedy of Haiti has been her inability to escape her origins.

The island of Hispaniola, originally discovered and settled by the Spaniards, had by the latter half of the 18th Century altered considerably both in racial stock and in administrative control.[1] The frail, gentle aborigines whom Columbus had found on the island in 1492 had been so decimated by harsh enslavement and disease by the first third of the 16th Century[2] that the Spaniards, seeking to escape the condemnations of Father Bartolomé de Las Casas,[3] began extensive importation of African Negroes, whom

1

they believed to be more suited to the slave labor
of the plantation. These importations became so extensive that the Negro population soon far outnumbered
the white. Moreover, the continual depredations of
French buccaneers, soldiers of fortune, and renegades
against the western third of the weak Spanish colony
eventually concluded with Spain's recognition by 1697
of France's virtual possession of this portion of the
island. Although this western portion never extended
very far inland—twenty-five, thirty, forty miles at
the most—the industry of the French Colonials worked
a miracle of wealth and accomplishment. By the middle
of the 18th Century, the colony produced more sugar
than the combined British West Indies, contributed
substantially to the overseas and international trade
of the French nation, and lined its valleys and
coasts with mills, irrigation ditches, busy roads,
small industries, and rich plantations graced by newly built mansions to house the newly transplanted
world of French manners and culture that developed
amid the heavy fields of sugar, cacao, rice, indigo,
cotton, and coffee.[4] By 1790 Saint-Domingue was
France's wealthiest colony—far more profitable than
Canada and her furs and missionaries had ever been—
and her population consisted of approximately a half-
million people. Colbert's mercantilist views found
closer realization in Saint-Domingue than they had
found elsewhere. By the time the Negro slave rose in
revolt, vast plantations filled the valleys of the
mountain ranges, small ports handled a flourishing
trade between France and the rum distilleries of New
England, and a tight social structure had been reared
that might well have been the envy of the planters
of Virginia and the Carolinas.

Yet, the social structure was not so sound as
it outwardly appeared, and in this sociological em-
bryo were to be found the ingrained and stultifying
difficulties of 1930 Haiti.[5] Haiti consisted by 1790
of three free classes: the *grands blancs*, or whites
who owned the great plantations; the *petits blancs*,
or whites who either worked for the *grands blancs* as
clerks and overseers or worked for themselves as
small planters, artisans, shopkeepers, lawyers, mer-
chant-shippers, or just followed lines comparable to
the white trash of the antebellum southern United
States; and the *gens de couleur*, who were free men
in whose veins ran African blood. The last class
really consisted of two groups, full-blooded Negroes

2

and mulattoes, and both became free largely as the result of the *Code Noir* promulgated by Louis XIV. As with the Spaniards and Portuguese, the French did not have the racial prejudice so characteristic of the Anglo-Saxon. Covering the extent of Negro slavery in the colonies, the *Code* extended to the manumitted bondsman the privileges of French citizenship:[6] he could own slaves or land and dispose of his property by will, follow the profession or trade he desired, vote, marry, or travel, as he preferred.[7] Neither Louis nor his ministers expected many slaves to be freed, but more were liberated than might have been suspected.

Primarily, those who were freed were mulattoes who tasted liberty because they were children of slave mothers and white masters who, finding them socially embarrassing, sent them to France for extensive education or to positions in the small towns of Haiti, or perhaps gave them small plantations in more removed sectors of the country. Born mulattoes, their descendants, seeking to mate with white rather than black, became quadroons, octoroons, or men whose prime purpose was to forget the drops of Africa that merged with the blood-stream of the European. Occasionally pure Negroes were to be found among the *gens de couleur* --freedom for faithful service, the reward of a mistress, the gift of a dying man to a beloved friend--but the *gens de couleur,* who later became known as *affranchis,* were basically separated from the great mass of the Haitian people by their mixture of blood. Well-educated, thirsting with ambition to take their places with the ruling whites, seeking to prove their superiority over the African slave mass, shrewd, and ever-increasing in numbers, they soon owned by 1791 approximately a third of all the land and a fourth of all the slaves in the colony. L. E. Moreau de Saint-Méry records that out of a population of 519,000 in 1790, only 40,000 were whites (*grands* and *petits*), 28,000 *affranchis,* and 452,000 slaves.[8]

Had the Frenchman in Haiti been as liberal as his brethren in France itself, the ugly patterns which plagued Haitian history in the years prior to 1930 might not have been set. But the white settler could not abide the growth of a threatening, and what he believed to be inferior, class. This was especially true of the *petit blanc,* whose only reasoned superiority in the colony lay in the color of his

3

skin, and whose position was rapidly challenged by the wealth and growing power of Africans. The *petit* could make no distinction between the African whom he whipped in the sugar fields and the African whose carriage and horses plowed the dusty avenues of Cap-Français, Les Cayes, and Port-au-Prince. Nor could French women tolerate the *affranchis* upon finding that young Frenchmen with a practical eye for gain were as willing to marry warm-blooded wealthy colored girls as patrician French women bred in the ballrooms of cultured but decidedly cooler white society. Nor were they particularly overjoyed at the ever increasing abilities of *affranchi* women in the arts of charity, literature, or physical adornment. By 1790, over the course of several decades, the *blancs* encouraged a rising flood of color prejudice that was hitherto not present in French life and that was to embitter the *affranchis* for generations to come. The more the *affranchi* tried to escape his African heritage, the more he was repelled by the white man; the farther he tried to flee from the slave camp, the more pointedly he was ever reminded of his ancestry. By 1790, when the two powerful classes of Haitian society, the ruling white and the desirous-of-ruling *affranchis*, were ready for civil war, the Revolution in France set the stage for a settlement of the issue.

The colonial assembly met in May, 1788, to consider sending delegates to the first Estates-General to be convoked since 1614. In this assembly, the *grands blancs* who controlled the situation did two things which Leyburn considers blunders because they called the attention of France to the state of conditions in Saint-Domingue: (1) thirty-seven deputies were named to represent Saint-Domingue; and (2) a list of grievances was drawn up with a request that the *grands blancs* be left free of French interference in the governing of the colony.[9] The petition and the deputies called attention, indeed, to the state of affairs in Saint-Domingue, especially the attention of the radicals in Paris who wished to abolish slavery in all French territories. The French National Assembly, which had promulgated the "Rights of Man," did not grant the Haitian slaves their freedom—opposition from the *grands blancs* was too great—but it did pass a resolution which ostensibly granted equal political rights to descendants of free men. The interpretation of the resolution was, however, left to the ruling class, which refused to concede

4

the *affranchis* anything at all. When Ogé and Chavanne
led a demonstration at Cap-Francais demanding rights
for the colored class, they were seized and executed
"with notable brutality" in March 1791. Matters were
complicated by the rising of the black slaves five
months later.[10]

No one knows for certain, and the accounts are
conflicting but the chances are that the *affranchis*
encouraged or perhaps stimulated the slave insurrection. Only by this method could they have frightened
the white planter into recognizing the common peril
and the need of *affranchi* assistance in dominating
the slave. Most likely, this was all that was intended. But, if the *affranchi* attempted a ruse to serve
his purposes, he produced something that soon went
beyond his control. The Negro stir became a vast
flood which within ten years' time drove the white
man from Haitian shores but at the same time left the
affranchi a hopelessly tiny stick swirling across the
surface of a great tidal wave that had neither his
assistance nor his sympathy. If he were formerly an outsider looking in upon a society he admired and wished
fervently to become part of, he was now equally an
outsider, but to a society he wanted no part of and
could not admire.[11]

After a bloody and ferocious two-year period of
insurrection in which unspeakable cruelties were in-
flicted by white upon black and black upon white,
(while the *affranchis,* who had discovered that the in-
surgent slaves had a tendency to be friendly with
them, tried to obtain control of the slave revolt to
their own advantages), matters were additionally complicated by the invasions of British and Spanish who
tried to put down the revolt before it spread to
Jamaica and Spanish Santo Domingo. Add to this the
rise of a radical party in Paris which determined to
liberate the slaves, thus arousing the fury of the
grands blancs, petits blancs, and *gens de couleur*
against Republican France, and the picture of Saint-
Domingue in 1793 is one of inter-class and inter-race
struggle, political cleavage, and national antipathies of a complexity rarely seen in the history
of any nation: Negro against colonial white; white
colonial against radical French; affranchis against
the colonial whites on the basis of colonial white
supremacy but in sympathy with the whites against
emancipating the slaves; the French, Negroes, and a

5

majority of colonial whites and *affranchis* opposed
to English and Spanish. Nor were the lines clearly
drawn between races and classes; if anything, the
lines were blurred and indistinct rather than clear
at any point. Within a year conditions indicated that
only a strong man could bring order out of the welter
of confusion in which Saint-Domingue found itself.
This man proved to be the former slave Toussaint
L'Ouverture.[12] By 1796 he had not only beaten the
Spanish and the British, but he stood as France's
governor-general in Saint-Domingue. Only one rival
stood between himself and absolute power in the
French colony, André Rigaud, the mulatto leader of
the *affranchis*. By 1799, after a brief conflict decided by Toussaint's superior capabilities and enormously superior numbers, the *affranchi* power was
broken and the Negro stood supreme on his own soil.

From 1799 until 1802 peace returned to Saint-
Domingue, and Toussaint became something of a symbol
of the purest ideals of the French Revolution.[13] Although a former slave, and barely literate, Toussaint
proved to have the shrewdness, kindness, stability
of character, and capacity for leadership that offered to bring his country out of the stormy seas of
rapine and lust into the tranquil waters of a calm
future. He set up a Constitution, divided the country
into military districts, set over each a commander,
checked the passions of his people against the whites
still left in Saint-Domingue, encouraged former white
settlers to return, and, through persuasion and force
both, herded the masses of blacks back to the plantations. Men like Dessalines and Christophe showed themselves particularly assiduous in bringing the ten-
year neglect of the fields to an end.[14] Shirkers were
buried alive, sawn between two planks of wood,
whipped and quartered, and subjected to ingenious tor-
tures. The emancipated slaves now found themselves
in Davis' words "once more slaves--slaves of a military state."[15]

Yet the ultimate result might have been salutary
had Toussaint been permitted his way. As it happened,
the emergence of Napoleon to power in France brought
about the Negro leader's fall.[16] The First Consul
could not abide having this "gilded African" rival
him within the French culture as the champion of the
rights of man, and in January, 1802, Napoleon's
brother-in-law General Leclerc arrived at Cap-

6

Francais with twenty-thousand veterans to restore white control to the island, his hands filled with paper promises from the First Consul. Whites and mulattoes in general hailed his arrival, but General Christophe, black commander of the city, was not quite so elated. The black troops resisted, and the War for Haitian Independence began. When it ended two years later, Toussaint had died of cold and starvation in a dank French prison in the Jura Mountains of Southeast France; Dessalines ruled an independent country known as Haiti (an aboriginal Indian name meaning "mountainous"); Leclerc was dead of fever; fifty thousand troops, or two French armies, had been consumed, one by fighting, the second by disease; the country lay prostrate with ruined trade, destroyed plantations, rotting fields, a frightened hungry population, burned towns and villages, and an enormous army that was to remain Haiti's chief expense through the one hundred and twenty-five years that were to follow; and a hatred of the white man that was not to be shaken for at least a century.[17]

Dessalines proclaimed independence on January 1, 1804, and then embarked upon an unabashed tyranny. He professed liberté, but this liberté meant liberty from France, and he failed to mention egalité and fraternité as part of his beliefs. Like Toussaint, a former slave, but, unlike him, unforgiving, and ruthless, he hated the whites (remembering how they had turned against Toussaint at the arrival of Leclerc), distrusted the mulattoes (even though his hope was to unite all Haitians of Negro ancestry), and sought ever to be on guard against the French. To these ends, he divided all Haitians into two classes, cultivators and soldiers, sent the cultivators to the ruined plantations and fields, sent the soldiers to supervise them, and lived by the philosophy of the mastery of the state over the people. Slavery had been abolished and the whip forbidden; in their places were serfdom and the even more brutal _liane_.[18] A new constitution was established in 1805 proclaiming Haiti an empire and Dessalines himself absolute monarch. All Haitians were proclaimed "blacks" in the effort to unite mulattoes and Negroes; and Dessalines even offered Pétion, Rigaud's chief general in the civil war with Toussaint, his daughter Célimène in marriage (which offer Pétion respectfully declined). Whites were massacred wherever and whenever they could be found by a ruthless

7

army, and that army was kept large beyond its needs, ostensibly to meet the ever-present danger of French invasion but actually for the maintenance of tyrannical power. "The laborers can be controlled only by fear of punishment, and even death; I shall lead them only by these means, my 'morale' shall be the bayonet" was his reply to a request for Roman Catholic religious education.[19] Two tasks the monarch set for himself--the fortification of Haiti against foreign invaders and the return of the country to its prosperity of French days. These two tasks he performed admirably. Unfortunately, he also performed them with great cruelty, a misfortune for a country with Haiti's particular background; where previously hard work had only the social stigma of the slave, now it became anathema altogether to a people who had already tasted the delights of laziness.

Inevitably, Dessalines proved himself all too human in conceiving Haiti's welfare to be synonymous with his own, and revolt broke out, particularly in the West where Pétion commanded. Leaving his home in the valley of the Artibonite, he rode with a few officers to Port-au-Prince. Upon reaching Pont Rouge on the outskirts of the capital, October 17, 1806, he was assassinated by the very troops he was to command. He lay for hours where he fell, until buried by an old peasant woman who could no longer endure the stench.

Christophe fully expected to become emperor of Haiti, but the South, dominated chiefly by mulattoes, threw its weight behind Pétion, and we have the spectacle of a Haiti divided against itself until 1820, the North controlled by the "Emperor Jones" and dominated by Negroes, the South governed by Pétion and dominated by the mulatto.[20]

Christophe and Pétion were as different in background, temperament, philosophies as men may be, and their respective areas were governed accordingly. Christophe, Negro, an ex-slave, illiterate, whose whole experience had been gained in the revolutionary and civil wars, and aware of no other system of discipline, was well-fitted to carry on the political principles of Dessalines. Though he did not vary the soldier-cultivator system which had brought so much prosperity to the country, though he did not lift the strict code of discipline from the backs of the black

8

serfs, though he hated the French no less violently, he did agree with Toussaint rather than with Dessalines in his recognition that Haiti needed the white men, their talents, education, techniques, especially the English, whom he particularly admired. Where Dessalines had been the slave-master, he was the stern patriarch; where Dessalines hated, Christophe feared--but also respected.

He established the elaborate *Code Henry*, an attempt to emulate the French pattern of setting down on paper complex machinery for human behavior, masterfully drawn and impossibly applied. Education was made compulsory under the English Lancastrian system then in vogue; laborers were given partial weekends off for rest and prayer, though they still were not permitted to move from the land or change occupations; a sound currency was established; the work day was limited to specific hours; foreign traders were encouraged as well as foreign investment; the printing of books was encouraged; and even rules set down for the regulation of the people's dress. Though the system of state-owned lands worked by cultivators remained unaltered, he did permit proprietors to lease state lands, pay a certain portion of the profits to the state and retain the rest. At his death, Christophe's treasury yielded a surplus of six million dollars in gold.

He crowned himself Henry I in 1811, but was wise enough to create a peerage as well to satisfy the ambitions of his powerful subordinates. Though he governed the great masses of the people through force, he dealt with his generals more gently, with an eye to their desires and an ear to their tongues. Though ignorant, he had, unlike Dessalines, a passion for culture which drove him to try "to make Haitians the most civilized, educated and creative people on earth."[21] But like Dessalines, his egomania, that treacherous servant of many great men, overwhelmed him and made him its slave.

As the magnificent palace of San Souci, rising in brick and concrete near Milot, represents Christophe's attempt during the early part of his rule to bring culture and glory to Haiti, so the Citadelle, a vast fortress constructed at the expense of thousands of lives, symbolizes the tyrant into which he, like Dessalines, finally degenerated. His

9

benevolence had been based on force, and only upon
the basis of increasing force could his problems be
solved. The hardships of the North soon equalled its
prosperity, and those hardships contrasted much too
vividly with the ease and tranquillity of Pétion's
mulatto-controlled South. Desertions to the South increased, both by mulattoes and Negroes; Christophe
imported Dahomets[22] from Africa, whom he used as a
private police force; nobles and common folk alike
were subject to the severest scrutiny; and taxes fell
upon strong and weak alike. In 1820, after suffering
a paralytic stroke, he escaped the revenge of his enemies by committing suicide in his palace of San
Souci, dramatically as ever, with a silver bullet.
Legend tells us that his queen and a faithful servant
dragged his body up the treacherous path to the
Citadelle and dumped it into a vat of quicklime.

Pétion, in his administration of the South, followed an entirely different line. Born in freedom a
mulatto, educated in France, cultured, intelligent,
he unwittingly set the pattern for Haiti's later history.[23] He is known as the Jefferson of the Republic,
and he bears strong intellectual resemblance to his
contemporary in the United States. He believed in the
ultimate capacities of the people; he understood the
need of the Negro masses for training in democracy;
he wished to unite mulatto and Negro; he refused to
follow the Toussaint-Dessalines-Christophe pattern
of great state-owned plantations run by the soldier-
cultivator system of forced labor, but preferred to
break up the government lands into smaller plots
which were either sold, leased, or given away to individual cultivators. Pétion set a policy of distributing land to the people which in a country that
does not follow the British rule of primogeniture is
national suicide. As each owner died, the land was
distributed among the sons, and so on and so on, until Haiti by the 20th century became a country of
tiny plots of ground no longer capable of producing
the sugar and coffee which were Haiti's staples and
her wealth, and barely large enough to support the
families to which they belonged. And in the process
he broke the power of the *affranchis* --or *élite* , as
they came to be called--the only class capable of running the country with any semblance of ordered democracy, forcing them from an economic position based
upon land to one based upon office-holding and commerce.

10

Unfortunately for Haiti, the years between 1807 and 1820 saw a country divided between two separate extremes of philosophy, neither one of which was by itself the solution to the economic and political problems that Haiti faced. Had Christophe the faith in democracy held by Pétion, or Pétion the passion for efficiency of Christophe and Dessalines, Haiti might have been set upon traditions of democracy and hard work. As matters turned out, she obtained neither tradition. When Christophe died in 1820, the country was re-united under John Pierre Boyer (who succeeded Pétion in 1818) under Pétion's pattern in the South.[24]

Boyer governed Haiti from 1820 until 1844, and his *élite* administration hardened the forces already crystallized in Haitian life: (1) The *élite* took the place of the whites as the aristocrats, distinguished not by landholding as in colonial times but by education, literacy, manners, office-holding, and wealth derived from government and commerce. (2) The civil service fell into the hands of the *élite*, while the army remained in the hands of the Negro, creating a bipolarization in Haitian politics. (3) The parceling of land continued, and wild coffee took the place of sugar and plantation coffee as the staple, with the result that the soldier-cultivator system fell into disuse. The last attempt at restoring prosperity to agriculture, Boyer's *Code Rurale* of 1826, which was the final attempt to restore the great plantations, failed miserably. The peasants "had...a taste of liberty with economic anarchy and they preferred this to compulsion and...signing of dubious contracts." Putting it another way, "Material gain is desirable, but not at the expense of liberty. Freedom means something, even in poverty."[25]

The term freedom, however, one must understand, meant something other than it meant in the northern nations. It did not mean freedom of enterprise, vigor of action; it meant the freedom to do nothing. The middle class which was so badly needed to build the nation simply never came into being. If it existed at all, it existed in the few whites who still lived in Haiti, whites who served much the same purposes for the country that the Jews served during the Middle Ages. The people were divided into rich and poor, cultured and uncultured, but they were not divided on the basis of the torpor which set in upon the population. The *status quo* became a sort of desir-

ed commodity that could not be altered without vio-
lating tradition and good taste. That some should be
wealthy, others horribly depressed, became as much
a part of Haitian life in the 19th century as the oppressive heat.[26] But at least the masses were no longer the pseudo-serfs they had been; they were now
peasants free to work their tiny plots of earth had
they the desire or the energy to do so.

From 1843, the year of Boyer's overthrow by a
group of young mulattoes, until 1915, the date of the
American Intervention, Haitian history became little
more than a series of revolutions, in which politics
became submerged in self-seeking, fundamental doctrines of democracy were lost, and great issues were
practically non-existent. The government revolved,
rather, between the *Ins* and the *Outs*. It was a government in which the *élite*, outvoted by a Negro majority
consisting of an illiterate 95 or 96 per cent of the
people and outmatched by an official Negro army and
thousands of Negro guerrillas (called *cacos* in the
North and *piquets* in the South) hiding in the mountains, sought to promote its interests either through
its natural arm, the civil service, or by backing
Negro revolutionists more amenable to its control.
Elections were corrupt, bribery common, ignorance
among presidents normal, and violence habitually
based upon the *cacos*, that natural spawn of continued
disorder, who occupied the heights at the beck and
call of any aspiring presidential candidate whose success might offer booty and adventure.

Ordinarily we think of revolutions in terms of
gigantic proportions: the overturning of an order,
the tearing down of a system to construct a newer and
better, the influx of new ideas. By this view, only
one revolution took place in Haiti, that of 1791-
1804. This revolution alone went to the bottom of
Haitian life. Those that followed affected less and
less the Haitian mass. Toussaint, Christophe, Pétion,
Boyer were the fashioners of government; those who
followed were merely disturbances upon the surface
of the waters, whose effects neither spread wide nor
sank deep. The violence at Cap-Francais (later called
Cap-Haitien), at Les Cayes, and at Port-au-Prince,
whether it turned right or left, produced little in
the way of benefits for the two millions lingering
in the thousand valleys of the country, hiding in the
hills, or grubbing for bread in the streets of the

towns. In this way, at least, Haiti did not imitate France, for in France's continual violence we do find a strong searching of the Gallic soul for a better life that does not seem to be manifested in Haitian political meanderings.

From 1843 until 1915, Haiti endured thirty-two heads of state. Rivière-Herard, the mulatto set up by the *élite* to replace Boyer, was overthrown in 1844 by the Negro army, instituting Negro control of the presidency for the entire period from 1844 until 1915, with the exception of Geffrard, Salnave, Boisronde-Canal, and Hippolyte. Guerrière stayed in power eleven months, his successor Pierrot eleven months, Riché less than a year. Soulouque, Domingue, Boisronde-Canal, Salomon, Légitime, Alexis, Simon, Oreste, Zamor, and Théodore were deposed by revolution; Salnave was tied to a pole and shot; Hippolyte died in office; Leconte was blown up in his palace; Auguste died by poison; Simon Sam retired under pressure; and Jean Vilbrun Guillaume Sam, the last of the presidents prior to the American Intervention in 1915, was torn to pieces by a mob in Port-au-Prince after murdering one hundred and sixty-seven of his political enemies in a prison blood-bath. Nissage-Saget alone, a mulatto, managed by some amazing quickness of mind to retire peacefully at the conclusion to his four-year term. In one hundred and eight years, twenty-four executives held office, seventeen were deposed by revolutions, two of whom were publicly murdered; two were allowed to retire peacefully from office; eleven served for less than one year each. From 1908 until 1915 alone, so violent and hopeless had Haitian politics become since the grand days of Toussaint that seven presidents were selected and deposed: Simon by revolution; Leconte by an explosion in his palace; Auguste by poison; Oreste by exile; Zamor by revolution (and was later murdered in the same massacre by which Sam destroyed his other political opponents); and Sam by lynching.

Whether one subscribes to the theory that history is the results of the actions of great men or the results of forces too deep and too strong for men either to control or modify to any great extent, or even if one denies any thesis to history, one cannot deny that by the time of the American Intervention specific forces endemic to Haiti and Haitian life had established themselves--forces that would destroy the

Occupation and that could not be overlooked by the commissioners of 1930 in any attempt to settle Haitian affairs and determine United States policy in that area. Strong man rule vied with group rule, dictatorship with democracy, the *élite* with the mass, the civil service with the army, the North with the South and West of Pétion's old regime, universal education with education for the few.

Few historians disagree that at the time of liberation, the hope of Haiti lay with the only educated class left in the country, the *affranchi*. Had the *affranchis* lent their culture, their superior knowledge to the world, their wealth and talents to the development of the country, they might have led the Negro along paths of education to a stable, prosperous modern democracy. Had they not despised manual labor, they might have formed a group devoted not only to literary and cultural pursuits but to the technical sciences which form the heart of any sturdy modern democracy. And had they been pure Africans this is precisely what they might have done. But they were not; they were the descendants of white parents who denied them, and psychologically they were whiter than the French who had now been either driven from the land or dead. Like the Jewish Torquemada who in fleeing from his Jewish'ness became more anti-Semitic than the most fanatic Inquisitors, the mulatto denied all connection with his Negro brother. For him the white aristocrat had never left Haitian shores; he himself was now the white aristocrat, and the black man was still his slave. The mulatto was a Frenchman heart and soul; he spoke French and not the native Creole, wore French clothes, aped French manners, and dressed his wife and children in Parisian fashions; he was educated in Gallic literature, wrote French codes and constitutions, and selected law for his profession; his food smacked of Normandie and his wine of Bordeaux, the Champagne, and the Loire. And the cleavage which had arisen in colonial days between white and mulatto now became between affranchi and the Negro mass a great chasm only to be transcended by the most miraculous processes. The mulatto had escaped massacre because the Negro slave had considered him to be African; he accepted freedom from massacre gratefully but he would not accept its concomitant, being African. Nor would be accept anything that might destroy his single advantage over the mass: his education—with all that this implies in matters of

the sheer ability to read and write, create and inter-
pret legislation, keep commercial records, publish
newspapers and journals, maintain an awareness of
world conditions, and accumulate wealth. Education
for the masses of the people, the only real hope for
a strong modern nation, would have destroyed the sin-
gular strong point of the mulatto, and against this
he set his face.

The *élite* spoke continually through Haitian history for parliamentary government, which superficial-
ly at least seemed to substantiate its claim that it
spoke for democratic government. But without mass
education, parliamentary government meant only
representative government for the *élite*, which was
another way of enabling it through a controlled legislature to offset the strong powers of a Negro president placed in office by a Negro army. Haitian
politics of the period before 1915 was a constant
struggle between the Negro army and the *élite* for positions of strength, each totally selfish, while the
mass of the people sat unchanged and ill-considered
--if considered at all--in its tiny plots on the moun-
tainsides and in the valleys of the nation. True,
there were two parties (the Liberals representing the
élite and the Nationalists representing the Negro
army leaders), but the Liberals were not liberal and
the Nationalists were not concerned with the national
interest. Without the help of the *élite*, the only
class capable of bringing about a genuine democratiza-
tion and technical modernization of the country,
Haiti was severely handicapped. "The Liberals squan-
dered their opportunities in 1822, 1843, 1859, 1870,
and 1876... Thereafter no serious effort was made to
establish responsible government, and the problem of
subordinating the military to the civil power remained unsolved."[27]

Had the *élite* controlled the army, Haitian history before 1915 might have been, despite its oligar-
chical despotism, at least relatively free from violence. But the *affranchi* had missed his opportunity
to raise armies during the wars of the 1790's, leaving the major fighting to black generals. By the time
Boyer took command of a united Haiti in 1820, so many
Negro generals of experience existed that they could
not easily be retired. Nor was a shabby, ill-
uniformed, worse paid, illiterate army the place for
the cultured mulatto who preferred the conversation

15

of the law office and the government post; and when we consider that the primary source of recruits was the rural Negro whom only Negro officers could understand and control, we see that by Boyer's time the army was largely to be in command of its own situation. The revolution of 1843 had been a movement of mulattoes, that of 1844 one of the army, and from that time forward until the Intervention, only three genuine mulattoes (Nissage-Saget, Boisronde-Canal, Auguste) held the presidency. The *élite* could not stand against the guns of the army, poor as those guns may have been, and they withdrew into their aristocratic shell to try less obvious methods of retaining power.

The army offered an ideal situation to the illiterate Negro who wished either advancement in life or security. It gave him employment, the spoils of war, some excitement, a feeling of importance, and a sense of belonging to something. It was the only way to advancement for a man who was barred by the *élite* from economic and social progress. Boyer spoiled things for the army, however, by getting France to recognize the independence of Haiti in 1838. Until that time, a huge army was demanded by the generals and the presidents to defend the country against the ever-present danger—so they said—of French reinvasion. After 1838 no such danger was imminent. Laziness, lack of training, a laissez-faire attitude encompassed the military, together with a sense of disintegration, until the Negro generals discovered, as did the Roman armies on the frontiers or the Praetorian Guard two millenia before, that they might raise an emperor by merely lifting him upon their shields.

Overmilitarization has been as much a drain upon the Haitian population as the yaws, hookworm, and yellow fever. Men, fearing to go to market lest they be impressed into service by one general or another on the road, preferred to remain in the hills while their women travelled to the towns and trading centers. The small revenues obtained by the government often went primarily to line the pockets of generals. Crops went into the ever hungry maw of foraging troops. If it furthered the careers of a few young blacks who had pretensions of military honor, the army destroyed the lives of thousands of young men who despised the miserable existence it offered.

Candler[28] tells us that in 1842, when the population
was still less than a million, the district governments had nine generals, sixty-three colonels, forty-
eight lieutenant-colonels, nine captains, one lieutenant, and twenty-eight medical officers; in the
standing army were thirty-three colonels, ninety-five
lieutenant-colonels, eight hundred twenty-five captains, six hundred fifty-four lieutenants, five hundred seventy-seven sublieutenants and ensigns, six
thousand eight hundred fifteen noncommissioned
officers, twenty-five medical officers, and twenty-
eight thousand soldiers. With no foreign enemy to
fight, they controlled the districts in which they
were located, plotted, counter-plotted, and welcomed
the adventure of occasional forays against the *cacos*
in the hills or the special delights of revolution.
The mulatto hated the Negro Army clique, yet it was
his own fears that kept it going, like the rattle-
snake chasing its tail; had the *élite* been willing
to open up other channels of advancement to Negroes,
the army would have lost its main attraction. But to
do this would have meant mass education and the
destruction of the *élite* advantage anyway, so the mulatto accepted the army as a preferable evil and
tried to mitigate its effect upon his life.

Historians have a way of stating that the times
find the man. They found the man in Toussaint, but
such a man was not to be found again. The first and
best of the Haitian rulers, he had the understanding
of his people that Dessalines and Christophe did not
possess, firmness of will that Pétion and Boyer lacked, and perhaps the insight into his people of no
other Haitian leader after him. Dessalines and
Christophe forced their people--and not for very
long; Pétion catered, for all his ideals, to *élite*
interest; Boyer's long twenty-five years of control
was a mere waiting for the storm, with no significant
achievements to call leadership. And when the storm
came in 1844, we see launched a line of incompetents
in the presidential chair. Haitians worshipped the
strong-man ideal, but the problem lay in finding the
strong man to fit the ideal. Far from being strong,
the presidents competed with each other for weakness
and immorality, culminating in the administrations
of Domingue, Auguste, and the second Sam.

Domingue's so-called government serves the example. Nissage-Saget, as we recall, by some twist of

fate, managed to retire without a revolution at the close of his term of office. He selected in May of 1874 Michel Domingue, a Negro general in command of the Southeastern Department, and appointed him commander of the army. Domingue was elected--"elected" in the sense that no one objected at the time--on June 11, 1874, for a term of eight years. He immediately turned over the government to his nephew, the unscrupulous Septimus Rameau, who lost no time in looting the treasury. He floated a loan from France for twenty-six million francs, most of which found its way into the pockets of Rameau and his friends. Revolt brewed, and Rameau ordered the arrest of General Brice, Montplaisir Pierre, and Boisronde-Canal, three very influential men in the country and three whom Rameau particularly suspected of rebellion. Brice was killed in his office, Pierre in his own house after a long defense in which, according to Sir Spencer St. John, he killed seventeen soldiers, wounded thirty-two, "mostly mortally," and could only be subdued by the employment of artillery.[29] Boisronde-Canal, warned in advance, escaped. On April 15, 1876, Rameau was murdered while in the process of trying to get government funds out of the country for his proposed exile, and Domingue set hurried sail for Jamaica. Jamaica, indeed, became between Boyer and the second Sam the happy hunting ground of exiled leaders of Haiti--exile based on pilfered funds from the Haitian people. Boisronde-Canal, succeeding Domingue, was the only president who seemed to possess a sense of responsibility, but after a serious riot in July of 1879, in which men were slain, he resigned and left the country in disgust.

This is not to say that the men who held the presidency were basically immoral. To say this would be to have an unclear picture of the era. So natural had the confusion and rapacity become to Haitian politics that the presidency was not looked upon as a trust for the benefit of the nation; it was the prize which went to the victor, to be used for the victor's advantage. That the government had too little money to do any good for the people, but more than enough to make poor men wealthy seemed to be the philosophy.

But even assuming that the governing groups were truthfully concerned with the benefit of their country, the problem of obtaining sufficient revenues

with which to implement progressive ideas still had
to be solved. The country had no commerce; apart from
wild coffee she had nothing to sell. She had no resources in minerals, no cattle or sheep ranches, no
longer any of the great cacao and sugar plantations
which had made her so wealthy before the revolution
of 1791. Her greatest wealth was in her agriculture,
but as has been observed, Pétion's policy of split-
ting up the great plantations into smaller and smaller plots of ground, together with the Haitian tendency to divide inheritances equally among sons,
destroyed the plantation system and with it the only
source of large revenues. Agriculture had sunk to
little more than that which Haitian women and old men
laboring under primitive conditions with primitive
instruments could produce. Sugar was no longer shipped abroad, and just enough was produced to satisfy
small local needs, while the tilling of the soil, the
construction of fencing, the breeding of live-stock
were neglected. The only cultivation worthy of the
name was the growing of garden vegetables. Coffee,
cotton, and bananas grew in a semi-wild state, rural
homes were shacks with thatched roofs, sanitation was
non-existent, and manual labor even among the Negro
masses was shunned by everyone except the women.[30]
The stigma of slavery after 150 years had finally
penetrated down from the élite into the lowest rungs
of the racial ladder. Erosion of the land and care-
lessness in the protection of the once rich Haitian
forests were gradually destroying the land that was
still valuable. With such conditions and a virtually
bankrupt treasury, graft seemed to be the only worthwhile pursuit of a president.

Many Haitians, especially young men who have
been to the United States or Europe, blame the general torpor of the average Haitian, which certainly
is a force to be reckoned with. At the end of 1923,
the American High Commissioner Russell declared that
not only were 95% of the people illiterate but that
they were immoral as well and had the mentality of
a child of not more than seven years of age reared
under advantageous conditions.[31]

The Haitian as an individual, whether mulatto
or Negro, did not seem to be any different than any
other man, regardless of race, who had to spend his
life in the tropics under a sun 130 degrees in the
shade a good part of the year and over a hundred the

19

remainder.[32] This was a problem beyond the control
of the Commissions of 1930 but a vital one that had
to wait for science and not politics to solve. The
industrial nations lie in the temperate zone, and
if we have difficulty in the United States in bringing
technology and civil rights below the Mason-Dixon
line, how much more difficult developing them in
an area two thousand miles farther south? Add to
the problem of climate tropical diseases unknown
farther north,[33]a geography that resembles a crumpled
piece of paper,[34]an overpopulation problem that makes
Haiti one of the most densely populated countries in
the western hemisphere,[35] and an isolation that can
only come from being a tiny patch of French culture
and language in a vast oasis of English, Spanish,
and Portuguese, and we have a few of the major forces
with which W. Cameron Forbes had to contend in that
winter of 1930.

For the Haitian of the 19th century, the solution to his country's problems was to be found in
lengthy constitutions and codes. Haiti created fifteen constitutions during the 19th century alone.
Each one, created by either a mulatto president or
by a mulatto working at the request of a Negro president, was remarkably detailed, painfully constructed,
and masterful in the fluency with which the parts
fitted into the whole. Nor were the numerous Codes,
such as Christophe's *Code Henry* or Boyer's *Code
Rurale* less carefully reared. The trouble was that
they did not work. They did not work because they
were not suited to the Haitian situation. They were
French systems as badly suited to the Haitian condition as the French constitutions have been unsuited
to the Gallic. The American people hammered out in
the hot July months of 1787 a constitution which,
despite its defects, arose out of the patterns of
American colonial life; Haitian constitutions have
not been indigenous growths but rather ready-grown
foreign plants set down in a hostile soil. Where
the British and American constitutions were products
of peoples they governed and suitable thereby insofar
as any man-made product may be suitable, the Haitian
constitutions have neither been the product of nor
suitable for the people governed. Where the Founding
Fathers in Philadelphia refused to copy *in toto* the
British pattern of democracy, the Haitian mulatto,
blinded by his devotion to French culture and his
passion to be a genuine Frenchman, borrowed with an

almost fanatic devotion the very product of France which has always been her poorest export.

Toussaint's constitution of 1801 did not separate the colony from France, but it established the strong-man doctrine of the governor-general's superior position over any legislative body and set the groundwork for the Toussaint-Dessalines-Christophe cultivator-soldier system of forced labor. Dessalines' constitution of 1805 (1) established the empire with himself as emperor, (2) continued the forced labor provisions, (3) tried to unite the mulatto and Negro, as we have seen, by calling all Haitians "blacks," (4) required all *affranchis* to take up a trade in the effort to create the needed middle class which successful trading nations must possess, (5) and contained the famous clause, "No white man shall set foot on this territory as master or as land-owner," a phrase which remained in Haitian constitution-making until that of Dartiguenave in 1918. Pétion, using the Constitution of the United States as an example, sought in 1806 to create a strong president who could be re-elected but could not obtain dictatorial powers or remain in office for life. Christophe answered Pétion with one in 1807 for the North, and another in 1811, in which he proclaimed himself King, Haiti a monarchy, and created a peerage.

It was, however, Pétion's second constitution, that of 1816, that remains the most influential one in Haitian politics. Tired, weary, and somewhat disgusted with his people's lack of will for achievement and the failure of the mulattoes to see further than their own interests, he amended the constitution of 1806 to adopt the principle of the life presidency with the right of the incumbent to choose his own successor. The results could not have been worse, for upon the union of the North and the South in 1820, the principle of the benevolent life president led too easily to the retention of power by incompetents. Were the *Outs* satisfied that the *Ins* could be retired from office at the close of four years, the urge to revolution might more often have been drowned in patience, but the prospect of being interminably deprived of the fruits of corruption was much too much to ask of the ambitious.

Influential as Pétion's second constitution was,

the most valuable constitution in 19th century
Haitian politics from the standpoint of progress toward democracy was that of the young mulatto revolutionaries of 1843. Here we have an attempt to attain
a proper balance between legislature and president,
the direct election of the president by the people
(which implied building a strong educational system),
the subordination of the military to the civil arm,
honest elections, and a legislature that alone would
exercise the right of making laws. The army, predom-
inantly Negro and illiterate, did not care for such
radical reform because it would not submit its almost
unrestricted actions to the whims of the *élite*; the
mulattoes, because they feared that giving an honest
vote to and establishing an educational system for
the masses would deprive them of their chief advantages. Leyburn calls this constitution "completely
unrealistic," as it was, but had the ideals of the
ruling classes been different, it might have formed
the foundation for a constitution actually moulded
to serve the practical needs of the nation.[36]

The Negro army revolt of 1844 brought a new constitution and a series of ineffective documents that
contributed little to the betterment of Haitian
politics. Each succeeding one became little more than
a statement of policy by those in power. This has
been, in effect, what Haitian Constitutions precisely
are--statements of party platform (if one may apply
that term to Caribbean politics), one-sided statements of action, rather than an all-encompassing
framework in which all parties, all groups, all elements agree to work and resolve their differences.
Would one be overstating the case to say that Haiti
has had so many constitutions that she has not really
had any?

Riché returned to Pétion's document of 1816 modified by that of 1843 in that the president was not
to be selected by his predecessor for life but was
to be elected, but not by the people, but by the
legislature in joint session; Soulouque, in the grand
tradition of Louis Napoleon, over-threw all pretense
of democracy and created the Second Empire; Geffrard
returned to Riché's creation; Salnave in 1867 modified Geffrard's work by inserting the provision that
no legislation might be passed without at least two
thirds of the members of both houses of the legislature present, which made it possible for any group

to hinder legislation through absence, a device which Salnave used to try to keep himself in power for life. Thereafter no president tried to revive Pétion's "term for life" concept, though many still aspired to the role.

Domingue created a constitution in 1874, Salomon one in 1879 and another in 1886, Hyppolite one in 1889, which lasted until 1918.

Nor were the Codes any the more successful. The *Code Henry* of 1812, the *Code Rurale* of 1826, and the Code of Salomon in 1883 were doomed to failure. The *Code Henry* (spelled on the English form by Christophe to show his admiration for that country) consisted of seven parts: Civil, Commercial, Shipping and Maritime, Civil Process, Criminal and Police Process, Agricultural, and Military. The agricultural section seems to have been Christophe's, but the rest of it, despite Christophe's preference for English forms, was decidedly French. If northern Haiti showed prosperity under Christophe, its prosperity was not the result of his Code but the result of the rigid system of discipline which any dictatorship may achieve within relatively short periods of time.

The fact is that the mulattoes who were responsible for the writing of these codes and constitutions, regardless of whether Negro or Mulatto sat in the presidential chair, did not dare create an instrument which if carried to idealistic fulfillment would have given universal suffrage to the masses of the population, free elections honestly tabulated, a president truly sensitive to the desires of the people, and the dissemination of education throughout the country. The reason why no Constitution was devised that would be acceptable to all was that there was no group among the rulers—Negro army or mulatto civil service—that would sacrifice part of its interest to the betterment of the nation. The constitutions devised reflect not the patriotism of the sincere Haitian, but the selfish passions of groups in power who wanted to stay in power—sometimes mouthing the glowing liberté, fraternité, egalité, but spoken with a sneer and a touch of contempt. The constitutions had the trappings of the democrat and the heart of the sweat-shop boss. The rulers had little faith in the people, and where their *interests* in addition *favored* an ignorant mass, how could one truly expect liberalism to triumph? The genuine ideals of the young mulattoes of 1843 were all too quickly tossed aside as much too dangerous and all too sincere, which was perhaps worse.

Yet, in all fairness, could Haiti, just a few short steps removed from slavery, step promptly into ordered democracy and respect for democratic traditions, when 19th century Europe had as little or less regard for such traditions? Prussia lived under her illiberal constitution of 1850 for almost seventy years; Russia did not have her first Duma until 1906; Louis Napoleon separated France from her democratic constitution of 1848 with the touch of his fingers; as late as 1882, only 7% of the Italian population had the vote. Even England had to pass through the destruction of Stephen's reign, the Wars of the Roses, the Puritan Revolution, and the Revolution of 1689 before she achieved a reasonable measure of constitutional stability. On the other hand, even were Haiti's constitutions created with honesty instead of with clever mind and deceptive tongue, they would have had to be implemented by sincere legislatures, interpreted by well-trained judiciaries, and enforced by patriotic, self-sacrificing executives, few of whom existed in 19th century Haiti.

On March 4, 1915, Vilbrun Guillaume Sam, who had engineered his own revolution, became president. No sooner did he enter the office than Dr. Bobo, emerging from the safety of the Dominican Republic, began the traditional revolt. In the course of the sordid affair, Sam was personally attacked, taking refuge in the French legation at Port-au-Prince. General Oscar Etienne, Sam's friend, herded 167 political enemies into prison and then shot them down, killing all but one or two who managed to escape by feigning death. The crowds rose in fury. A few members of the mob entered the legation, actually "smelled Sam out" by the antiseptic on his bandages, found him hiding in a corner under a bed, and threw him to the waiting mob. Sam was literally ripped to pieces and the parts of his body mutilated in the streets. General Etienne was dragged from the Dominican legation and shot. On July 28th, 1915, Admiral Caperton landed forces in obedience to the following message from Secretary of State Lansing:

State Department desires that American forces be landed

24

Port-au-Prince and that American and foreign interest be protected; that representatives England, France be informed this intention; informed that their interests will be protected, and that they be requested not land. In acting this request be guided your knowledge present condition Port-au-Prince and act at discretion.[37]

The landing brought a measure of order to the capital. Caperton's purpose was to get a president elected who would be amenable to permitting the United States' settling of Haiti's internal difficulties. With Sam dead, the question of a president revolved about two men: Philippe Sudre Dartiguenave and the infamous Dr. Bobo. On August 8, Captain Edward L. Beach, Caperton's Chief of Staff, held an audience with the two candidates. The following conversation gives a picture of the character of Haitian politics:

"Gentlemen, it seems likely that one of you will be elected President of Haiti. Haiti is in great trouble; she has suffered much. The United States has come to Haiti as a good friend, interested only in Haiti's welfare, in her happiness, in her prosperity. The United States has determined that revolution and disorder and anarchy must cease in Haiti; that unselfish and devoted patriotism must characterize thereafter the acts of the Haitian Government. Senator Dartiguenave and Dr. Bobo, realizing this momentous crisis in Haitian history, with the eyes of Haiti and of the United States upon you, do you promise that if elected President of Haiti you will, in your official acts, be guided solely by earnest devotion to Haiti's honor and welfare?"

"I will so promise," replied Dartiguenave. "I have no other ambition than to be of service to my country."

"I promise," exclaimed Dr. Bobo, rather theatrically. "I would be happy to lay down my life for my beloved country."

"Senator Dartiguenave, in case Dr. Bobo should be elected, will you promise that you will exert every influence in your power to assist him for Haiti's good; that you will join with him heartily and helpfully and loyally?"

"If Dr. Bobo is elected President, I will give him the most loyal, earnest suport in every effort he may make for Haiti's welfare," replied Dartiguenave, with simple dignity.

25

"Dr. Bobo, if Senator Dartiguenave is elected President, will you help him loyally and earnestly in his efforts to benefit Haiti?"

"No, I will not!" shouted Bobo. "If Senator Dartiguenave is elected President I will not help him. I will go away and leave Haiti to her fate. I alone am fit to be President of Haiti; I alone understand Haiti's aspirations, no one is fit to be President but me; there is no patriotism in Haiti to be compared with mine; the Haitians love no one as they love me."[38]

On August 12, Dartiguenave was elected to the presidency by the National Assembly, and then the United States proceeded to make a treaty with Haiti based upon Theodore Roosevelt's corollary to the Monroe Doctrine: "International police power applied to Latin-American countries guilty of flagrant cases of chronic wrongdoing or an impotence which results in a general loosening of the ties of civilized society."[39] Under heavy pressure from Lansing, Dartiguenave signed the treaty on September 16, 1915; the National Assembly, equally reluctant, approved it in the face of American seizure of the Haitian cus-tom-house and revenues, and the United States Senate approved the treaty in May, 1916, but by executive agreement the terms of the treaty had been put in ef-fect on the preceding November 29.[40]

The treaty of 1915 was more forceful in placing Haiti under American control than the Platt Amendment with Cuba had been, or the treaty of 1907 with the Domini-can Republic, in regard to those nations. Perhaps the State Department felt that it had been too lenient in dealing with the internal affairs of Cuba and the Dominican Republic. In any case, this treaty stated --and Haiti agreed completely to its terms under the administration of Dartiguenave--that Haiti must not alienate its territory to any foreign power or place its sovereignty under the control of any foreign power; its national debt could not be increased with-out the approval of the United States; all Haitian debts were to be tabulated and classified, and paid from funds made available by the general receiver; that this general receiver was to be nominated by the United States before appointment by the President of Haiti; and that certain officials of the Haitian government were to be appointed only after due nomina-tion by the President of the United States, such as

26

engineers of public construction and sanitation, financial advisers, officers of the newly established native constabulary, and so on. The general receiver, now at the very center of American reform policies, was to apply all his collections of revenues to the expenses of his office and that of the financial adviser first, then to the "interest and sinking fund of the public debt," and third, "to the maintenance of the Haitian constabulary," the balance "to go to the Haitian government for current expenses." Expenses of the receiver general and the financial adviser, be it noted, were not to exceed 5% of the customs revenue, unless by agreement of the Haitian Government and that of the United States. Article XIII together with Article I indicated that the United States was to aid the Haitian Government not only in clarifying its finances but also in undertaking engineering projects which would be necessary for the sanitation and public improvement of the Republic.

The treaty, finally, was to exist for ten years, but could be extended ten more, which it was, so that the effective date of the expiration of the treaty was 1936.[41]

Results of American Intervention until the year of the Haitian Commission of 1930 are not included within the scope of this chapter. The details of these years are adequately treated in Millspaugh and the Reports of the High Commissioner.[42] A few pertinent points are necessary, however, for an understanding of the reasons for the agitation which occurred in 1929-1930.

In 1918, a new Constitution went into effect. This Constitution was approved by a plebiscite on June 12, 1918, which was highly influenced by the gendarmerie. The gendarmerie of the government urged the voters to approve the Constitution, took charge of balloting, and, while ensuring the honesty of the voting, virtually predetermined the result by its mere presence if nothing else.

Among the many changes, administratively, which the new Constitution set up, the most important for the purposes of this book are the following: a legislature was to be established which would be elected by popular vote and which would in turn elect the President; but this legislature was to be elected

27

only on the call of the President of the Republic.
Nor could the "call" come at any time; it could only
come on the 10th of January of an even-numbered year,
which year was to be fixed by the sole discretion of
the President. In the meantime, all legislative power
was to be exercised by the Council of State, a body
of 21 citizens selected by the President, himself,
kept filled by the President, and which would have
the power to select the President of the Republic on
the expiration of his term of office, which was four
years. This meant, in brief, that the government of
the nation lay in the hands of the Council of State
and the President of the Republic, each of which
selected the other, and that so long as the system
remained in effect, a legislative assembly, popularly
elected, might never meet. The purpose, obviously,
was to give the Haitian and American Governments time
to educate and prepare the people for self-government
in the light of Anglo-Saxon democratic traditions.[43]

Unfortunately, from the first, dissension arose.
The *élite* and many members of the so-called lower
classes strenuously objected. Foreign Minister Borno
was selected for the presidency in 1922, and again
in 1926. Though he apparently seemed to work for the
betterment of the nation, he approached the 1930 elections thoroughly unpopular and thoroughly opposed by
the many parties which had arisen throughout Haiti
and the major cities.

Adding to Borno's unpopularity was the appointment by Harding of John Russell to the newly created
post of High Commissioner. The purpose of creating
this post was to unify under one direction the entire
American governmental personnel in Haiti, with the
further object of placing all American officials in
Haiti under the State Department in Washington. His
functions were many, but generally they may be summed
up in the suggestion that he give direction and guidance to the Haitian Government. He was to be something of a "big brother" to the Haitians, but with
the "big stick" ever present, should it be needed,
of the American marines and the American officered
Garde. He was to investigate, report, and supervise
the work of the treaty officials. In the words of
President Harding, he was ambassador extraordinary
"to represent the President of the United States in
Haiti for the purpose of investigating, reporting upon and supervising the performance of their duties

by the treaty officials in order that the purpose of said treaty may be fully accomplished." Unfortunately, Haitians regarded Borno and Russell as exercising what may loosely be called a "joint dictatorship," making Borno all the more unpopular as representing the elements that would turn Haiti, for all its faults --and many Haitians recognized its faults--over to the interests of a foreign power.

To credit the opposition parties with doctrines would be as much a delusion as to declare they had none. Yet, the truth is that the real difference between the Administration and the Opposition was that the Administration was "in" and the Opposition "out." The *"Outs"* could bear their lot so long as they felt that Borno would call for legislative elections in 1930, which he declared he would not do. During his last administration, 1926-1930, the presidential term had been changed by the Council of State to six years. This meant that if the Council elected Borno to the presidency again, he would hold office from 1930 through 1936, the date of the expiration of the American Intervention Treaty. Borno wanted the Americans to remain since his unpopularity would have ushered him out of office some time ago had not American marines kept him there. He knew, so reasoned the Opposition, that American Marines had to be kept in Haiti if he were to remain in the driver's seat, which meant that when the treaty expired in 1936, as President of the Republic, he would negotiate another for perhaps an additional thirty or forty years.

A students' strike broke out on October 31, 1929, at the Central School of Agriculture. Mobs arose in Cap-Haitien and Port-au-Prince. At Cayes, a strike occurred among the school children. Martial law was proclaimed on December 4, 1929, but the worst disturbance was yet to come. At the aforementioned Cayes, a mob of 1500 advanced toward the town, where they were confronted by a line of marines. When the peasant leaders demanded the release of three prisoners, the marines refused. The peasants closed in upon the troops. At first the men fired over the heads of the mob. Their second volley killed ten and wounded twenty-four others.[44]

The country now threatened upheaval. The Opposition knew that unless 1930 saw national legislative elections, Borno might remain in power with American aid indefinitely. This was their time for action. In

The Hoover Commissions to Haiti

the light of this background, President Hoover decided to send a special investigative commission to Haiti to report on conditions and make recommendations for future action by the United States Government.

Many good things may be said for the Occupation; it established a program that included construction of highways, the building of agricultural and technical schools, the honest administrations of revenues, the substitution of a well-trained and equipped gendarmerie for the ill-clad, ill-fed mob that hitherto represented the Haitian Army, the institution of a health program that went far toward eradicating the centuries old diseases of the people, and the establishment of efficient government. The fatal flaw, as Forbes was to discover, was that none of these things were done at the behest of, by, and through the Haitian people themselves. The value that came to Haiti came not by the sweat of the Haitians themselves, not by the self-sacrifice and energy of the Haitian mass, but by the gift of a very rich uncle. We failed in Haiti because we did nothing more than substitute efficient rulers for the old, inefficient ones--and the old, inefficient ones were anxious under the guise of liberty to get back into control again. We failed in Haiti because we tried to impress our concepts of democracy upon a people in whom the old forces were still alive and ably at work.

What made Haiti so important in 1930 was that the problem that beset Haiti and Forbes at that time is ever more alive with us today in the 1980's. How do we get a nation to gear itself for struggle, to gather its resources and its energies, and to lift itself *by its own resources* into a 20th century of civil liberty and economic prosperity?

NOTES

Since complete citations are given in the bibliography, the author employs short form footnoting in all chapters.

1. Comparatively little has been written in English about Haitian history. Those works by English-speaking authors dealing generally with Haitian history from its beginnings to 1915, which are particularly useful, are, as follows:

Brenda Gayle Plummer, *Black and White in the Caribbean: Haitian-American Relations, 1902-1934*, a 1981 unpublished doctoral dissertation at Cornell University.

H.P. Davis, *Black Democracy; the story of Haiti;* Hubert Herring.

A History of Latin America; James G. Leyburn, *The Haitian People;* Arthur C. Millspaugh, *Haiti Under American Control, 1915-1930,* chapter one, in particular; Ludwell Lee Montague, *Haiti and the United States, 1714-1938;* Mary Wilhelmine Williams, *The People and Politics of Latin America;* Rayford W. Logan, *The Diplomatic Relations of the United States with Haiti.* Of these, the Davis, Leyburn, and Logan volumes are especially clear in their presentations.

French-speaking historians whom the reader may wish to consult are Dantès Béllègarde, *La nation haitienne* and *Haiti and its People;* Abel Nicholas Leger, *Histoire diplomatique d'Haiti* Jacques Nicholas Léger, *Haiti: Her History and Her Detractors;* Thomas Madiou, *Histoire d'Haiti;* Louis Élie Moreau de Saint-Méry, *Description topographique, physique, civile, politique et historique de la partie francaise de l'ile Saint-Domingue* (probably the best source-book for the period before the revolution); J.C. Dorsainvil, *Manuel d'historie d'Haiti;* R. Lepelletier de Saint-Rémy, *Saint-Domingue: Etude et solution nouvelle de la question haitienne.*

2.   Herbert M. Krieger, "The Aborigines of the Ancient Island of Hispaniola," *Annual Report of the Smithsonian Institution for 1929* (Washington: Smithsonian Institute, 1929), p. 478. Krieger claims that only six or seven hundred were living by 1533.

3.   See Las Casas' *Very Brief Recital of the Destruction of the Indies,* which, though perhaps questionable in its statistics, is substantially correct with regard to the sufferings endured by the native inhabitants.

4.   Montague, *Haiti and the United States,* p. 5.

5.   Leyburn, Chapters One and Two.

6.   See particularly Art. 59, *Code Noir.*

7.   Unfortunately there was a divergence between the liberal provisions of the Code and practice. Under Louis XV not only were the provisions not generally enforced, but discriminatory laws were passed.

8.   Moreau de Saint-Méry, Vol. I, p. 285. One should note the specific meanings of the following: (1) *mulatto:* those Haitians with some element of white blood. Although the mulatto is supposed to be half Negro, half white, the quadroon a quarter Negro and three quarters white, and so on, the term mulatto was generally applied to anyone with some portion of his blood white, especially if his skin were light. (2) *affranchi:* those Haitians,

31

both mulatto and Negro who had been freed in colonial days, were educated, owned slaves, and for the most part aped French manners and customs. (3) *élite*: the general term for the Haitian aristocracy; elusive in any specific meaning, it came to signify all Haitians who could trace their ancestry back to freedom in colonial times, were educated, wealthy, spoke French rather than Creole, and followed gentle pursuits such as law, commerce, landholding. Although the *élite* includes pure Negroes, they are relatively few in number since the constant pressure of the *affranchi* was to marry the light-skinned. The *affranchi* woman had a horror of having a child darker than herself, with the result that the *élite* has had a tendency to become lighter-skinned over the course of Haitian history. Writers on Haitian history are likely to use the terms *mulatto, affranchi, élite* interchangeably, although, as indicated, differences do exist.

9.   Leyburn, pp. 20-21.

10.   Davis, Chapter Three, *passim.*

11.   As Madiou has pointed out, the mulatto was in a very real sense lost. He could not enter the white man's world, and he dared not the Negro's. He travelled between two worlds, was a member of neither, and to a great extent was a man without a country. Behind his mind may be the strange suspicion that like the white man, he is not really an Haitian at all. But where could he go? In what nation would he be accepted? The white nations would treat him as an inferior, and he preferred not to merge with the black. France? Here he would be welcome as a Frenchman, no better, no worse, and he would lose his privileged status. So he remains Haitian.

12.   Toussaint was born a slave at Breda near Cap-Francaise approximately 1746. Despite his condition of servitude, somehow he learned how to read and write, and displayed such abilities of leadership that his master made him superintendent of the other Negroes on the plantation. During the revolt of 1791, he joined the leaders of the Negroes, Jean-Francois, Biassou, Boukmann, and Jean Jannot as a physician to the troops, but only after he first aided his master to escape the general massacre of the whites. Jean-Francois arrested him for partiality to the whites, but he was liberated by Biassou. On the death of Louis XVI, many of the leading blacks, including Toussaint, joined the Spaniards, who had invaded Saint-Domingue, and here Toussaint gained the military reputation that lifted him to the command of four thousand black troops. Upon the liberation of the slaves by the Republican government at Paris, Toussaint deserted to the French with all his troops, turned on the Spaniards and the English who had invaded Saint-Domingue, and drove

both of them out. By 1796, he was generally considered by whites, blacks, and mulattoes the only man to restore order in the colony. Only the mulatto chieftain Rigaud still questioned him, and in civil war Toussaint emerged the victor. From 1799 until 1802, Toussaint set his hand to rebuilding the colony, with himself acting as governor-general. However, Napoleon's determination to bring Saint-Domingue into closer relationship with France frightened the blacks into fears of renewed slavery, and war broke out anew, this time war for liberation from France herself. Toussaint did not bring this struggle to completion. Invited to a dinner for the purpose of discussing Haitian affairs, apparently in complete trust of his French hosts, especially French honor, Toussaint was placed in chains and shipped to France where he quickly died of cold and starvation. The final liberation of Haiti was achieved by Toussaint's chief lieutenant, Dessalines.

See Ralph Korngold's *Citizen Toussaint* and Harriet Martineau's novel *The Hour and the Man*. The latter idealizes Toussaint and was enormously admired by Wendell Phillips.

13. So great a symbol of liberty and the unlimited possibilities of Man did he become that Wordsworth wrote on his death:
"There's not a breathing of the common wind
That will forget thee; thou hast great allies;
Thy friends are exultations, agonies
And love, and man's unconquerable mind."

Leyburn comments, however, that "he had moments of inordinate vanity, and would brook no interference. His henchmen had to endure merciless tongue-lashings. His own people's freedom, about which he was publicly so solicitous, was in many respects little better than slavery." (pp. 26-27)

14. The system probably originated in the mind of Dessalines.

15. Davis, p. 56.

16. Saint-Domingue had in addition to its natural wealth, a military significance to Napoleon as a base toward building a new empire in the New World, i.e. Louisiana.

17. See generally T.G. Steward, *The Haitian Revolution, 1791-1804*.

18. The long supple branches of certain indigenous vines were no less vicious, but in the mind of Dessalines at least the symbolism had been erased.

19. Toussaint's constitution declared the Roman Catholic religion the only publicly professed faith in Haiti, but Dessalines' of 1805 refused to admit a dominant religion.

20. Two excellent studies by Duracine Vaval are "Alexandre Pétion: 1'homme et sa vie," *Révue de la Société d'Historie et de Géographie d'Haiti*, Vol. III, No. 7 (July, 1932) and "Le Roi d'Haiti Henri Christophe," in the same journal, Vol. II, No. 3 (June, 1931).

21. Selden Rodman, *Haiti: The Black Republic*, p. 17.

22. These were Africans imported by Christophe from Dahomey as a special bodybuard and police force. During the latter part of his reign when, like Dessalines, his benevolence had evaporated in the heat of his egomania, Christophe tried to impress several foreign dignitaries with the loyalty of these Dahomets by ordering a platoon of them to march off the parapet of the Citadelle.

23. Of the four great blacks—Toussaint, Dessalines, Christophe, Pétion—Pétion was perhaps in a sense the greatest, and in another sense the weakest. His greatness lay in his military genius and the purity of his ideals; his weakness, in a readiness to bestow the gift of genuine democracy upon a people utterly unprepared either by tradition or education to receive it. As Dessalines and Christophe moved too slowly in the direction of liberalism, Pétion went too fast.

24. Leyburn admires Pétion, but states that "his country was rich when he came to power and poor when he died; united in 1806 and divided in 1818. Candor compels his admirers to admit that many of the calamities of the social and economic history of Haiti can be traced back to Pétion's administration." This would appear to be an oversimplification of the problem. That the country was united in 1806 and that Christophe had a full treasury does not prove the validity of the Dessalines–Christophe system. Christophe was as much responsible for the division of the nation as Pétion, while the question regarding the treasury is not so much whether it was empty or full as how evenly was the wealth distributed throughout the population.

25. Rodman, p. 19.

26. See the report of Samuel Hazard, a correspondent of the *New York Herald*, who visited Haiti in the middle of the 19th century. He speaks of a period a generation after Boyer, but his comments are still applicable.

27. Montague, pp. 18–19.

28. John Candler, *Brief Notices of Hayti*, p. 91.

29. Sir Spencer St. John, *Haiti, or the Black Republic*, p. 121.

30. The Haitian woman has been the heart and soul of labor in Haiti. The mulatto despised manual labor because of its connection with slavery and the African homeland; the Negro male found it, on the other hand, almost impossible to follow for the reason that the turbulence of the times constantly demanded his presence in the army. Either he was actually in military service or he was in danger of being impressed. In desperation, the majority of able-bodied young men hid in the hills while their women tilled the fields and brought the produce to market.

31. General John H. Russell, *Report of the American High Commissioner for 1925*, p. 4. Millspaugh answers this comment indirectly: "(W)hether such generalizations were or were not helpful it is true that Haitians in the mass had not yet advanced far enough in understanding to identify their personal interests with good or bad government; and their relative number suggested that some change must be wrought in them. Their wants were mainly for the bare necessities of tropical and primitive existence —a thatch-roofed hut, a modicum of clothes, food naturally grown and easily obtained, crude and sensual social life, and sexual satisfaction. To an American they appeared indolent, shiftless and poverty-stricken. Actually, they were for the most part care-free and contented, and possessed nearly everything in life that they had learned to want. To transform a person of this type into a functioning democratic citizen would apparently necessitate his learning to want certain things that he had not hitherto wanted—among them good government—and to be able to discriminate between good and bad government, as well as between good and bad leadership." Millspaugh's comment appears much sounder. *Haiti Under American Control*, pp. 137-138.

32. Wallace Thompson, "Climactic Influences in the Caribbean," *Current History*, Vol. XXXI (February, 1930), pp. 915-918.

33. See Dr. Camille L'Hérisson, "Diseases of the Peasants of Haiti," *American Journal of Public Health*, Vol. XXV, No. 8, (August, 1935). Very useful is Dr. Robert P. Parsons' *History of Haitian Medicine*.

Hookworm, malaria, yaws, cardiac and pulmonary infection, venereal disease, dysentery, cancer were so prevalent during the period before the American Occupation as to be accepted by the people as part of the normal processes of living. Forbes' Commission found that the health service of the Occupation was the only element appreciated generally by the people.

34. A legend exists to the effect that when Napoleon once asked what the geography of Haiti was like, one of his officers crumpled a piece of paper and threw it on a table before him.

35. Haiti has the highest density of population in the Western Hemisphere. Of twenty-two Western Hemispheric nations, Haiti is the twenty-first in size (only El Salvador is smaller), yet she must support a population of several millions. In the 1930's she had a population of approximately three million living in a mountainous country of 10,204 square miles (density 294.9), while the United States had 132 million people living in a relatively fertile area of 3,025,701 square miles (density 43.5). Twenty to thirty years later, the problem had grown worse for Haiti. According to the United Nations Statistical Yearbook for 1958 (based on a 1950 census), Haiti had a density of 319 persons to the square mile, compared to that of 57 for the United States. Each year, as the soil of the valleys becomes exhausted and the population increases, Haiti draws closer to disaster socially and economically.

36. Leyburn, p. 239.

37. U.S., Congress, Senate, *Inquiry into Occupation and Administration of Haiti and Santo Domingo.* Hearings before a Select Committee on Haiti and Santo Domingo, 67th Cong., 1st Sess., pursuant to Senate Res. 112, p. 1277. Hereafter referred to as *Hearings.*

38. *Hearings,* p. 316.

39. See generally Henry Fowler Pringle, *Theodore Roosevelt.*

40. Discussions of events leading up to the treaty and the treaty itself are to be found in Davis, pp. 149–188; J.A.H. Hopkins and Melinda Alexander, *Machine Gun Diplomacy,* pp. 71–94; Millspaugh, *Haiti under American Control,* Chapter 2.

41. One may soundly question whether Haitians or Americans at the time of the making of the treaty actually expected American troops to be out of Haiti by 1936. The expectation was more likely that the Occupation would extend indefinitely. The ten-year element was a sop to Haitian pride, perhaps making the Occupation more palatable.

42. Millspaugh, pp. 64–167; Russell, *Reports of the American High Commissioner,* 1923–1929.

43. For the text of the constitution, see *Hearings,* pp. 1551–1562.

44. *New York Times*, Dec. 8, 1929; *Report of the American High Commissioner* for 1929.

The Hoover Commissions to Haiti

Chapter 2

Drafting of the
Forbes Commission

In his message of December 3, 1929, President Hoover voiced his concern over conditions in Haiti and his fears for the future of the American Occupation.[1] Four days later he asked Congress for approval of a "commission to Haiti to review and study the matter in an endeavor to arrive at some more definite policy than at present...Our representatives in Haiti have shown great ability and devotion, and have accomplished signal results in improvement of the material condition of that people. Yet our experience has revealed more clearly than was seen at first the difficulties of the problem, and the entire situation should be reviewed in the light of this experience." He asked that the commission be constituted without delay and with an appropriation of $50,000 for expenses.[2]

The dislike of the Haitian ruling classes for the American Occupation was not without sympathy in the United States. The Congressional debates indicated the spirit with which many Americans regarded our interference in Haitian affairs and in Caribbean politics in general. Even accepting Wilson's viewpoint that intervention was necessary in Haiti in 1915 to prevent German infiltration during the First World War, the dangers of that conflict were now gone, and many Americans were of the opinion that we no longer belonged in a foreign land. Harding himself in 1920, expressed the Republican attitude when in campaigning for the presidency he referred to the Constitution of 1918 as a document "jammed down their throats at the points of bayonets."[3] The Caco War of 1919-1920, in which American marines stamped out the Caco insurrection of Charlemagne Peralte, evoked the feeling that we were stamping out human liberties. "In spite of the intentions and verbal assurances of Americans, the course of events to 1921 was such as to strengthen the suspi-

cion that their real purpose was to destroy Haitian
independence and exploit Haitian resources for their
own benefit."[4] In 1920 the Navy Department itself
made several investigations, such as those of Rear
Admiral Harry S. Knapp, Generals George Barnett and
John A. Lejeune of the Marine Corps, and Assistant
Secretary of the Navy Franklin D. Roosevelt, and
went so far as to set up a court of inquiry under
Admiral Henry T. Mayo to investigate complaints of
Haitians against arbitrary actions of individual
marine officers. Although the court vindicated the
accused, smoke of suspicion lingered heavily in the
air. Dr. Carl Kelsey's study, *The American Interven--
tion in Haiti and the Dominican Republic*, done at the
request of the Latin-American Division of the State
Department, was a defense of the Occupation and American policy; but this did not prevent repeated attacks
in Congress, the liberal American press (particularly
The Nation and publications of the National Association for the Advancement of Colored People), and
private writings. In 1921, twenty-four American lawyers submitted a report to the State Department entitled "The Seizure of Haiti by the United States,"
in which they condemned the Occupation, its ultimate
effect upon the intrinsic concepts of democracy,
and urged strongly its being brought to a speedy
conclusion.[5]

The most significant wave of criticism came
with the McCormick Committee in the Fall of 1921.
After extended hearings which attempted to pierce
the soundness of the Intervention, the achievement
to date, and the prospects for the future, the Committee finally decided, as had Kelsey, that on the
whole the Occupation was worthwhile. It did feel
that mistakes had been made in the actual handling
of individual phases of the Occupation, but it did
not disagree at all with the Occupation in principle.[6]

The attacks, however, did not cease; rather
they increased. Private travelers such as the Women's
International League for Peace and Freedom (consist-
ing of a travelling committee of five women and one
male college professor), Blair Niles (Mrs. Robert
Niles, Jr.), and the team of J.A.H. Hopkins and
Melinda Alexander helped keep the embers glowing.
In April, 1922, the National Popular Government
League handed Secretary of State Charles Evans Hughes
an address indorsing the anti-Occupation views of

twenty-four lawyers who represented the Foreign Policy Association. Senators Norris, King, and Borah
attacked the Government's Haitian policy in June,
1922, during a discussion of Senator King's appropriation bill amendment which provided that no part
of appropriations be used to support marines in
Hispaniola. The railroad concession controlled by
the National City Bank of New York, the Rodenberg
option, American agricultural concessions in Haiti,
the revival of the *corvée* system by which peasants
were forced into road-building for specified times,
were attacked as examples of flagrant American imperialism. The feeling was voiced that the United
States had drifted from its original purpose and
had entered upon another that was harsh and blind.

Hoover, however, was a man of strong convictions. He could never have been swayed from the current policy in Haiti had he been convinced of its
soundness. Other considerations certainly filled
his mind. First, our efforts in the Dominican Republic, Cuba, Panama, Nicaragua, and the Philippines
had placed an enormous strain upon the American taxpayer with no visible benefits to either taxpayer
or nation. Second, the Depression which had just
set in during the Fall of 1929 did not endear expen-
sive occupations or overseas adventures to an already
economically disturbed people. Third, our protectorates were neither appreciated by the peoples protected nor productive of lasting results--at least the
sort of results envisioned by the Roosevelt-Wilson
ideal. No sooner had Washington withdrawn the marines
from Nicaragua in 1925 than the Liberal and Conservative parties of that small nation were at each
other's throats, and in 1927 American forces again
were sent to restore order and supervise an honest
presidential election. In the meantime, Americans
were being killed fighting the guerrilla general
Augusto Cesar Sandino while Nicaraguans and Latin
Americans generally applauded each clever escape
of the fugitive leader. Cuba showed no signs of ability to maintain internal order despite our repeated
interventions under the Platt Amendment; Panama had
not profited by American tutelage; and the turmoil
in the Dominican Republic since our naval forces
departed in 1924 indicated that political habits
in that portion of Hispaniola had undergone no radical change. Indeed, the only apparent result of our
interventions seemed to be that we had earned among

41

Latin American nations a reputation for imperialism.

Fourth, the great powers were meeting in London to discuss disarmament. At the same time, the Philippines clamored for independence. Once the Philippines became independent and the United States no longer bound to defend them, the British feared that the less friendly Japanese fleet might likely enter southeast Asian waters, too close to British possessions. If such were the case, then Britain could no longer adhere to the Washington Conference ratio of 5-5-3 for Britain, the United States, and Japan respectively. Considering that Britain would then be forced to split her navy three ways to protect possessions in three oceans, the existing ratio could only give her a Pacific fleet inferior to that of the Rising Sun. Were the United States to follow a policy of withdrawal from lands which could never possibly become integral states of the Union, then the Philippines would be as much a part of this policy as the Caribbean, and for the above-mentioned reasons Britain was vitally concerned. Britain pressed Secretary of State Stimson for information, and Stimson, Hoover. A report was essential in regard to Haiti so that policies evolved there might be applied to the Philippines as well.[7]

Fifth, Hoover himself may be included in the critics of the Occupation for larger reasons. Our war with Mexico in 1846-48, our action in slicing Panama from Colombia in 1903 (despite our belated atonement to Colombia by a twenty-five million dollar payment in the Treaty of 1921), our "dollar diplomacy" in the Caribbean, our refusal to follow the decisions of the Central American Court which we ourselves had set up to arbitrate controversies in that area, together with rising tides of both leftist and rightist extremes south of the Rio Grande, convinced Hoover that, "unless we displayed an entirely different attitude, we should never dispel the suspicions and fears of the 'colossus of the North' nor win the respect of those nations."[8] During the few months intervening between his election to the Presidency and the taking of office, Hoover made a trip to Latin-America, covering Honduras, Salvador, Nicaragua, Costa Rica, Ecuador, Peru, Chile, Argentina, Uruguay, and Brazil. He was particularly upset by the turmoil in Nicaragua, which American troops there could only allay but not solve. Signifi-

cant is the following passage from the fourteen addresses he made on that trip:

> I come to pay a call of friendship. In a sense I represent
> on this occasion the people of the United States extending
> a friendly greeting to our fellow democracies on the
> American continent. I would wish to symbolize the friendly
> visit of one *good neighbor* to another. In our daily life,
> good neighbors call upon each other as the evidence of
> solicitude for the common welfare and to learn of the
> circumstances and point of view of each, so that there
> may come both understanding and respect which are the
> cementing forces of all enduring society. This should
> be equally true amongst nations. We have a desire to main-
> tain not only the cordial relations of governments with
> each other but the relations of *good neighbors*.

> I have come on a visit as a neighbor. I have thought that
> perhaps I might symbolize the goodwill which I know my
> country holds toward your own. My hope and my purpose
> and my aspiration are that better acquaintance, larger
> knowledge of our sister republics of Latin America, and
> the personal contact of government may enable me to better
> execute the task which lies before me. [9]

In his address of April 13, 1929, he said:

> ....it ought not to be the policy of the United States
> to intervene *by force* to secure or maintain contracts
> between our citizens and foreign states or their citizens.
> Confidence in that attitude is the only basis upon which
> the economic cooperation of our citizens can be welcomed
> abroad. It is the only basis that prevents cupidity en-
> croaching upon the weakness of nations—but, far more
> than this, it is the true expression of the moral recti-
> tude of the United States. [10]

In his Memoirs, he further states:

> ....To give proof of my determination to end force inter-
> ventions....I requested authority from the Congress for
> an official commission to examine the situation in Haiti
> and advise when and how we were to withdraw—in effect,
> how to extricate ourselves from the mess into which we
> had been plunged by the Wilson administration. [11]

Two questions arise at this point: One, did
Wilson intervene in Haiti primarily to preserve the
private interests of private American citizens in

that troubled country, or were his purposes more
wrapped up in the sincere desire to instruct Haitians
in the methods of democracy, insure stability in
a country not far from the American coast, and prevent the infiltration of Germans who represented
to Wilson the direct antithesis of everything democratic? Two, if Hoover had already made up his mind
that we should withdraw, why did he bother to send
a commission to Haiti? The answers lie in Hoover's
uncertainty. Before he would withdraw the Occupation,
he had to be advised by someone whom he absolutely
trusted and in whom he had deep confidence that
Wilson's policy had been wrong to begin with, that
little had been achieved, that withdrawal was a wise
American procedure, and that the precedent set by
withdrawal would in the long run be of benefit to
the American people. Only a commission could serve
these purposes.

During his administration, Hoover's use of the
commission was the subject of many jibes. In reality
Hoover created fewer commissions than any of the
presidents since 1900. Theodore Roosevelt's administration was responsible for 107, Taft's for 63,
Wilson's for 150, Harding's for 44, Coolidge's for
118, and Hoover's for 42. Of these, 22 were set up
by Congress, 20 by the President.[12]

In a talk at Johns Hopkins in 1920, Hoover divided public questions into two classes: (a) those
in which one has "sufficient facts, figures, and
common experience to give certain indication of the
course of constructive action"; (b) those which are
so complex, which arise out of so many political,
social, economic factors, and are influenced by as
many more, that any solution is not really a solution
but rather an exercise in "pure judgment guided by
adherence to national ideals." David Hinshaw states
that Hoover felt the most dangerous animal in the
country to be the man filled with the emotion and
desire to pass a new law. "He is prolific with drama
and the headlines. His is not the road to the fundamental advance of liberty and the progress of the
American people at this time in our history."[13]

Hoover used the commission system because he
thought it to be the surest means of obtaining facts
about a situation and reaching a reasonable judgment
on the basis of those facts. The appointment of a

commission to Haiti was the thirteenth commission appointed thus far in Hoover's administration. Previously he had appointed the Federal Farm Board, and then commissions to investigate crime and law enforcement, child welfare, the reduction of expenditures in military establishments, Southern patronage, waterway development in California, the construction of a bridge across San Francisco Bay, fixing the boundary of the Yellowstone National Park, conservation of the public domain, a commission to represent the United States at the Althing celebration in Iceland, one to report on national illiteracy, and the last to make a survey of national trends.[14]

In the House the question of Hoover's Commission was debated primarily by G. Huddleston (Ala.), C.L. Beedy (Me.), J.W. Palmer (Mo.), A.H. Greenwood (Ind.), S.S. Arentz (Nev.), H.W. Temple (Pa.), F.G. Johnson (Neb.), M.R. Wood (Ind.), J.C. Lithicum (Md.), O. DePriest (Ill.), R.W. Moore (Va.), R. Crosser (Ohio), H.M. Fish, Jr. (N.Y.), and M.D. Hull (Ill.). In the Senate, the chief debaters were C.A. Swanson (Va.), J.J. Blaine (Wisc.), G.W. Norris (Neb.), T.L. Oddie (Nev.), and S.D. Fess (Ohio).[15]

The discussions went smoothly enough for the most part in both House and Senate. One or two points of controversy, however, strike our interest. Several members in the House wanted a bi-partisan commission because they felt that this type was more likely to give an unprejudiced report. Crosser replied that bi-partisanship alone would not ensure an impartial report. He wanted men of proven democratic leaning. "If the Commission to be appointed by the President consists only of members who believe in the benevolent despotism doctrine or, in other words, of members who always assume that other people are not capable of governing themselves, then we can be sure that the Commission will come back and report that we should continue to govern the Republic of Haiti." Hull asked Crosser whether he wanted "a commission prejudiced in advance? Crosser answered no, "but I do not want them prejudiced against the principle of fundamental democracy. I would like to see appointed members with clear convictions as to the justice of democratic principles, but that does not mean they would be prejudiced in regard to the evidence which might be presented to them. It is easy to ascertain whether or not a man believes in democracy or believes in autocracy."[16]

Hull suggested that the Commission consist of six men, three who believed in democracy for Haitians, three who did not subscribe to this doctrine. But Crosser objected. Hull then suggested that men be chosen without preconceived opinions. Crosser replied that men who have not very clearcut, definite views in regard to the justice and wisdom of the principles of government by consent of the governed--that is, of democracy--would not be very well qualified to investigate the wisdom or propriety of the occupation of Haiti by the United States.

Fish held that the members should speak French and that at least two of the members should be colored citizens. DePriest supported this suggestion. He compared self-determination in Haiti to that of the Negroes in the United States, remarking that he had received hundreds of telegrams asking that American Negroes be sent on the Commission. The trouble was that the Haitians themselves objected to having American Negroes on the Commission. "It was explained," said the *New York Times*, "to this government that the Haitians observed a lack of sympathy on the part of Americans of their race and could not, therefore, welcome such a commission if one had been named."[17]

Huddleston finally arose in complete objection to the Commission, stating that anything the Commission was to discover was already well-known to the Congress and to the American people. For him the Occupation had been a mistake, and it had been prosecuted not for the benefit of the Haitian nation or the much-flaunted "political tutelage" principle, but for the sheer satisfaction of the greed of American businessmen. The indictment was severe: (1) Americans bought up the Haitian national debt at great discount and then refunded and increased it to forty million dollars, all now owned by the National City Bank of New York. (2) Americans cheaply purchased bonds of the national railroad and paid the two million dollars in interest out of funds of the people of Haiti. Americans now had two million dollars and a bond issue of three and one-half millions on a railroad that earned seventy-five thou-

sand dollars per year. The Fall transaction in Teapot
Dome, said Huddleston, was honest compared to this.
(3) Americans owned the best harbor in Haiti. (4)
Foreign ownership of land was permitted for the first
time in the Constitution of 1918, and Americans now
owned some of the most fertile land in the country.
(5) American businesses profited enormously in Haiti
from the abundance of cheap labor ($.20 per day).

He went on to state that he found incongruity
in the demand of these very members of Congress that
American Negroes in the South be permitted to vote
but denied in the same breath the right of Haitian
Negroes to run their own country.

For Huddleston, the history of Haiti was known,
other investigations had taken place, any textbook
would give more information on the country than a
commission could discover, the Department of State
had been in close contact with Haitian life and politics anyway, and furthermore, he felt the Occupation
had been begun by Executive action and should be
settled by Executive action. His address approached
the ludicrous as he described a dignified Commission
in top hats and tails prowling about mountains and
valleys for a few days, peering into family huts
and rural pots, and then finally sitting down to
write a report which was to enlighten the world.
Huddleston did not think any commission ever really
did any good or accomplished anything. The average
man in Washington, in his opinion, would know more
than the Commission could discover. "I know what
they are going to report," he said. "You could write
the report in advance. We *had* a Senate investigation
in Haiti. The report was a partisan report. I do
not mean partisan according to political parties
but according to the habit and thought and reaction
toward the situation."

On the other hand, he believed that genuine
harm might result, that the Commission could be another nail in the coffin of Haitian autonomy.

Who can tell what the end will be? Oh, but you say that
the Haitians are not fit to govern themselves. No! They
are not; and four hundred years from now they will not
be fit to govern themselves unless they make haste with
great speed to overtake us in the meantime.

> ....We can't live as an imperialism abroad and democracy at home, tyrant in foreign countries and free people in the United States. We cannot hold securely upon our liberties here and take them away from people that live in other parts of the world---poor or ignorant whatever they may be, the consequences will come back to us--the recoil will fall on us.[18]

Nevertheless, the House passed the resolution December 9th, 1929.

In the Senate Blaine inquired as to the period of time the Commission was to investigate. Was it going to investigate conditions prior to the time of Occupation, during the Occupation, just at the present time? If at the present time and during the Occupation, then there was an implication that Hoover's Republican predecessors in the Presidency might have been at fault.

Swanson replied that he did not know what Hoover was going to do in this respect and that the Senate had no right to direct him anyway. Foreign affairs were in his hands. "All I know is that he is the first president who has ever manifested a real desire that an investigation be undertaken to enable him to reach a conclusion as to what ought to be done." He went on to explain that Harding felt no necessity to send a commission, since the Occupation still had a long while to run, nor even Coolidge. But by Hoover's administration the evidence appeared clear that by 1936, the date at which the occupation was to end, Haitian politics were not going to have been improved very much during American control.[19]

McKellar questioned the right of the President to appoint a commission, feeling that this was purely a Congressional duty, but Borah and Smoot pointed out that historically this had always been his right. The discussion, as a matter of fact, showed, in opposition to McKellar, that it agreed with Huddleston's implication in the House that the Chief Executive had absolute right to appoint a commission, had always had that right, and did not need Congressional approval or permission. Huddleston had implied in the House that Hoover was trying to make matters appear as though the Congress were authorizing the Commission in the effort to shift responsibility for future American mistakes in Haiti from his own

48

shoulders to those of the Congress. The Senate went so far as to amend the original resolution so that in its final form the Congress did nothing more than authorize funds necessary for the operation of a commission actually appointed by the President. This was a minor point, but illustrated Senate strategy.[20]

The resolution, as amended, passed the Senate February 1, 1930. The House agreed with the amendment, and the final resolution read, as follows:

> ....That there is hereby authorized to be appropriated the sum of $50,000 to cover any expenses which may be incurred by the President in making an investigation by commission or otherwise of the conditions in and a study of the policies relating to Haiti. Such expenditures may include the expenses of any commission appointed, the compensation of employees, travel, and subsistence, or per diem in lieu of subsistence, stenographers and other services by contract if deemed necessary, rent of office in the District of Columbia and elsewhere, the purchase of necessary books and documents, printing and binding, official cards, and such other expenses as the President may deem necessary.[21]

It was a rather innocuous resolution, but it threw responsibility for resultant difficulties squarely where Congress wanted it to be--on the heads of President Hoover and his Commission.

On the whole, the newspapers treated the usefulness of the Commission idea with a variety of opinion: While the *Constitution* of Atlanta, Feb. 8, called it "another step toward development of a new policy in the Caribbean," the *Salt Lake Tribune* on Feb. 28, ridiculed: "Voodoo land beckons investigators....Down to the land of mumbo-jumbo."

Hoover ultimately used two commissions: one, composed of white men, to leave at the end of February; the second, composed of colored Americans, to leave after the political upheavals had been reasonably settled. To be chairman of the first commission and to set the tone for a revision of American foreign policy toward Latin America, he selected William Cameron Forbes, whose monumental achievement had been in the Philippine Islands and whose record of amity with alien cultures had been admirable.

Forbes' life covered what many people in these later years of the 20th Century like to call the best period of American history. Born in 1870 when the last bugle sounds were closing the struggles that threatened to destroy the Union, his life witnessed the rise of the American industrial genius, the emergence of the United States as a world power, her achievement of world leadership; and it closed, as did those of Adams, Clay, Calhoun, and Webster, in times as dangerous for the continued existence of the nation as they were in the years which immediately preceded his birth. In a sense, he went full cycle. Yet he is not remembered in particular measure, either by historians or the general public. He is one of those innumerable men of American democratic life who enter public service with the best that is in them, make their contribution, and quietly pass away with little more than a brief mention of their names. They either are soon forgotten or become the tiny shadows gently flickering in and out of the lives of the well-known personages who have captured the historical stage.

Forbes was a man of energy and zeal who had an intense belief in the destiny of American democracy. The grandson of John Murray Forbes, who had made a fortune in the China trade during the days of the Clipper ships, and on his maternal side the grandson of Ralph Waldo Emerson, he carried in his heredity the shrewd business ability and incredible gift for observation of the one and the passion for learning of the other. Outspoken both publicly and privately, enormously rich, aristocratic, a lover of fine homes and the noble sport of polo, a talented writer of books on business *and* polo, he presents a complex personality which swings between the reaches of conservatism and liberalism and finally settles down at the liberal end. He was the patrician as liberal, so much so that he considered his governorship in the Philippines his greatest monument in life. Republican in his party affiliations, he was on intimate terms with Theodore Roosevelt, Taft, Coolidge, and Hoover, respected the second Roosevelt (to whom he was a distant cousin) if he did not quite always agree with him, and despised Woodrow Wilson to the very bottom of his bones. For him, Wilson was the false prophet of democracy, the blatant demagogue whose chief interest was himself and the development of an esoteric cult dedicated to an altar at which

Wilson himself presided as High Priest. Haiti, for Forbes, was just another of Wilson's terrible blunders.

Educated at the Milton Academy and the Hopkinson School, he entered Harvard University, where in addition to a self-imposed heavy program of reading and study, he developed a strong interest in class football, which was later to bear results in quite a different line.[22] Upon graduation in 1892, he entered the newly organized Stone and Webster Engineering firm, became officer and director in several Boston banks, and then, just before the turn of the century, joined the family business, J.M. Forbes and Company, Merchants, located opposite the Old State House at the head of what was once King Street.

Football first made his name known to Theodore Roosevelt. Harvard had been doing poorly in its annual games with Yale, and Forbes asked President Eliot for the chance to coach the Harvard team. His fury and vitality threatened either to break the team completely or push it to victory. In 1900, after Forbes' remarkable win over Yale, Theodore Roosevelt is recorded to have begun a speech with the words: "Ladies and Gentlemen, I believe the score was 17 to 0." In this manner was the stage set for Forbes' entrance into public life. "Wanting a change of scene and desirous of measuring myself against a major job, in 1902 I asked President Theodore Roosevelt if he could use me in connection with the building of the Panama Canal."[23] He also asked President Eliot to write a letter of recommendation, in reply to which Eliot sent the following to Roosevelt:

Dear Mr. President:

W. Cameron Forbes (Harvard A.B. 1892) is just the right sort of man for membership in the Canal Commission. His business experience has been very appropriate. Neither money nor pressure would swerve him one hair from the line of public duty; at the same time he is pleasant and serene in dealing with people. He would take any unavoidable risks for an adequate object, but his judgment is good about risk, and also about plans, measures, and men.

He comes of first rate stock and remembers it.[24]

Roosevelt liked Forbes' qualifications and would

have used him, but administrative delay prevented
Forbes' appointment to that particular commission.
Instead, Roosevelt asked him to take a place on the
Philippines Commission. When Roosevelt became President on the death of McKinley, he selected Taft,
a member of the Philippines Commission, for his Secretary of War. Luke E. Wright filled Taft's vacancy,
and Forbes was asked to fill Wright's position, that
of Secretary of Commerce and Police.

This was not what Forbes or his family had con-
templated. The government was under attack from the
anti-imperialist press, Forbes had had no experience
with colored peoples, especially those of Catholic
persuasions, and frankly, he doubted his ability
in this type of public service. He finally accepted,
but only after enduring the pangs of his own conscience, awakening the sense of duty he had particularly inherited from his mother, and listening to
the admonitions of those he respected. H.L. Higginson
wrote: "Even if you should not return, we should
mourn you, but we should be glad you had done the
right thing and we shall be very proud of you."[25]
Other forces were upon him demanding that he stay,
such as the death of his father in 1897, his grandfather, J. M. Forbes, in 1898, and his uncle, Malcolm
Forbes, in 1904, which really placed the burden of
the huge family interests upon his own shoulders.
But in the end his idealism won the struggle and
he took the job. He asked Roosevelt if he had any
instructions, and Roosevelt replied, "If I had to
give you instructions, I would not have appointed
you." The words were mildly reproachful, and Forbes
never forgot them.[26]

As Chief of Constabulary, he had charge of the
military police, six thousand men of the Post Office,
the Coast Guard numbering some twenty steamers and
launches, government business among the innumerable
islands, the light house service, all corporations,
franchises, transportation, roads, harbors, and telegraph services. So aroused over the lack of adequate
transportation within the main islands did he become,
that he entered upon a plan of highway construction
that earned him the title of "The Roadbuilder" in
the Philippines. Indefatigable, filled with the energy of youth and a rising sense of personal destiny,
he set two major tasks for himself: knowing the islands and learning the Spanish language. Within a

year's time, he is reported to have been making speeches in the native tongue of the people, and he eventually became the best-travelled American administrator in the Philippines.

Serving as Chief of Constabulary, then Vice-Governor under Smith, and later Acting Governor during the early months of 1909, in this last year Forbes finally became Governor of the Philippines under Taft, in which capacity he served until 1913, when he was summarily dismissed by Woodrow Wilson. When the latter dismissed him, he did so in a curt manner which rankled Forbes:

> Washington, August 23, 1913. Harrison confirmed August 21. The President desires him to sail September 1. Harrison to accept and take office September 2. The President desires to meet your convenience. Should Harrison take linen, silver, glass, china, and automobiles? What also would you suggest? Wife and children will accompany him. Please engage for him servants you leave.[27]

Forbes never forgave Wilson. He could not understand his being dismissed merely because a Democratic administration had come into power, and there was never any question concerning his competence or ability. Wilson never explained his behavior.[28]

Whether Forbes' dislike of Wilson influenced his work in Haiti or not cannot be determined. Probably it did not, for he was not the sort of man to permit his emotions to run away with him. But he did consider Wilson's 1915 action a blunder. The following letter to William Allen White, written after the Commission's trip to Haiti, gives a significant view of Forbes' attitude toward the man who had given assent to the Occupation:

Dear Mr. White,

> ...My grievance against Wilson is that he seemed to me to be utterly insincere, a straight out and out phrase-maker, interested in the sound of his tones, and careless with their meaning. His utterances might be said to be more or less oracular but as to his idealism, I cannot see it. He took and wrecked our whole Philippine machine, scattered the trained men to the four winds and then went and butted in on Haiti and Santo Domingo, put men to run them entirely untrained for the job of concil-

iating dependent peoples, and made the kind of mess of it which you and I have seen.

He declared for freedom of the seas. And what does freedom of the seas mean? The Germans yelled with one voice: That is what we are fighting for. Englishmen say they have no objection to freedom of the seas. The question was interpretation of what that meant. Did it mean liberty or license? Did it mean the right of pirates to ply their wares as between belligerents, blockading ports, all the rest of the things that enter into the question of freedom of the seas—all left to the imagination and in my judgment intentionally so. The phrase was pleasing to the ear of the phrase-maker and to the unthinking among the world's hearers, a group which includes a great many big-hearted women whose emotions are more powerful than their intellects. Many of this sort are to be found among our family and friends, pacifists who continue endandering the peace of the world by an effort to assure peace by unwise methods.

Self-determination of small peoples—what did that mean? It meant the North was in the wrong in the Civil War, and yet people who would rather have their tongues pulled out by the roots than admit such a thing went around hugging themselves and shrieking self-determination as if it were a panacea for all world ills. I think no phrase unthinkingly turned out by any other charlatan has made so much mischief in so short a time as that one did. And yet, when Wilson came to draw his League of Nations Covenant, as our phrase-maker termed it, self-determination was found to be twisted around into a period of tutelage for weaker peoples, they not to be consulted as to whether they are in need of help nor as to whom the tutor is to be. And so we got our mandate system, utterly in conflict with the principles enunciated by our "idealist," too proud to fight.

I think the story of our Mexican situation under Wilson almost the most shocking thing to be found in our history—General Pershing sent down into Mexico, not allowed to take possession of the two railroads that flanked him, not allowed to shoot, ordered to go in and catch Villa with his hands. I happen to know personally what Pershing thought of it, and he is an able and practical man. The petulant taking of Vera Cruz, with the silly statement given out that he proposed to settle the land problem in Mexico at that time, was another asinine performance of our "idealist." The ostensible object was to

54

obtain a salute for the Flag, which he did not get.

Go right through Wilson's record and you will find first one and then another of these rhetorical outbursts, each one entirely at variance with some practical course of conduct later. I haven't heard of a single case in which he did a decent thing by one of the dollar-a-year men who served him during the War. The unanimous feeling of those I have talked with--and I haven't gone out of my way to talk to any of them--was that Wilson was person- ally a skunk. I remember Mrs. Douglas Robinson telling me of her brother rapping the table on one occasion and in a loud voice informing the whole group sitting around that his sister had told him he mustn't call the President a white-livered skunk.

There are many things in the administration of Wilson of which I approved. His selection of men to run the World War was pretty good, apart from the Secretaries of War and Navy, the first of whom knew enough to keep his hands off and the second of whom was a buffoon. But Pershing, Hoover and Davison were ten-strikes. I entirely approve of his not letting Roosevelt go to the other side to fight. Roosevelt wasn't a trained soldier and Wilson had plenty of trained soldiers to send. Roosevelt ought to have known enough to realize that it was a young man's job and a trained man's job and no place for an elderly politician. I can't believe but that Roosevelt did know it and tried to get the job, not for political glory, but with some ulterior object, such as stirring Wilson into action by arousing public opinion. Also, I think Wilson was right in not sending General Wood to take com- mand in Europe. Wood was senior to Pershing and was not friendly to him and his presence in Europe would unques- tionably have been an embarrassment to General Pershing. That, however, does not excuse the very clumsy manner in which Wood's desire to go overseas was treated, nor does it justify the failure to use him in this country in a capacity commensurate with his abilities. There were at least a half-dozen jobs, which could properly have carried the rank of lieutenant-general, for which Wood would have had an opportunity to put his experience...to good advantage. The contemptible procedure of allowing him to train a division and then recalling him just as he was stepping aboard the transport, letting the people think that it was General Pershing's doing that he was not sent over--was to my mind indefensible from every point of view and merely one of several dozen schoolmaster gaucheries with which Wilson's record is smooched.

But when you come right to it, can a man as mean-spirited as Wilson was and as you show him to be in your book in little personal ways, be a true idealist? There must be magnanimity of heart if there is to be magnanimity of mind and the fact that Wilson's egoism had ingrown to such an extent that he could not abide criticism, opposition, or, what is worse, credit for a success going to one of his subordinates even if deserved, marks him to my mind as lacking in one of the essential elements of greatness to a degree I feel sure posterity will not overlook.[29]

In any event, Forbes was not the type of man to sulk. He could dislike a man, but he would not lose himself in defeatism. And yet, on the other hand, he could not remain in a country run by Woodrow Wilson. When, in 1914, the Maine Court offered him the sole receivership of the Brazilian Railway Company and a chance to throw himself into work of an entirely different nature from that of the Philippines--and on second thought, perhaps not quite so different in many respects--he leaped at the opportunity. For six years he labored at the operation of the Railway, which had a valuation of three hundred million dollars, with thirty-eight different corporations in five South American countries, and with branches and properties extending from Brazil into Uruguay, Paraguay, and Bolivia. His efforts to make it into a profitable undertaking turned out to be successful. Most of the stockholders were British, Belgian, and French, and as he made money for them he felt that he was in addition helping the war effort. During the progress of the European War he crossed the Atlantic six times and the English channel seven, with an almost reckless disregard for danger.

With the return of the Republican Party to power in 1921, Harding sent Forbes with General Leonard Wood as a member of a commission to the Philippines to report on Democratic rule--or "mis-rule," as Forbes calls it in his "In Retrospect"--and on the readiness of the area for independence. Seven months later, in May, 1921, the report voiced opinions which were, notably, far different in relation to the Philippines from those made nine years later when Forbes considered Haiti. The 1921 report stated that the Filipino people were happy and peaceful and keenly aware of the benefits of the American rule. The movement for independence, however, was strong, more among Christian Filipinos than non-Christian. "We find a general failure to appreciate the fact that independence under the protection of another nation is not true independence." The Filipino government was as yet weak and inefficient, but the character of public officials good. Forbes attributed this inefficiency to "lack of inspection and to the too rapid transfer of control to officials who have not had the necessary time for proper training." Generally, the Filipino capacity for self-government was found to be solid, although their politics were muddy, their justice departments lacking in confidence, and their economics shaky.

Continued occupation of the country was recommended. To withdraw, the report stated, would be a betrayal of the Filipino people, a misfortune to the American people, a distinct step backward in the path of progress, and a discreditable neglect of our national duty.[30]

Why Forbes did not accept further public service during the 1920's is not clear, particularly since he was friendly with Secretary of State Hughes whom he had given strong support in 1916 during the campaign to oust Wilson. Whatever the reason, he returned to private life, purchased a ranch in Sheridan, Wyoming, and threw himself wholeheartedly into an active business career which centered about the J. M. Forbes and Stone and Webster firms. He also began to experience poor health. Years of living in the warm climates of the Philippines and Brazil had made him incapable of enduring the rigorous New England winters he had loved as a child, and he started spending winters first in Thomasville, Georgia, and then Taylor, Honduras, where he watched the interests of the United Fruit Company of which he was a director.

His chief interest during these years, was the writing of his monumental *The Philippine Islands*, which appeared in 1929. Hoover had known Forbes personally since the days of the Wilson Administration, was intimately acquainted with his work, and had become even friendlier with him as a result of their mutual friendship with Calvin Coolidge. *The Philippine Islands*, scholarly, definitive, and unusually well-written with Forbes' gifts for descrip-

57

tion and observation, convinced Hoover that Forbes
was not only one of the men for his commission to
Haiti, but the person to direct the group. Hoover
apparently had no intention of sending a group of
youthful idealists to the area; what he wanted was
a collection of seasoned men, mature in thought,
and experienced in the rough and tumble of practical
affairs, each successful in his own right, whose
reasoned judgments, mitigated as little as possible
by emotion, would form a clear basis for (1) settling
the internal affairs of Haiti quickly and to the
best advantage of all concerned (2) determining a
United States future policy toward Haiti and, by
implication, Latin-America. The goals, by necessity,
were somewhat misty; the methods of achieving those
goals were scarcely glimpsed.

On January 30, 1930, Forbes received the following telegram:

> January 30, 1930
> The White House
> Washington, D.C.
> Hon. William Cameron Forbes
> Gulf Stream Cottage
> Delray, Florida
>
> Confirming previous communication the President hopes
> you will dine and spend the night at the White House on
> Wednesday, February fifth.
>
> > George Akerson,
> > Secretary to the President

Forbes recorded in his half humorous style the course
of events which ultimately brought him to Haiti:

> On arrival at Washington, where I was invited to stay
> at the White House, I was not met by the White House car;
> I suspected some mistake and took the taxi up. Upon arri-
> val, I found Mr. I. Hoover, the head usher, had read my
> telegram carelessly, assumed that I was coming from the
> North and figured the Miamian would get in at three and
> ordered accordingly. I had already had my lunch on the
> train and with some difficulty explained to the attendants
> that I was expected. They dug up the repentant I. Hoover
> and I was shown to my room where I washed off evidences
> of travel and mosied over to the State Department, where
> in the absence of my old friend Harry Stimson—now in

58

London endeavoring to work out a disarmament agreement
--the Under Secretary, Joe Cotton, received me and broach-
ed the question of going to Haiti.

Apparently I was to be chairman of the Commission which
was to be organized largely to suit my taste, and whom
did I want? I found very soon that this phrase "to suit
my own taste" was largely verbal, as what my taste was
to be was laid out for me in no uncertain terms. Henry
Fletcher, an old friend and an able fellow, had already
been drafted as second in command. This pleased me great-
ly. A man by the name of Elie Vezina, a French-Canadian
resident in Woonsocket, Rhode Island, was to represent
French-speaking and culture and also the Roman Catholic
Church. Democrats and the opposition were to be represented in the person of James Kerney of Trenton, New Jersey,
an editor and warm personal friend of Woodrow Wilson,
unlamented, about whom he had written a book and about
whose failings, I afterward learned, he harbored few illu-
sions. Another member of the Commission was to be William
Allen White of Emporia, Kansas. And all these had been
invited to serve as had been the President of the University of Virginia. Did I want a lawyer? And if so, whom?
Immediately I thought of Jerry Smith. Splendid! I called
him up on the telephone but he said immediately it was
utterly impossible and that was that!

I personally felt the need of a good lawyer, as I had
no legal training, and I knew I would be bombarded with
legal and constitutional questions as they told me Port-
au-Prince was hopping with lawyers, a favorite profession
among the Haitian elite, who despised materialism and
looked down upon tradespeople or those who worked with
the hands. In fact they were obsessed with the idea common
to the uneducated or partly educated that the object of
an education was to obviate the necessity for work, an
attitude of mind I had been very familiar with in the
Philippines.[31]

Forbes did not get his lawyer, or anyone else
he desired. The only one he officially demanded and
got for his staff was Robert C. Redmayne, who had
been his personal secretary since 1914; Cotton filled
up the remainder of the Commission and its staff.

That same evening in Washington, he had dinner
with the President, found out what Hoover wanted
--although Hoover preferred to deal in generalities,
leaving Forbes untrammeled by too many instructions

--and recorded the following:

> I had a cozy chat with the President for over an hour. He is not a bit theoretical or visionary. He sees things exactly as they are. He honestly wanted to get out of Haiti and let them run their own affairs; and he honestly doubted whether it would prove possible. The United States is lousy with great-kind-hearted and woolly-headed enthusiasts who judge every community by their own. And who try to figure out what we should do to situations like that in Haiti by taking what they conceive to be the Christian position of doing by others as they think they would like others to do to them.
>
> Where these good souls fail to be Christian is in their lack of tolerance. And I verily believe that were a group of these to be placed in authority to clean up a situation such as acceptance of their own recommendations would create in Haiti, that they would be so stirred up by the misery, injustice, torture, and anarchy, they would make the conduct of the trained, experienced, and restrained Army and Navy (Marine) officers seem very mild in comparison. This however is hardly capable of proof for fortunately this kind of unbalanced person is seldom selected for caring for a situation of that sort...
>
> President Hoover...had...a perfectly clear conception of the difficulties likely to be encountered but with it a wish to let Haitians work out their own salvation even with more or less disorder and substantial loss in the efficiency of the government. He also had a realizing sense both of the merits of the Marines and of their limitations. [32]

Henry Prather Fletcher was well-known to Hoover as former Undersecretary of State and as his confidant and adviser during Hoover's November, 1928, trip as President-elect to Latin-America. During a formal banquet in Buenos Aires, President Irigoyen informed the visitor that he was not accustomed to formal speaking and that the Argentine Secretary of State would speak for him, to which Hoover replied that in that event "Mr. Fletcher would reply for me." [33]

Fletcher, as events turned out, did not find a reply necessary, but Hoover could not have selected one more skilled and experienced in diplomacy. Born in Greencastle, Pennsylvania, April 10, 1873, he

was educated at Chambersburg Academy, and then entered in 1894 the practice of law. The Spanish-American
War saw him in Colonel Roosevelt's Rough Riders a
well-respected private, whose devotion to the military appeared more and more to lead him away from
the dusty routine of purely legal pursuits. Thereafter his life became a continuous change from one
government post to another. From 1899 to 1901 he
served as First Lieutenant and Battalion Adjutant
of the 40th United States Infantry in the Philippines, Second Secretary of the United States Legation
at Havana in 1902, Second Secretary of the United
States Legation at Peking from 1903 to 1905, and
Secretary of the Legation at Lisbon, Portugal, 1905-
1907. In 1907, he was back at Peking, remaining there
until 1910.

His wealth of experience in Latin-American affairs, at least in Spanish America, came with his
appointment as United States Minister to Chile from
1910-1914, United States Ambassador to that country
from 1914 to 1916 under Wilson, and immediately thereafter Ambassador to Mexico during the difficult years
from 1916 to 1920, when that country was torn by
the early struggles of the social revolution precipitated in 1910 by the mystical Francisco Madero.

Not the type of man whose usefulness ended with
the advent of a new administration, when the Republi-
cans took command again in the 1920's he became Undersecretary of State 1921-1922, Ambassador to Belgium
until 1924, and Ambassador to Italy until 1929, when
he resigned from that post in protest against the
Fascist government.

His career following the appointment to the
Haitian Commission found him Chairman of the Republi-
can National Committee from 1934 to 1936; General
Counsel until June, 1944; Special Adviser to the
Secretary of State July, 1944; a member of the Ameri-
can delegation to prepare plans for the International
Organization at Dumbarton Oaks; and Special Adviser
to the Secretary of State on foreign subjects.

As second in command, his first-rate knowledge
of Latin-America surpassed that of any other member
of the commission, including that of Forbes himself.
Fletcher was a quiet man, soft-spoken, given to deep
reflection, with a devotion to the job that Forbes

particularly liked. Of the five men, he was the only career diplomat, and his advice and judgment carried great weight.

James Kerney, the noted New Jersey editor, had been a close personal friend of Woodrow Wilson, although he liked to call himself a progressive independent. He was born April 29, 1873, the son of recent immigrants from the west coast of Ireland, educated in Trenton, New Jersey, where he attended parochial school and occasional night classes. For a time he did just about anything he could find--he painted wagon wheels, was a stenographer, then a reporter in New York City, Philadelphia, Trenton, and Newark. The difficulty of his early years never dampened the natural spark of his quick Irish wit or the geniality of his disposition, but if anything, ignited them and gave him a somewhat joyous outlook on everything he did.

He became editor of the *Atlantic City Press* in 1902, then the next year editor of the *Trenton Evening Times*, which he eventually purchased. With the acquisition of the *Trenton True American* in 1912, the *Trenton Sunday Advertiser* in 1912, and the *Trenton State Gazette* in 1926, he virtually exercised a monopoly over journalism in that city. Realistic, he preferred the commission form of government, which carried over to the use of the commission in many other aspects of administration. A member of the State Civil Service Commission from 1908 until 1911 before he became a newspaper owner and publisher, he later returned to public service in 1918 as Director of the American Committee on Public Information in Paris, for which he won the Legion of Honour, served on the Haitian Commission, and was lay judge of the Courts of Errors and Appeals and Pardons from 1931 to 1933.[34]

He had originally opposed Woodrow Wilson in the race for the New Jersey Governorship in 1910, but later became not only his firm supporter but his close friend. His *Political Education of Woodrow Wilson* (1926) still remains a fairly valuable insight into the machinery of Wilson's mind. Forbes declares in his journal that he enjoyed many hours discussing Wilson with Kerney, and that the latter finally admitted that Wilson did have shortcomings. But one suspects that Kerney was more tactful than anything else.

Forbes admired Kerney for his achievement in life, his ideas, his charm, his wit, but apparently found him more charming than capable in the actual labors of the Commission. The truth is that Kerney was not a well man. He suffered during the Haitian venture the first of the series of heart attacks which eventually brought about his death on April 8, 1934.

William Allen White, the "Sage of Emporia" and a personal friend of Hoover's, was probably better known to the American public through his articles in the *Emporia Gazette* than any other member of the Commission. He knew little about Latin-America, had apparently small acquaintance with the problems of Haiti, but had a reputation for deep human sympathies with the under-dog. One suspects his being chosen more for the humanitarian impulse he was likely to give the Commission than for any intellectual contribution he might make.

Born in Kansas, February 10, 1868 of Puritan stock through his father and pure-bred Irish through his mother, White studied at the University of Kansas, but left to edit the *El Dorado Republican*. In 1891 he became Kansas City Editorial writer on the Star, and four years later purchased the *Emporia Daily* and *Weekly Gazette*. His article "What's the Matter with Kansas?", his attack on Populism in 1896, and the almost ceaseless stream of articles and books that flowed from his pen made him before long the best-known editor in the nation. Where Kerney preferred the fast pace of metropolitan journalism, White chose the quiet nonchalance of small-town living. Between the "sage of Emporia" and Forbes' grandfather, the "sage of Concord," there might have been a good deal in common. The years from 1891 up to the period of the Haitian Commission and beyond until his death in 1944 saw a steady production of short-stories, sketches, novels, political essays, biographies, editorials, and autobiographical material. Included were two biographies of Calvin Coolidge--one in 1925 and one in 1938--as well as the one which Forbes himself could not welcome, the *Life of Woodrow Wilson*, published in 1924. That Forbes could possibly work for any length of time with two admirers of Wilson was a tribute to his

63

New England sense of tolerance and fair play. White did, however, belong to the liberal wing of the Republican party, and this may have in some fashion excused his heresy in Forbes' mind.

During the First World War (1919) White had gone to France as an observer for the Red Cross, and the same year had been selected as a member of a Commission to Prinkips in Russia, but apart from these two appointments, had had no official touch with diplomatic life.[35] His main attribute, apparently, was that he had a fervent desire to do right, to see the right prosecuted, and perhaps he provided the emotional balance to Forbes' and Fletcher's calm and studied intellectual approach to the Haitian enigma.[36]

Despite this, when White years later was asked about his public service in reference to a biographical sketch of himself, he replied with excessive humility: "I have served on one or two travelling commissions of no great importance." That he said this either indicates the genuine humility for which he was famous or else his failure to understand the place the Forbes Commission held in the formulation of a new American foreign policy.[37]

Elie Vezina had been a student of Haitian politics for some time. Although born in Canada, he moved in 1889 at the age of nineteen to Chicago where he became an American citizen. A journalist by profession and active in politics, he eventually settled in Woonsocket, Rhode Island, where he became well-known through his activity in community affairs and his secretaryship of L'Union St. Jean Baptiste d'Amerique, an organization claiming 16,000 members. Hoover named him to the Commission because of his ability at the French tongue, his contact with French culture, his Catholic religion, and a life-long interest in Haiti that had given him a knowledge of Haitian history and education that would be of inestimable value to the other members of the Commission. His primary task lay in making a report on Catholic schools in Haiti, as an American Catholic sympathetic to French culture might view them. (In the fall of 1930, the Moton Commission made a more comprehensive report on Haitian education, but the Moton Commission was Protestant and Negro in composition.) Holder of the Legion of Honor, a Knight of the Order of

St. Gregory, Vezina was probably the quietest and least noticeable member of the Commission.[38]

A sixth member appointed was Willis Abbott. He never communicated with the Commission, however, and never appeared despite the telegram from Cotton to Forbes: "Abbott is a full member of the President's Commission. His appointment has been announced. His status is complete."[39]

Generally, the newspapers agreed that the members of the Commission were well-selected. *The Kansas City Journal-Post*, Feb. 9, stated: "It will be seen that the Commission is not only equipped to ascertain facts but it will be able to give full publicity to its findings. Mr. White is always sure of a multitude of readers and Mr. Kerney is not without experience in preparation of printed words. This is badly needed, because of the literary assaults that have been made on American performance of necessary but distasteful duties in the Black Republic." The *New York Times*, Feb. 8, declared: "Mr. Hoover on last Tuesday said the Commission would be composed of 'men of unbiased minds,' who 'would work out in broad vision' the 'sequent steps which will lead to the liquidation of our responsibilities and at the same time assure stable government in Haiti' after the marines leave the island.'" The *Dallas Morning News*, Feb. 8, felt the members to be well-qualified. Their experiences "amply qualify them for the task."[40]

Though Forbes has been credited with the actual job of choosing an adequate secretarial and advisory staff, setting up time schedules, and arranging for transportation to Haiti, these matters were really handled by Cotton and James Clement Dunn, who had been selected earlier as Counselor to the Commission. Dunn was relieved of his duties in the State Department a month before. During his eleven years with the Department of State, he had had a good deal of experience in Haitian affairs, was Charge d'Affaires at Port-au-Prince for two years, and Cotton felt he would be helpful to a commission in Haiti. Dr. Victor G. Heiser of the Rockefeller Foundation went along on Forbes' personal request as Medical Adviser. Rees H. Barkalow of the American Diplomatic Service, although he had never been in Haiti, was chosen Secretary and Disbursing Officer. He was fluent in French and generally handled the Commission's funds, the clerical staff, and made arrangements for trips inside Haiti. Charles H. Marshall was Secretary. Chosen for his knowledge of French, he was the contact between the Commission and the Haitian people, received petitions and representations from the Opposition parties, and handled all translations of documents. Warren H. Kelchner, Assistant Secretary, had just been appointed to the American Foreign Service. His job was that of assembling research material, which he had been doing for the previous two months. A noted scholar on the Haitian situation, he had made a complete index of the report of the Senate inquiry of 1921. Cotton placed him in charge of the library and documents that accompanied the Commission. Fernand L. Dumont was interpreter of the native *patois* or Creole which 95% of the Haitian masses spoke. Richard T. Strong was Stenographer-Secretary, and Redmayne was Forbes' personal Stenographer. In addition there were a number of women stenographers.

On the 24th of February, the five members assembled in Florida, proceeded to Key West, and on the morning of the 25th, set sail on the *Rochester* for Port-au-Prince. The ship had been the old *New York* of the Battle of Santiago fame, and Forbes' personal cabin supposedly that of Admiral Sampson himself. Each of the members carried the rank of Ambassador. Kerney joked with White, Vezina stood quiet and alone, Fletcher perused the newspapers, and Forbes busily talked with members of his staff.

That evening at sea Forbes took the advice of Huddleston of Alabama and took a good book to bed. It was H. P. Davis' *Black Democracy: the story of Haiti*, which had come off the presses a year or two before. He could not have done better reading. It was one of the trunkload of books, papers, reports, and documents which Cotton had sent down at the last moment.

NOTES

1. *The Congressional Record.* Proceedings and Debate of the Second Session, 71st Cong. Vol. LXXII, Part I, p. 21.

2. *Ibid.*, p. 232. Also see *House Document* 139, pp. 232, 236.

3. *The Congressional Record*, Vol. 62, Part IX, p. 8963

4.   Millspaugh, *Haiti Under American Control*, pp. 95–98.

5.   *Ibid.*, pp. 229–232; also, *Senate Report* 794, 67th Cong., Second Sess. A good deal of the criticism of the American Occupation was sparked by articles in Oswald Villard's *The Nation*, which began in 1920 a strong campaign of condemnation of the Wilson program in Haiti. See *The Nation*, Vol. CX (February 21, 1920), p. 226; Vol. CXI (July 17, August 28–September 4, September 25, 1920), pp. 64–65, pp. 236–238, pp. 265–267, pp. 295–297, pp. 307–310, pp. 345–347.

6.   This was a select committee of the Senate composed of Medill McCormick, Tasker L. Oddie, Atlee Pomerene, and Andrieus A. Jones. In its report, the Committee stated: "There are certain elements in Haiti which can balk and perhaps delay the rehabilitation of the country. They can not prevent it. They can do much to further it. The obvious duty of patriotic Haitians is to uphold their own Government in effectively co-operating with that of the United States under the treaty, and so hasten the day when Haiti may stand alone. The alternative to the course herein suggested is the immediate withdrawal of American support and the abandonment of the Haitian people to chronic revolution, anarchy, barbarism, and ruin." By the time of Hoover's administration, the current of thought seemed to have passed to the view that nothing less than complete and total annexation of Haiti would correct Haitian politics. See *Report of the McCormick Committee*, Senate Report 794, June 26, 1922.

7.   W. Cameron Forbes, Journal, Second Series, Vol. III, 1930–34. Unpublished. Hereafter referred to as the Haitian Journal. Forbes did not keep a day by day account, but wrote as important events or thoughts occurred to him, with the result that exact determination of the precise times to which he refers is often difficult.

8.   Herbert Hoover, *The Memoirs of Herbert Hoover*, Vol. II, p. 210.

9.   *Ibid.*, p. 213.

10. *Ibid.*, p. 333.

11. *Ibid.*

12. William Starr Myers, ed., *The State Papers and Other Collected Writings of Herbert Hoover*, Vol. II, p. 158.

13. David Hinshaw, *Herbert Hoover: American Quaker*, pp. 190–

192.

14. William Starr Myers and Walter H. Newton, *The Hoover Administration: A Documented Narrative*. See generally.

15. Mr. Fish introduced *House Resolution 85* initiating a study of Haiti. This became *House Joint Resolution 150* as introduced by Mr. Porter, requesting a Committee to visit Haiti. Later, as amended by the House, it became *House Joint Resolution 170*. In its final form, it emerged as *Public Resolution 37*. See *Congressional Record*, Vol. 72, Parts I–III. Mr. Porter: Committee on Foreign Affairs, p. 772. Reported back, p. 835. Made Special Order, p. 905. Debated, p. 908. Amended and passed House, p. 923. Referred to Senate Committee on Foreign Relations, p. 993. Reported with Amendment, p. 2093. Debated, pp. 2137, 2774, 2846. Amended and passed Senate, p. 2852. House agrees to Senate Amendment, pp. 3027, 3040. Examined and signed, pp. 3091, 3123. Presented to President, p. 3208. Approved (*Public Resolution 37*), p. 3591.

For general discussions of Haiti prior to the Forbes Commission, see the following:

> *House Document 35*, 27th Cong., 3rd Sess.
> *Senate Executive Document 113*, 32nd Cong., 1st Sess.
> "   "   "   *25*, 34th "   3rd "
> "   "   "   *37*, 36th "   2nd "
> "   "   "   *17*, 41st "   3rd "
> "   "   "   *64*, 49th "   2nd "
> "   "   "   *69*, 50th "   2nd "

For discussions bearing directly on the Forbes Commission, see *The Congressional Record*, Vol. 72, Message of President, pp. 232, 286; expenses of Commission, p. 3209; remarks in House relative to affairs in Haiti, pp. 316, 621, 629, 676, 688, 811, 814, 823, 908; remarks in House on *House Joint Resolution 170*, p. 3040; remarks in Senate on affairs in Haiti, pp. 286, 2137, 2774; remarks in Senate on *House Joint Resolution 170*, p. 2846.

16. *The Congressional Record*, Vol. 72, p. 909.

17. *New York Times*, February 7, 1930.

18. *The Congressional Record*, Vol. 72, p. 923.

19. *Ibid.*, p. 2851.

20. *Ibid.*

21. *Ibid.*, p. 2852.

22. He enjoyed poetry throughout his life. Unlike the Anglo-Saxon and more like the Latin American statesman whose second profession is that of the poet, Forbes loved to read poetry more than write it. He tells us in his "In Retrospect" that he once in his youth wrote a poem which he called "Life and Death." He showed it to George Santayana, and asked for the great man's comment. Santayana replied that it was very good, but that it was "not the work of a great poet but it was the work of a gentleman." Forbes never wrote poetry again, but he continued to love poetry, read verse, and keep scrapbooks of bits of poetry cut from newspapers and magazines. In his dying moments, in the Fall of 1959, his younger brother Edward relates that he sat by the bedside of the failing man quoting at random first lines from the quatrains of the "Rubaiyat" while Cameron completed each quatrain. It was his consolation in his earthly trials, and his peace in the moments before death.

He also had a fondness for comic songs. When his spirit was troubled or he had problems to solve, his mind would wander over half-forgotten melodies. One of these tunes was "Move My Armchair, Faithful Pompey," which had been his father's favorite and which the elder man had picked up as a soldier during the Civil War.

In 1950, reaching the age of eighty, Forbes dictated a brief resume of the salient features of his long life. The manuscript is brief, and from time to time he would replace certain pages as his memory corrected itself or he felt he could improve upon his writing. He called the manuscript "In Retrospect," and it remains unpublished.

23. Forbes, "In Retrospect," p. 6.

24. Ibid.

25. Ibid.

26. Ibid.

27. Victor G. Heiser, *An American Doctor's Odyssey*, pp. 53-54.

28. Heiser, who worked closely with Forbes in the Philippines, says of him: "I have known all the governors-general of the Philippines and, in my opinion, the one most gifted in administrative ability was W. Cameron Forbes. He laid a firm founda-

tion for sound government which might totter in political earth-
quakes but would not fall. His nine years of service...did
much to create the forces which would eventually make the
Islands fully rounded and self-sustaining economically. Improvement of harbor facilities and reduction or abolition of Harbor
dues did much to stimulate commerce. His brilliant achievements
in all these fields ranked with those of Lord Cromer in Egypt
...He ran the Philippines as a business; politics were allowed
to play no part...Forbes started in to develop their material
resources. But before this could be done, roads had to be constructed. The military caminos which the Spanish had built
for conquest had long fallen into decay and disrepair. Forbes
built new ones, also for conquest, but this time intended to
seize the treasures of Mother Earth...So persistently did
Forbes bend his energies in this direction that, half-jokingly,
half-affectionately, he was dubbed Caminero Forbes. Wealth
began to flow along with roads which he had opened. His efforts
resulted in raising sugar production from fifty thousand tons
to a million and a half a year and in developing the copra
industry to an extent hitherto undreamed of. Wherever we went
in southern Luzon we used to see the silvery white hemp fibre
hanging out to dry...Forbes encouraged gold-mining...Forbes
did much to advance the Philippine tobacco industry against
the bitter antagonism of American corporations already interested in the Cuban product...Forbes' interests were not alone
material. He had a strong sociological bent, particularly toward penology...Such was the power of Forbes' personality that
it pervaded every department. The esprit de corps was raised
to so high a pitch that all labored joyfully and without regard
for their own interests; even the office boy was heart and
soul a part of the movement and fairly convinced that if he
were not there at eight o'clock in the morning the wheels would
stop." (*An American Doctor's Odyssey*, pp. 50–53). For two recent assessments of Forbes' work in the Philippines, see
Robert M. Spector, "W. Cameron Forbes' studies in the Philippines: A Study in Proconsular Power," *Journal, Southeast Asian
History*, Vol. 7, No. 2 (September 1966), and Peter W. Stanley,
"William Cameron Forbes: Proconsul in the Philippines," *Pacific
Historical Review*, Vol. 35, No. 3 August 1966).

The Manila Merchants Association, which had not been particularly friendly to Forbes during the administration, stated in
its publication that Forbes' governor-generalship was "one
of the most notable achievements in colonial government that
has been recorded on the pages of the world's history." ("In
Retrospect," p. 13)

29. Forbes, Haitian Journal, pp. 93–96.

30. On p. 345 of his *Philippine Islands*, revised in one volume, Forbes states: "President Harding sent the mission to the islands primarily to study and report upon their readiness for independence, and to render judgment whether 'the Philippine Government is now in a position to warrant its total separation from the United States Government...'" Major-General Leonard Wood was chairman of the commission and Forbes second in command. Others on the staff were Col. Frank McCoy, Chief of Staff; Mr. Ray Atherton, representing the State Department; Lieutenant-Colonel Gordon Johnston; Major Edward Bowditch, Jr.; Lieutenant-Commander Stewart F. Bryant, who represented the Navy; Professor H. Otley Beyer, University of the Philippines, an ethnologist who had dedicated himself the specific study of the Philippines area.

For the final report, see Forbes, *The Philippine Islands*, Vol. II, Appendix, pp. 542-543.

31. Forbes, Haitian Journal, pp. 8-10.

32. *Ibid.*, p. 12

33. Hoover, *Memoirs*, Vol. II, p. 213.

34. *New York Times*, April 9, 1934; *Nation*, April 25, 1934.

35. *New York Times*, January 30, 1944; *Newsweek*, February 10, 1947; David Hinshaw, *The Man from Kansas*; William Allen White, *Autobiography*; D.C. Fisher, *American Portraits*.

White's reply to Cotton's request that he be a member of the Haitian Commission reads, as follows: "Your telegram to Governor Forbes. Tell him that I shall go with full kit and accouterment, excepting possibly dancing bells, gas mask and shroud, with the sartorial tonnage sufficient to warrant nineteen guns for which affiant shall ever pray. W.A. White." (Forbes, Haitian Journal, p. 9)

36. Forbes, Haitian Journal, p. 83.

37. Stanley J. Kunitz and Howard Haycroft (eds.), *Twentieth Century Authors*, p. 1513.

38. *Providence Journal*, Feb. 8, 1930.

39. Forbes, Haitian Journal, p. 138.

40. For various views of the finally constituted Commission, its preparations for departure, and the popular outlook on conditions in Haiti at the time, see the *Boston Herald*,

Springfield Republican, *Topeka Daily Capital*, *New York Times*, New York *Herald-Tribune*, *Richmond Times-Dispatch*, *Wheeling Intelligencer*, Charleston *News and Courier*, Louisville *Courier-Journal*, *San Francisco Chronicle* for Feb. 8, 1930; New Orleans *Times-Picayune*, *Hartford Daily Courant* for Feb. 9, 1930; Port-au-Prince *Le Matin* for Feb. 7, 1930.

Chapter 3

The Internal
Political Settlement

The *Rochester* arrived within sight of Port-au-Prince at 2:30 p.m., the 28th of February, a half-hour before the officially scheduled time of arrival. To prevent upsetting reception plans, Forbes asked that the ship delay for the required time before proceeding into the harbor.[1]

Forbes' Journal tells us that the crowds were large, the reception warm, and the route from the wharves to the city lined with demonstrators carrying posters and signs asking for the end of American occupation. If violence occurred, he made no mention of it.

The Commission was driven from the wharf to the American Legation, where it was joined by the American High Commissioner General John H. Russell, and then to the Hotel Excelsior. Actually, Port-au-Prince had no adequate hotel. The building where accommodations had been made was a large, white, poorly constructed frame house, with the high ceilings and wide verandas so typical of the tropics. The first floor consisted of four large corner rooms off a long corridor or hallway, the second of five smaller rooms and a tiny office. The bottom four rooms became the sleeping quarters of the ambassadors, the upper six the working areas. Forbes chose one or two rooms which he, Fletcher, and three secretaries could use for offices; the other members of the Commission used the remaining rooms.

After a moment or two of rest and refreshment, the five men were taken to see President Louis Borno. Borno seemed to be happy to see them. He and his ministers spoke approvingly of the work of the American Occupation and the accomplishments of the Haitian people since 1915. Because of the need for continued

American assistance, they generally appeared insistent that American marines remain on Haitian soil. Forbes noted Borno's light skin, excellent manners, nervousness, and rather annoying habit of punctuating his comments with sudden harsh bursts of quick laughter each time he wished to make a particular point. He did not make a good impression upon the Commission. William Allen White, in a vein inappropriate to his normal great gift for human sympathy, remarked in a letter to his wife: "He is thin, tall, toothy, and most disagreeable, and lives entirely apart from reality...He has a little sneering laugh...I kept pinching myself—and Kerney said he did also—to realize that I was not listening to a stage melodrama. It just did not seem possible that any man should be so patent a stage villain." [2]

White, Forbes, and the other members of the Commission modified their first impressions of Borno in the course of their stay in Haiti, but in the first flush of their meeting, they were still under the influence of Borno's critics both in Haiti and in the United States. White and Kerney, well before their departure from the United States, had been of the opinion that Borno was an arch-tyrant, trampling upon the bodies of his people with the support of American marines. As a matter of fact, White and Kerney were convinced from the start that the Commission should recommend clear steps to withdraw United States forces immediately from the black republic. So much did they fear that the Commission might be too conservative or too cautious or perhaps be swayed by the double-talk of the incumbent president that, even before they joined the Commission, they spent a day together at Palm Beach planning some strategy toward effecting their aims.

Forbes was less impassioned. He had had too much experience to allow himself the luxury of judging before he had command of the facts. Neither White nor Kerney could move him to condemn Louis Borno as the villain he so obviously seemed to be. Emotion did not rise swiftly with Forbes, particularly when he soon became suspicious of the motives of the Haitian opposition parties.

Millspaugh speaks well of Borno, despite the general antipathy toward him in both the Haitian and the American press. A member of the *élite*, light of skin, he had been distinguished "for his intelligence, culture and high character." Before entering public service he had gained the reputation of a capable lawyer, served in virtually every position of the Haitian Cabinet and been three times minister of foreign affairs. As minister of foreign affairs, Borno had signed the treaty of September 16, 1915, as well as the act which extended that treaty. Although he had been called a puppet of the United States Occupation, in reality Borno was genuinely convinced that Haiti needed a period of tutelage under American leaders. As late as 1925 he stated that he could not call general legislative elections because he did not believe that Haiti was ready to govern herself. His refusal to play the part of puppet was evidenced by his refusal to accept a new land title law which both the High Commissioner and the Financial Adviser wanted in 1927, because he felt that it would be unconstitutional and impracticable. Like most of the presidents of Haiti, Borno made the error of believing himself indispensable to the office; he did not go so far, perhaps, as to identify his own interests with those of the nation, but he did believe that Haiti desperately needed the policy which he alone could render. Honest in his own dealings, precise, and patriotic, his chief fault was an over-sensitiveness to the taunts of public opinion. The very keystone of his policy --a close relationship between himself and High Commissioner Russell--became the subject of the strongest vituperation. He believed that this close relationship would most impress the Commission; strangely enough, this aspect of his administration least favorably impressed them. [3]

On leaving Borno, the Commission visited Sansariq, Minister of Foreign Affairs, then returned to the Hotel Excelsior, where it was paid a return visit by Sansariq accompanied by Louis Borno's son.

The Commission ate at the Hotel, the members being cautioned not to eat anywhere else because of the danger of dysentery. In the beginning a bit of difficulty was experienced because the servants insisted upon garnishing all food with native lettuce. Though the hot and humid weather dulled appetites and made clothing wet and sticky, Forbes and Fletcher, who had had experience in such climates, were less discomforted than the others. James Kerney, whose keen Irish wit was such a delight to Forbes, throughout the mission, always seemed to have a story to turn discomfort into laughter, but for Forbes the discomfort was more mental than physical. His Journal records:

> Our Commission, with Marshall, Dunn and Heiser, ate at our hotel, our meals all being served on a porch overlooking a small yard beyond which was a highway down which and up which traffic was continually passing. Negro men and women from the interior always completely if not elegantly dressed, mounted on donkeys or very miserable ponies, appeared from the interior with packs or panniers and loads, the little donkey often carrying a load and a full-sized negro or negress perched above. Some rode one animal and led another; and these were often most interesting types. It was tragic to think that it was the welfare of these people our American occupation had protected and assured, and that our work in so far as it would lessen this control would inevitably inure to the disadvantage of these poor country people; and yet they are immeasurably superior to the so-called *elite* here who affect to despise them and propose to despoil them and, producing nothing themselves, are for the most part drones. [4]

To Dr. Moton he wrote after the Commission's work was over in Haiti: "The whole situation to me is a tragedy--a tragedy because I don't see any good ending to it."[5]

In all the long years in the Philippines, Forbes had never experienced the sense of despair that he felt in Haiti. Where Haiti was tiny and over-populated, the Philippines were large and with great areas for expansion; where Haiti had been free since 1804 and the fresh optimism of newly won freedom had vanished, the Philippines were bursting with zeal for the future; no deep race problem existed for the Philippines; the land was rich.

The first or second night the Commission was invited to an American club in Pétionville, a thousand feet or more in the hills, where they dined with General Russell. The next afternoon Russell gave a large reception to the Commission, to which he invited the leading men of Haiti--prelates, ministers, "business-men, navy men, and worlds of marines with their ladies." The Commission was told that

American men--soldiers and civilians--got along well socially with the *élite* until considerable numbers of American women arrived, and then the color line was drawn sharply and definitely. Apparently American women of the 20th century were not much different from French women of the 18th. Forbes did not notice a color line at the party, however, for "negroes, wholly black, rubbed shoulders with whites and mulattoes of all shades." General and Mrs. Russell told him that they had made a determined effort to cultivate Haitian society regardless of color, had invited members of the *élite* to their own home, had gone to theirs for meals, and had kept in close contact with the prominent families of Port-au-Prince. That Forbes was impressed is evidenced by his words: "I don't doubt General Russell did his best to play the social end of his difficult part to the limit."[6]

Indeed, Forbes was favorably impressed with General Russell all the way through. He felt him to be a sincere man doing an almost impossible job, and he resented the inferences in American newspapers that Russell was little more than a joint dictator working with Borno to impose military government upon an unwilling people. He tried to judge the two men as he found them himself, and in the final report to the Secretary of State, both Russell and Borno received good treatment.[7]

Russell drove Fletcher, White, and Forbes about Port-au-Prince, showing them the wharves of the Haitian-American Company, the technical schools set up by the United States Government, the General Hospital, railroad, sugar central, a maguey plantation still watered by an aqueduct of French colonial days, and an American agricultural school. During most of the drive, Russell talked optimistically of Haiti's future, explaining not only points of interest but the need for more time if the American tutelage was to bear fruit.[8] He did not say so directly during these conversations, but Russell believed --as did Borno--that withdrawal of the American Occupation would destroy the flower in the bud. After only fifteen years, for the first time in Haitian history, progress was being made; to withdraw now would throw the country back into her traditional disorder and destroy any chances for democratic and technological growth. Indeed, this was to be Forbes' dilemma. He knew that upon the proposals of his re-

77

port on Haiti would be based Hoover's policy in that country and perhaps in the rest of Latin-America.[9]

When the Commission was appointed, Haiti was big news (although soon to be pushed off the front pages in favor of the London Disarmament Conference) and the newspapers were well-represented in Port-au-Prince with correspondents: Brennan of the Associated Press, Frans of the United Press, Denny of the *New York Times*, as well as correspondents from the *Baltimore Sun* and the Roman Catholic Press. The pressure was on to find an immediate political settlement at least, and this Forbes proceeded to do as his first object.

Aboard ship just before arrival, the Commission had prepared a statement which announced that hearings would be conducted at which everyone, for or against the present government, was invited to speak. Included were comments that the United States government pledged itself to withdraw its forces as soon as possible and supplant American civil officials with Haitians. The withdrawal comment had been inserted by Forbes against his better judgment by the pressure of White, Kerney, and possibly Fletcher. Assistant Secretary of State Cotton objected to any mention of withdrawal. White became angry as he had apparently been under the impression that this was the purpose of the Commission. In Forbes' view, the sole purpose of the Commission was to gather information and make recommendations; it had no power to guarantee anything. On the day of arrival, February 28th, the Commission issued its statement regarding the proposed hearings, but made no mention of the withdrawal of United States forces.

The result was a boycott by the Opposition of the proposed hearings. At this point, however, White made his first contribution to the Commission. Pierre Hudicourt, one of the *élite* leaders of the Haitian Opposition to the government, and a friend of Oswald Garrison Villard of the *Nation*, was assured by Villard of White's liberal tendencies and that if anyone were going to obtain the withdrawal of the American Occupation, this particular member of the Commission was the man. Hudicourt decided to present himself at the first hearing and was sufficiently impressed thereby to use his influence to terminate the boycott.[10]

78

The hearings had been set up to begin on Saturday, March 1, 1930, at the presidential palace, in a large luxurious hall with an abundance of long windows elegantly draped. Forbes sat in the center, Vezina at his left, Fletcher at his right, and Kerney and White beyond Vezina to the left. Forbes, Vezina, and Fletcher generally kept regular attendance at the interviews, but Kerney and White preferred to use much of their time during the ensuing week in travelling about Port-au-Prince talking to the people in the streets. These interviews continued, with the exception of Sunday, March 2nd, through the following Saturday, March 8th.

Any one who wished, as indicated by the Commission, was permitted to speak, but the majority of those who eventually presented themselves appeared to be of the *élite* class. They were well-educated, followed law or journalism as a profession, generally, and possessed light skin.[11] No representation from the great mass of black skinned rural Haitians appeared, which seemed to distress Forbes very much. He did not feel that he was listening to the voice of the Haitian people but only to the literate few who spoke not for Haiti but for themselves. The hearings were held in French—the language of the *élite* —rather than the popular Creole, but were translated into English for the benefit of the non-French-speaking members of the Commission. First taken down in shorthand, the material was later typed for the benefit of the record. In addition, Forbes had the habit of dictating each night to Redmayne the general gist of the interviews which occurred on that particular day.

The first day was particularly significant because only two people appeared before the Commission, Pierre Hudicourt and Ernest Chauvet, for neither one of whom Forbes apparently developed a liking. As a matter of fact, since the Opposition Parties, which considered Borno a traitor to Haiti and the Commission a mere tool of the Borno-Russell administration, had boycotted the Hearings, one would assume that Hudicourt and Chauvet appeared for the sole purpose of "sounding out" the Commission and confirming the Opposition's view.

Mr. Hudicourt was brought in to the hearing by Mrs. William Hill Weed, daughter of an ex-

Congressman from Connecticut who formerly visited
the Philippines with the Taft Commissions, and who
now represented the *Nation*. Although Hudicourt did
not care to take part in any formal hearing, he did
spend more than an hour talking with various members
of the Commission--first Fletcher, then White,
Vezina, and finally Forbes. No reporters were present, and he spoke to each individually and privately
in a low voice.

He wanted President Hoover immediately to an-
nounce that elections for a National Legislature
should be held, although the special time for the
calling of such elections under the constitution
had already passed. He stated flatly that he was
a lawyer himself, and a successful one, and that
since the Borno-Russell administration had on past
occasions disregarded the constitution when it had
suited their purposes (he was not specific on this
point), he saw no reason why Borno and Russell should
not ignore the strict clauses of the constitution
when it suited the fervent wishes of the Haitian
people that they do so. Again and again, he urged
immediate announcement by the Commission of such
an election. Should it do so, then, he felt, the
Haitian people would surely be convinced of the independence and sincerity of the members. When Forbes
asked him what he would do were he elected President
of the Republic, he replied that he certainly would
not permit the High Commissioner to dictate to him,
nor stand for any interference with the administration of the government.

The main grievance Haitians had against the
Americans in Hudicourt's opinion was racial, that
Haitians were humiliated by the treatment given them.
"He said when his wife and daughter drove in their
car they were not recognized. Asked if that could
not be eliminated by the selection of officers who
would not conduct themselves in that way, he said
that it was a thing that could not be remedied by
law; that there was an inherent sentiment, and that
as long as we sent American marines so would that
sentiment be harbored by the Haitians."

Forbes asked him what Americans had particularly
merited the dislike of the Haitians. Hudicourt mentioned Dr. Freeman, head of the Service Technique
and Duncan the engineer. Duncan, he said, was organiz-

80

ing voodoo dances to be shown the Commission when
going about the country in order to demonstrate their
barbarous characteristics. When he said that these
voodoo dances were prohibited by law, Forbes said
entirely seriously that the Commission was a law-
abiding body and that if these dances were prohibited
by law he would not permit them to be performed, for
we "would not countenance any infraction of the law."

Hudicourt complained that the Americans treated
the Haitians with condescension, with no credit for
the excellence of their work, "that there had been
good Haitian doctors, even before the American intervention, but the Americans were unwilling apparently
to admit it...American engineers sent Haitians out
to do field work on construction of roads, and then
denied them any credit, and also held them down to
the lower positions and took every occasion to represent them as being incompetent and untrustworthy."
When he complained that Americans were not being
fair to Haitians, Forbes replied that each should
be fair to the other, that in the many memoranda
and complaints he had seen or heard, no credit was
given by Haitians for American accomplishments. Forbes
wanted credit given to the United States for such
"progress as could be proved to have been made."

Hudicourt--and later Chauvet--was anxious to
know just why the Commission was in Haiti. Was its
purpose merely to make another informative report,
or was it going to correct past mistakes with the
intention of planning proper future developments?
Forbes assured Hudicourt that the Commission had
no intention of raking up the past nor of devoting
itself to situations that had developed in the past,
but wished to study the present situation and formulate plans for the future. At this Hudicourt seemed
delighted, and he proceeded to prepare an announcement to the press that the Commission was in Haiti
to prepare plans "in accordance with the wishes of
the Haitian people." Forbes refused to permit this,
because "while we hope we will be able to meet some
of their wishes we are very sure that we cannot meet
all of them, and we do not want to represent that
that is what we are here to do. We represented to
him that we want *to ascertain* the wishes of the
Haitian people." [Italics inserted.]

Chauvet called a short time later asking for

an opportunity to present his views. "He was a stout and somewhat soiled individual who owns a paper called the *Nouvelliste*, and represented many times that he had been in jail himself four times. He was very positive about the misunderstanding the newspaper had in regard to our first announcement; and later prepared a correction in which he announced that we are an administrative body planning to correct evils which he saw in the situation. This was utterly contrary to the fact and to our representation to him, which indicated something which we could readily see in his face--that was his unreliability." [12]

Forbes later commented that "One Pierre Houdicourt [sic.] spent an hour talking privately with me. He was a candidate for the Presidency, God save the day, and was very bitter and showed, I thought, little sense and marked unfitness for the office to which he aspired."[13] White and Kerney, however, were much more favorably impressed by Hudicourt.

As the days wore on, Forbes realized that few among those who held power in Haiti--and this excluded the great mass of the black, illiterate, Creole-speaking people--wanted Borno. Americans, the *élite* generally, and finally the Archbishop himself stood against him. Only the Marines and General Russell kept him in the presidential chair.

The country was seething with Borno's latest action. Just before the Commission had set sail for Haiti, Borno had dismissed four members of the Council of State and appointed four others more amenable to himself. Lately he had been having difficulty, went the rumor, even with the members of a council whom he himself had appointed, and had become frightened at the possibility of the Council's electing another candidate for the presidential elections that year. The Opposition, fearing that Borno would be elected for a third term, thought dangerous any occurrence that might conceivably aid the present administration's remaining in power. Upheaval had not yet come to Haiti, but Forbes felt that, unless the Commission worked quickly, the more radical elements in the Opposition would gain control of affairs. And in the meantime, the mobs increased in number and mobility. The first hearing served only to arouse the radicals to a suspicion that the

Commission would do nothing but talk and listen and record. At this juncture, William Allen White gracefully eased the tension.

Hudicourt had become rather friendly with White, had introduced him to a number of leading men and women in Port-au-Prince, and White enjoyed hospitality in the homes of several of the best families. On March 2nd, a parade had been planned by a group of *élite* women to lay a wreath at the statue of Dessalines, but a government regulation prevented parades or demonstrations of any sort without permission having been granted at least three days before. The request had not come through on time, and the Borno government refused permission. White was asked during one of his visits to an *élite* home what he could do. He relayed the information to Forbes and earnestly requested that permission be granted. Forbes said he could do nothing, but would ask Russell. Russell declared that, although the regulation forbade parades or public ceremonies unless the required time interval had elapsed, he would give permission.

That afternoon of March 2nd, White lunched at the home of Pierre Hudicourt--" I never had so sophisticated and as beautiful a meal in my life...It was French food with delicious sausages, pickled fish, tomatoes in oil, garnished fish salad, breast of roast turkey, gravy with onions, potatoes, ice cream, cake and coffee." He attended services at the church where the parade was to begin, then walked back to the Excelsior Hotel, where he watched the marchers go by. At regular intervals the marchers would stop, hail him, and then continue. White's letter to Charles M. Vernon gives the picture in his inimitable style:

> The *élite* of Haiti were heading the parade which means mulatto, octoroons, quadroons, and other multiple roons into the sixty fourths and ninety sixths, but all frankly calling themselves Negroes, though some of them were blonder than you and a few had light straight hair with blue eyes. They were--if I must say it--good looking and in many cases most beautiful women. This church parade was a woman's parade and started in the swell neighborhood of the town at the aristocratic Catholic church. Suddenly from out of the line, or out of the sidewalk, or out of the crowd, I never knew which, appeared a gaunt, wrinkled,

poor old peasant woman in a blue cotton dress. She ran
toward me and either fell, or kneeled, or prostrated herself, Heaven knows which, it was so quickly done, before
me. The parade stopped and began to jam and form a crowd
around her. The fashionably dressed leaders began to glare
at the old woman. I reached down and helped her up with
both hands. She thrust toward me as she rose a little
homemade Haitian flag made of two pieces of paper pasted
together. She said something to me in either French or
Creole or *Patois*, which I couldn't understand and which
I knew I must not assent to for that reason, being there
more or less in an official capacity. But I smiled my
prettiest smile and shook my head, and then she ran back
into the crowd toward where the line should be and was
glared at more or less by the well-dressed women. She
stood for a second or two trembling and frightened, and
to reassure her and to reassure the crowd that I was in
no way embarrassed by the incident, I waved at the crowd
touching the tips of my fingers to my lips in as affec-
tionate a gesture as I could make and conciliatory withal.
For as much as two or three seconds the crowd stood dumb
in amazement that any white man from America, and that
white man with ambassadorial rank who had just taken a
salute with nineteen guns, would do such a thing. Then
a roar or applause broke out and the reporters knew that
an incident had happened. [14]

The Press reported that White had kissed the
old lady's hand, and this is the way it hit the news-
stands in the United States. In reality the reporters
had not seen precisely what he did. Nor did White
correct them. For him the story was essentially correct; had he thought at the moment of so doing, he
would have, most likely, done so.

After this incident, especially since it came
at the start of the Commission's work, Forbes' task
was incredibly easier. White wrote in this same letter to Vernon that it was thereafter "pie for the
Commission. We could do anything we wanted to with
the Haitian opposition which had been teetering on
the brink of revolution and bloodshed until that
hour, having somewhat lost faith in all Americans."
This over-states the results, but at least the Opposition felt that the Commission consisted of sincere
men actually planning to do something constructive.

On the other hand, to American critics this
incident appeared as though Borno and Russell, afraid

of popular gatherings, had forbidden all public demonstrations, and that Russell had given permission
on this particular occasion because he feared the
effect on the Commission. Forbes tried to correct
this misconception by stating that the Commission
had nothing to do with granting permission to hold
the parade, that this lay purely within Russell's
prerogative, and that the Commission was not in Haiti
to correct dictatorship but merely as a presidential
civil advisory body. His statements had little result
in nullifying sentiment, however, and White emerged
as the hero of the whole business.

Now, Forbes issued a call for representatives
of the Opposition parties to meet with the Commission
to state grievances and to discuss how the present
controversy might be settled. In the meantime,
Russell, sensing that the Opposition intended to
force the issue of national elections and a new president, "even at the sacrifice of lives," proposed
a plan which endeavored "to effect a compromise
between the Opposition and the present administration
if such a compromise could be legally accomplished
within the provisions of the Treaty of 1915." This
plan, ultimately, with modification, became the basis
for the return of the Haitian *élite* to power.

Russell saw the handwriting on the wall—the
present system could not work. Borno refused to call
for national legislative elections for the present
because he said that he did not believe Haiti ready
for self-government, but the Opposition believed
that this was his way of retaining power. On the
other hand, the Opposition demanded national legislative elections and a new president because it wanted
Haitian destiny in the hands of Haitians; but Borno
believed that the Opposition merely wanted Haitian
destiny back in the hands of the greedy self-seeking
politicians from which it had originally been taken.
The only solution, then, to Russell's mind, that
would be satisfactory to Borno and the Opposition
would be to have the Council of State elect a provisional president acceptable to both Borno and the
Opposition, and have this provisional president call
for national legislative elections at the next legal
date (January 10, 1932), with Borno and the Opposition using the intervening two years to plan legitimate legislative campaigns. Russell thought Emmanuel
Ethéart, the president of the Court of Cassation,

and a close friend of Borno's, would be acceptable
to the latter, and he hoped that as "an elderly man
of high standing morally, socially...professionally
...and...not...active in politics," he would be acceptable to the Opposition. Furthermore, to set the
Opposition at rest, Ethéart (or whoever became provisional president) would before his election address
a communication to the representative of the United
States in Haiti (Russell, presumably) clearly stating
that "immediately following the national elections
in 1932, he would convoke the National Assembly in
extraordinary session and submit his resignation
and that he would in no event serve as Chief of State
after that time."[15]

According to Russell, he presented his plan
to Borno and Borno "was enthusiastic."[16] Why Borno
would be enthusiastic is difficult to see. By agreeing to Russell's plan, he was putting himself out
of office and returning himself to civilian life
(as well as to the dangers to which a former unpopular politician might be subject). But he really had
no more choice than did Russell. Unless the Opposition obtained a new president that year (1930) who
was pledged to re-establishing a National Assembly,
bloodshed would result, and the mere presence of
the Commission indicated Hoover's reluctance to permit
further bloodshed on Haitian soil. Even were Borno
to pledge himself to national legislative elections
in 1932, the Opposition would not tolerate his continuance in office. He had lost the support of the
élite.

No one knows how long Russell may have argued
with Borno, but the results were inevitable.[17] Borno
finally agreed to the plan. As to his reasons we
may only speculate. Perhaps the plan offered his
only hope for future political life. If Ethéart were
elected president for the purpose of holding elections two years hence, Borno might still retain
enough power and influence to turn the legislative
elections to his favor. On the other hand, perhaps
he merely bowed to the force of circumstances. He
is said to have remarked on one occasion, "Put not
your faith in Princes or the United States," but
of this we have no proof.

The representatives of the Opposition finally
met at three o'clock on March 6th. The Commission

found facing it five reasonably well-educated men:
George Leger, "an attorney of fine presence and good
standing; a slight man, rather light of skin"; Simon
Pradel, "mulatto, prominent lawyer"; Antoine Rigal,
"darker of skin, but white-haired" and "President
of the Federation of a number of 'patriotic' leagues"
(there were eight of them); Pierre Hudicourt, "mulatto, attorney, very bitter toward the present government"; Justin Sam, "Negro, student at St. Damien's
[sic], leader of Students' Movement." [18]

Russell's plan was unsatisfactory to them because E. Ethéart, as a friend of Borno's, was unsatisfactory, and, because, on any account, the Opposition
refused to have the president elected by the Council
of State, which from their point of view was little
more than a group of oligarchs whose sole purpose
was to retain power, or keep Borno in power. Furthermore, the main question seemed to be that of national
elections for the legislative assembly. General
Russell, Colonel Cutts (commanding the Occupation
marine forces), and General Evans (commanding the
Garde) held with Borno that no legal national elections could be held before January 10, 1932, and
that the election of a President should be made by
the Council of State. The most that Russell would
concede at this point was that Borno eliminate himself as a candidate, and that some "neutral" candidate, as he proposed in his plan, be elected by the
Council. The meeting came to an impasse, and Forbes
adjourned the discussion to a later time.

The crowds were becoming more and more hostile.
As the Commission was to discover, the Haitian mass
cared little for the efforts of the American people
to stabilize the country. The only service the
Haitians appreciated was the medical service. As
for the rest, they looked upon Borno and Russell
as joint despots whose every action, however good
in itself was a device to solidify the hold of a
foreign government upon Haitian soil. Everywhere
the Opposition had gained control of the crowds,
and long lines of men, women, and children, bearing
placards, swarmed past the building where the Commission met. Just how fully the Opposition had mastered
the crowds was to be seen by Forbes later on the
Commission's trip through the interior of the country
to Cap-Haitien.

Forbes urged Borno--through General Russell --to issue a "calming statement" to the Haitian press, and then called the Opposition parties' representatives to a second session held on March 7.

At this second meeting, Forbes modified the Russell plan.[19] The Opposition parties were to present a slate of "neutral" candidates, one of whom would be chosen by President Borno as acceptable to him. This candidate would then first be elected by the whole Haitian people in general elections (to satisfy the Opposition parties) and then elected by the Council of State (to satisfy the requirements of the Constitution of 1918). This neutral President would in turn supervise national legislative elections as soon as possible. Although the Opposition leaders did not care to permit the Council of State to vote (from their point of view the Council had long since been the puppet of the executive), they finally acceded to Forbes' wishes in the frantic effort to stem increasing violence.

Forbes telegraphed the plan to President Hoover that same day, the 7th, and received acceptance the 8th.[20] Yet, Borno still had to be satisfied; he was as much opposed to the new plan as the Opposition had been to the first. His objections mainly centered about the question of electing the National Legislature. Allowing a temporary president to be elected by both the Opposition and the Council of State met his approval after long persuasion by Russell, but holding elections for the Assembly before January 10, 1932, was anathema for him. Nor was his reasoning unsound. Were the United States to recognize elections held before the time permitted by the Constitution of Haiti, the effect upon Haiti and the rest of the governments of Latin-America might be injurious. This would be tantamount to saying that the American people would recognize illegal governments and successful revolutions whenever the occasion demanded and the net result would be the discouragement of constitutional government.

Forbes was caught between the demands of legality and those of expediency. After conference, the Commission finally decided that the new president, once elected, would call for national legislative elections "as soon as possible."[21] For Russell and Borno, this phrase meant "not until 1932"; for

88

Leger and the leaders of the Opposition, it meant
"during 1930." Forbes evidently satisfied the Opposition leaders by telling them that he would bend his
efforts toward getting the State Department in
Washington to agree to holding illegal elections
in 1930, while Borno seems apparently to have been
forced to accept the plan by rapidly growing awareness of his unpopularity and the little support existing for his position. The ambiguous phrase "as soon
as possible" was reluctantly accepted by both sides,
and plans were set in motion for the presidential
elections.

Another point of difficulty arose--minor, but
irritating to Borno. Was the new president to be
called "temporary" or "provisional"? The Opposition
circulated the statement that a provisional government was to be established. Borno declared that the
neutral president was not going to be provisional
since he would be a legally elected president with
all the powers of the Constitution conferred upon
him, but merely temporary. The word "provisional"
cast a stigma upon the preceding administration which
Borno could not abide.

Forbes sent an informative telegram to Hoover,[22]
and then set about finding a neutral candidate. Since
Emmanuel Ethéart had declined the honor of being
candidate for the temporary presidency, the Opposition obtained authorization to compose a list of
neutrals.

Forbes in his Journal notes that Borno had evidently hoped that in some way the United States
would recognize his services and perpetuate him in
power. At his four meetings with the Commission he
usually dwelt upon the great accomplishments of the
American Intervention, the particular achievements
of Borno himself, and the incapability of the Haitian
masses in governing themselves. He did not cease
to stress the terrible misfortunes, the complete
chaos that would engulf Haiti with the withdrawal
of American forces. Though Forbes and the Commission
were aware of the cogency of Borno's arguments, and
even admitted Borno's views well-taken, Forbes found
himself rapidly coming to the belief that the path
to wisdom lay in American withdrawal not only from
Haiti but from all the so-called protectorates. He
felt that with or without mistakes, the Haitian

people could only learn how to run their nation
democratically by actually doing it. His later report
to the president stated that only rapid Haitianization of the Haitian government would bring satisfaction to the people of that tormented land. As a practical measure in teaching Haitians how to run their
government, he failed to see the usefulness of the
Occupation; people only really learn by doing and
the Americans appeared to be doing most of the doing.

Forbes sent his official statement to the Press
on March 9th.[23] A copy was sent to Borno by
1:30 p.m. Sunday, two and one-half hours before being
given to the Press, so that Borno could make any
objections he wished to make in advance. He made
none, and the notice went as originally written to
the local press at Port-au-Prince and to American
newspapermen at Hinche.

On March 9th, leaving Dunn in the capital, the
Commission started its long proposed trip north into
the interior of the country. Forbes remarks that
everywhere the Commission went--Pont Beudet,
Mirabelais, Las Canobas, Themonde, Hinche, St.
Michel, Massaide, Cap-Haitien--it was greeted by
the same signs calling for the end of American occupation, Borno's regime, and for the return of government by a representative legislature. Everywhere
the Opposition, as it did in Port-au-Prince, seemed
to have complete command of the mobs. After a while
the Commission grew tired of the same slogans, the
constantly repeated cries, so that the agitation
had little further effect on the visitors.

> Our path lay through a number of towns and by the time
> we had passed through two of them it became evident that
> there had been an organized effort to create an atmosphere
> and we deduced the work of propagandists who, we soon
> learned, had preceded us and then very stupidly organized
> demonstrations. Everywhere were banners of paper, the
> Haitian colors, red and blue, with a strip of black pinned
> or glued to them, to indicate mourning for lost liberties.
> Everywhere were signs held up to us all in exactly the
> same words and asking for the same things: "Desoccupa-
> tion," "Suppression of the Alcohol and Tobacco Tax,"
> "Withdrawal of the Marines," "Suppression of Borno,"
> "Legislative Assemblies," etc., etc. Always the same and
> usually shown by people who had not the remotest concep-
> tion of what it all meant.

At Cap-Haitien the maid-servant in an American house told her mistress that she had to be out on the streets because an American officer was coming to count the people of the town, and that they must all be out so that they could be counted. One very stout and well-fed negress held to our agonized eyes a placard which read: "Save us or we perish." We felt her best chance of perishing was from apoplexy. [24]

Forbes could have been impressed by sincere demonstrations, but he felt that these were little more than stage demonstrations by professional demonstrators behind whom stood the *élite*.

At another point he gives the following interesting account:

....In every town we went we were greeted with the same reception; no music; everyone with the same paper banners, cut out of the same roll of paper; and with signs carrying the same inscriptions which the agitators who were going ahead writing the speeches for the officials and giving out flags and signs, all calling for the same things. It was a pitiable insult to our intelligence, and ultimately resulted in our cancelling nearly half of our trips as there was no use wasting time seeing the same tiresome silly things over again.

Our advance guard and business agent, who went ahead to arrange things for us with an officer of the Garde, kept seeing these agents and the crowds being rehearsed for their parts, which they didn't more than half understand. The natives speak a kind of patois, difficult for a Frenchman to understand, so the speeches had to be made in French, a tongue many of the towns people were not familiar with, and the head man of each town made his little address written out for him; and it made us sorry for them to see how they had to struggle to read and pronounce what was provided for them to say. At one town the presiding officer, wholly black, had endeavored to commit his speech to memory as had two friends; one of them stood on either side. Hardly a sentence could this poor man get through and he was prompted in a low voice by one or the other of his friends standing on either side. The crowds had been told to break out into applause at a certain point but they didn't get their cues or something else went wrong, for the strategic moment usually passed and then someone as an afterthought would remember that they had been told to clap and applaud, and he would

91

start with a ragged following, as one after another of
the assemblage would remember that they had been told
to clap. If there hadn't been tragedy underlying all this,
it would have been all opera bouffe. The seriousness of
it all lay in the fact that these poor dupes were really
asking for things that they should not have had, or,
better said, had only a small part. [25]

Forbes was no novice to trips of inspection.
His career in the Philippines had been marked by
the extensive journeys made first as Chief of Constabulary and then as Governor. He went by pack mule,
horse, wagon. Neither impassable road, nor forest,
nor torrent, nor disease prevented his travelling
throughout the islands in the effort to get to know
the people, both Christian and Moro. but then he
had been in his early thirties. Now he was sixty
years of age, Fletcher was sixty-one, nor were the
other members young men. The trip this time was too
quick. It was over a highway constructed by American
engineers, and it touched only the towns. By the
time the Commission reached Cap-Haitien, the members
were so exhausted that they met the *Rochester* at
that city and returned on it to Port-au-Prince by
way of Gonaives. The photographs which were taken
of the Commission show it only in little towns surrounded by official welcoming parties, or posing
with noted Haitians. There is no indication that
the Commission had any genuine contact with the Negro
people themselves, visited their hovels, or actually
saw them at their daily tasks. The trip was artificial at best. Forbes in the Philippines was Forbes
steeped in the blood, the tradition, the culture,
and the very soul of the Filipino; Forbes in Haiti
was a Forbes anxious to formulate an American foreign
policy and get out. The truth is that even if he
had wanted more time, Forbes could not have had it;
Hoover was anxious to get him home and pack him off
as American Ambassador to Japan. [26]

Word came at St. Michel that riots were breaking
out in Port-au-Prince. Dunn requested that at least
one member of the Commission return to the Capital.
Forbes refused the request, feeling that by complying
he might attach greater significance to the riots
than was desirable. Instead, he decided to shorten
the trip even further and return to Port-au-Prince
at the earliest possible time. The riots had come
about, Dunn explained, as the result of the following

notice sent out March 8th by President Borno to all the Prefects:

> It is false that a provisional government will be formed as the agitators are trying to make the people believe. The presidential election will take place April 14 by the Council of State and President Borno will not leave the National Palace until next May 15. Here you have the exact truth which must be made clear to the people. With regard to the legislative elections they will not take place before the nearest date fixed by the Constitution, which is January 10, 1932. [27]

The Opposition understood this to mean the complete negation of Borno's promise of presidential and legislative elections according to the Russell plan as modified by Forbes.

Actually, Borno did not mean this at all. Borno's explanation for his notice to the Prefects was

> (that) the Opposition had immediately telegraphed that they had won a great victory over him, that he was immediately going to be put out, and that a provisional government, agreed to by the American Commission, was to be established. The notices sent around by the Opposition were technically incorrect and wholly unwise. The Government was to be temporary and not provisional. No agreement had been reached for the abolition of the Council of State. On the other hand, President Borno's telegram to the prefects, instead of clarifying the situation, was also misleading and provocative of unrest and misunderstanding. [28]

Although Borno's notice confused the issue all the more, the Opposition apparently had faith in the Commission, for Dunn's telegram to Forbes in Cap-Haitien on March 10th indicated that things had quieted down in the Capital. Forbes and the Commission sent a telegram of information to Hoover announcing that the Commission intended to leave Haiti on the 18th, without waiting for the presidential elections to take place. The State Department through Acting Secretary of State Cotton objected to this, [29] but Forbes remained firm. Once the political settlement machinery had been set into motion, he saw no reason to remain. Supervising the elections he felt to be not the job of the Commission but of the more experienced Russell, who, as Forbes never would allow himself to forget, was the official representative of the United States Government in Haiti.

The Commission returned to a relatively peaceful Port-au-Prince on Tuesday, March 11th. The same day, in the pages of the government sponsored *Le Moniteur*, Borno made his official announcement of the details of the Russell-Forbes plan and his acquiescence to its details. But by adding that he would do every-thing in his power to aid every *constitutional* method of bringing peace and stability to Haiti, he implied unacceptance of the Opposition's interpretation of the plan--the calling for national legislative elec-tions *before* the legal date of January 10, 1932.[30]

Forbes knew that the leaders of the Opposition parties were inclined to be conservative. Despite the radical elements in the groups opposed to Borno, the conservative leaders had received votes of confi-dence from the parties they represented. "It was found," Forbes noted, "that their leadership was wholly contingent upon their ability to secure legis-lative elections earlier than the date provided in the Constitution, namely, 1932." [31] Previous to this trip through the interior, Forbes had been sympathe-tic to the wishes of the population for national legislative elections in 1930; now, he realized that unless this wish were granted, the conservative leaders with whom he and the Commission had been dealing--and who had been probably responsible for the relative tranquillity of the country--might lose control of their parties to the radical elements. He had no wish to face the results of insurrection such as he had encountered in the Philippines. Nor was his friendship with Aguinaldo in Manila wasted in all that he had learned as Governor-General of the Islands. [32]

The Opposition indicated that it could no longer be satisfied with the words "as soon as possible" with reference to these elections. Once the temporary president was elected by the people and the Council of State, it wanted the new president to call for legislative elections fifteen days after inaugura-tion. Forbes objected. He did not want to tie the hands of the new executive to so binding a command. Long argument ensued, but the Opposition finally compromised. The words "as soon as possible" were

to be permitted in the plan, but an interpretative
letter was to accompany the written terms of the
plan indicating that 1930 was the year to which "as
soon as possible" was generally believed to apply.[33]
Let the new president take office with the tacit
agreement that unless legislative elections take
place the same year, he alone must take the responsibility for a general uprising of the nation. Forbes
agreed to file such an interpretative letter, though
he knew that he did so without any prior approval
on this matter from the State Department. Such approval he hoped to obtain later; at the moment he
sensed the necessity for immediate agreement with
the leaders of the Opposition.

On March 15, the proposal agreed upon was published for the Haitian people. Each Arrondissement
was to designate on or before March 20, 1930, a delegate (except for the Arrondissement of Port-au-
Prince, which designated three delegates, and those
of Cap-Haitien, Cayes, Gonaives, Port-de-Paix,
Jacmel, Jérémie, St. Maro, Leogane, and Nippes, which
designated two)--a total of thirty-eight delegates.
The delegates were to meet at Port-au-Prince no later
than March 26, 1930, to form the Central Committee
which would be charged with the election of the candidate of the nation for the presidency of the Republic, this Committee to be presided over by the dean
of age. The candidate was supposed to be a political
neutral, acceptable to Borno and the Opposition,
pledged publicly and solemnly *before* the election
to call for national legislative elections to take
place not later than three months from the date of
the calling of the primary assemblies, pledged to
take the necessary measures to guarantee the freedom
of the ballot without restricting the exercise of
the right of universal suffrage, pledged to summon
the National Assembly in extraordinary session immediately after the elections and thereupon immediately
resign, and, finally, pledged not to be a candidate
for the presidency of the Republic at "this new and
definitive presidential election." [34]

The all-important interpretative letter together
with the Commission's acceptance of the provisions
were filed on the same day, the 15th. To the documents were affixed the signatures of the representatives of the Federated Committee of the Patriotic
Groups of Haiti (consisting of Le Comité Fédératif,

L'Union Patriotique, La Ligue des Droits de L'Homme et Du Citoyen, La Ligue D'Action Sociale Haitienne, La Ligue Nationale D'Action Constitutionelle, La Ligue de Defense Nationale, La Ligue de la Jeunesse Patriote, Le Parti National Travailliste, L'Union Nationaliste).

Now Forbes' problem lay in getting the State Department to agree to having national legislative elections in 1930, or, putting it another way, not to interfere with such elections should they take place before the legal date of 1932. He sent a telegram off on the 12th,[35] but the next day received an answer from Cotton objecting to such early elections.[36]

At four o'clock in the afternoon of the same day, President Borno asked to meet personally with the Commission. He once again spoke of his achievements in Haiti, the excellence of American efforts in that country, and his desire that the Marines remain there. He went on to say that he had formed a party of his own, the National Progressive Party. Of the five ministerial places in the cabinet of the new president, he wanted two places for his own party. Forbes replied that this was really up to the new president, that the next government would be coalition government, and that Borno's party would receive consideration along with the other parties in Haiti. Forbes suspected that Borno's requests were the result of promises made on behalf of friends who sought to retain their positions in the administration.[37] Borno appeared satisfied with Forbes' answer. At least, if Forbes was correct in his suspicion, Borno was now armed with a reply, which was probably all that he wanted in the first place. Borno knew that the Commission would have its way and he was resigned. The statement of the Archbishop of Haiti, to whom the Commission had paid an official visit, that he opposed the present regime and favored the new plan for the creation of a National Legislature, pushed out the last support from Borno's claims. All that the President could do was to give an explanation--an apology--for the notice to the Prefects which he had sent out while the Commission was touring the interior, and which had caused so much disturbance.

The Opposition now presented its list of neutral

candidates. Five names were presented: Dr. Felix Armand, Ernest Douyon, Dr. Jean Price-Mars, Fouchard Martineau, and Eugene Roy.[38] Though the names were listed alphabetically, the Opposition gently suggested that the last name would be quite acceptable. When Russell brought Roy's name before President Borno, the latter accepted Roy as satisfactory to him. The task was now to have the Opposition delegates approve him on March 26th, to be followed by his election on April 14th by the Council of State.

Forbes was worried, nevertheless. He knew that the whole purpose behind electing a temporary president was to call for legislative elections in 1930; but these were illegal, and, without approval from the State Department, such elections would not be tolerated. Although he could not convince Acting Secretary of State Cotton, he did manage to swing Russell around to his way of thinking, and Russell was the one who finally convinced the reluctant Cotton.

This letter was worded in such a way that the United States would not definitely promise to recognize 1930 legislative elections, but only to look upon such elections favorably with the idea that they *might* be recognized if conditions in Haiti warranted such recognition.[39]

Cotton could not object to this, and he replied to the Commission in the following confidential telegram, filed at the Navy Department at 8:30 p.m., March 14th, and received on the *Rochester* at 12:25 a.m., March 15th:

> We desire no public statement made as to the Department's opinion for the reason that we should regard the other construction of the Constitution as likewise permissible. We should not, therefore, like the pledge of a compromise President to call an early election to rest in any degree on our opinion, nor do we desire any moral duty to see that a pledge in that regard is carried out. It would seem, however, desirable, that the several factions with which you are in negotiation be informed of this position, making it clear that while we do not object to it, we do not insist upon it.[40]

Borno still continued to complain; he was never really brought to acceptance of unconstitutional elections. The fact is that Forbes, the Commission, and Russell (once convinced of the wisdom of the procedure) ignored Borno. Russell argued with Borno that once the new president was installed, Borno had no further responsibility anyway, but Borno continued to object on principle. In any event, only four things existed to which Borno's consent was needed—the election of Opposition delegates to the convention in Port-au-Prince (which was already taking place), the selection of a neutral candidate (which had been made), submission of the candidate's name to the Council of State, and election by that body. Apart from these particulars, Borno could be dispensed with. Indeed, his presence was more a source of difficulty than an aid in ironing out the Haitian problem.

On March 15th, the Commission made its statement to the press:

> The Commission is glad to announce that its plan made public on March 9 is now in a fair way to become effective. The federated groups had formulated and sent in a signed statement of the program satisfactory to the Commission and to President Borno. They have also suggested five names of candidates for the temporary presidency who would be acceptable to them. President Borno has informed the Commission through General Russell that of these names that of Eugene Roy was satisfactory to him, thus making Mr. Roy the coalition candidate.

The statement went on to declare the date of the Opposition convention to be March 20th (not the 26th) and to outline the details of the plan. It announced that the program had the sanction and approval of President Hoover (which was not quite true) and expressed thanks to all those involved in reaching this "happy solution of the problem." [41]

On the 15th, information was sent to the State Department, texts of all pertinent documents were later sent to Washington, and the Commission held a brief interview with Eugene Roy himself.

On the 16th, Forbes and the Commission left Haiti, arriving in Miami the 20th. On March 21st, Roy was nominated for the presidency by the convention of Opposition delegates at Port-au-Prince, and on April 21st, the Council of State elected him president. The Council was supposed to elect him April

14th, but as events occurred, a number of members
of that body refused to vote for Roy (despite the
fact that 14 out of 21 members stated they *would*
vote for him at the time he had been first suggested), and Borno postponed the date indefinitely. When
Borno's actions indicated that he might have had
intentions of nullifying the Commission's plans,
the State Department on April 12th warned him that
no one except Mr. Roy would be accepted as temporary
president by the Hoover Government. Borno accordingly
ejected ten members of the Council and replaced them
with ten men who were willing to go along with
Forbes' plan. Inauguration ceremonies took place
on May 15th with little disturbance, except at Port
de Paix. [42]

President Roy fixed National Elections for
October 14. Early in October, the United States
Government made the announcement that it had no intention of supervising the elections, that all American officials in Haiti had been instructed to maintain a strictly neutral attitude and not to indicate
by word or deed a preference for any individual,
and that American marines would be kept in barracks
on the election day. The elections came off with
little disturbance. [43]

One would be foolish to suppose that the Political settlement pleased Forbes as an actual settlement
of the Haitian internal turmoil. The settlement was
superficial, and no one knew this better than Forbes
himself. It merely allowed the Opposition to get
Borno out and get itself in. Throughout his stay
in Port-au-Prince, his trip through the interior,
his glance at Cap-Haitien, he repeatedly heard the
phrase "The Haitian people want..., the Haitian
people need..., the Haitian people..., the Haitian
people..." Yet one wonders--and so did he--if he
had ever really heard from the Haitian people.

Some time later, James G. McDonald, Chairman
of the Foreign Policy Association, published an article entitled "Progress in Haiti," in which he attacked the work of the Commission. [44] Forbes was disturbed
and wrote a letter to McDonald, refuting the latter's
comments point by point. McDonald had stated that
"constitutional institutions had been scrapped."
Forbes replied that technically they had been observed more than they had in the past. Not calling

for elections at all over the course of the thirteen
years since the adoption of the Constitution in 1918
seemed to Forbes to be far more against the spirit
of the document than evading the January 10th formality. Second, "rights of free speech and free press
have been ruthlessly ignored." But Forbes discovered
no infringement of the rights of free speech and
the press in Haiti. "Unless you have lived," he
wrote, "in a country with a press such as they have
in Haiti, you can have no conception of the lengths
to which they will go. Vitriolic abuse and misrepre-
sentation are their daily endeavor, partly with the
idea of levying blackmail, partly to indulge spite,
and conversely these papers will turn in favor of
an office-holder or candidate or aspirant for office
in return for a small stipend... They do not know
the difference between liberty and license." Of
course Forbes himself was the first to admit that
the government's claim of abuse of liberty was in
itself occasionally abused or used as a device to
silence critics of the administration, but little
doubt existed that the Haitian papers, particularly
those in Port-au-Prince, indulged all too often in
invective rather than in constructive criticism.
Third, "some of the public works have been more useful to the American occupation than to the Haitians,"
referring apparently to roads and docks, warehouses
and bridges, and other constructions that would prove
valuable to the military in squashing insurrection.
Forbes found this to be absurd and without proof.
Everything that had been done was done not with military motives in mind, he felt, but with motives of
benefit to the commerce of the nation. The major
buildings had been constructed out of money saved
from Haitian revenues by the American Receiver-
General. Fourth, "the American system is designed
to array the peasant leaders against the educated
and cultured classes." But this was meaningless.
The weakness of Haiti lay in her lack of a middle
class. Borno and Russell knew this. Mechanics were
unavailable, and the number of carpenters, black-
smiths, and skilled laborers was pitifully small.
If struggling to build a skilled middle class together with a class of trained artisans was seeking
to set the people against the cultured classes, then
Forbes admitted his guilt. Fifth, Forbes took exception to the statement that "ostensibly Mr. Roy is
to be named by the Council of State, but that is
only a face-saving device." Sixth, he resented the

slurs intimated by use of the phrase "the recall
of General Russell." To this Forbes wrote: "General
Russell is a competent conscientious official who
had rendered a great service to Haiti under very
difficult and disagreeable circumstances. He deserves
recognition, promotion, and applause." He stood too
far above mob passions to permit making Russell and
Borno the scapegoats for the Haitian venture of the
United States. He was deeply sympathetic to everything these two men had tried to do, especially
Borno. If anything, he blamed Wilson and the Haitian
ruling classes themselves.[45]

NOTES

1. Forbes, Haitian Journal, p. 27.

2. Walter Johnson, *William Allen White's America*, p. 421.
Also see Forbes, Haitian Journal, p. 29.

3. Millspaugh, *Haiti Under American Control*, pp. 106–107.
One should note that Borno's career prior to his becoming
President of the Republic was highly distinguished—perhaps
more than that of any member of the Commission, with the exception of Forbes himself. Born Sept. 20, 1865, Borno attended
the École Polymathique and Collège Saint-Martial in Port-au-
Prince. From 1887 to 1890 he was a member of the Law Faculty
of the University of Paris, 1892–94 a Professor at the Law
School of the University of Haiti, after which he entered public life. He was Charge d'Affaires and thereafter Minister
Plenipotentiary to the Dominican Republic from 1899 to 1908,
Secretary of Foreign Relations and Worship in 1908, Judge of
the Court of Cassation 1912–14, Secretary of Foreign Relations
and Justice, 1914–15, and in 1915 became Secretary of Foreign
Relations, Worship, Public Instruction, Labor, Finance. In
1919 he was appointed Director of the National Law School,
a position he held until assuming the Presidency of the
Republic, and during which time he was a member of the
Permanent Court of the Hague.

4. Forbes, Haitian Journal, pp. 34–35.

5. *Ibid.*, "Letter to Dr. R. R. Moton," April 10, 1930,
pp. 74–76.

6. *Ibid.*, pp. 36–37.

7. *Ibid.*, "Letter to Elie Vezina," May 19, 1930, pp. 92–93.

Also see *Report of the President's Commission for the Study and Review of Conditions in Haiti.* Forbes had a great fear of injuring the reputations of Borno and Russell, both of whom he felt had sincerely tried to do a good job, and, in his opinion, had been successful—or at least as successful as any men could be in such trying conditions. One of his deep regrets about the whole business was his feeling that he had ruined the careers of these two men. See Notes, this volume, pp. 110-113, footnote #45.

8.   On pp. 32-33, Haitian Journal, Forbes records Russell's conversation: "I heard him talk very interestingly of various plans for the improvement of the people. Asked whether it was not possible, in view of the fact that within a moderate time it was going to be necessary to turn over the government to the Haitians, to prepare the Haitian officers in charge of the various services, he said he thought the idea...perfectly feasible and...desirable...It was pointed out to him that if this were done now while he still retained such control as would enable him to direct their affairs..., that he could in six years build up a service with men trained to the job, whereas if such a body of men were not available at the end of six years and the Americans were withdrawn, leaving untrained Haitians to supervise and manage, there would be much less chance of their being able to do it successfully. To this General Russell agreed.

We went out over the road along the southern shore of the bay upon which work was proceeding upon a rather extensive scale, the boulevard being straightened, widened and surfaced. In view of the sharp reduction in revenues now going on due to the low price of coffee, this somewhat rather unnecessary expenditure seemed unjustified.

From General Russell's account of his own social activities it seemed as though he had made every effort to give social consideration to the natives, going to their houses, making calls, and inviting them to his house. The large social question of the treatment of the colored people by officers in the Marine brigade was not discussed.

The General showed special interest in the matter of land. He said that there was no homestead law, no law covering the matter of squatter's rights, and that the right of the people to the land they were using was merely the right of occupance. There was no land title law, and Mr. Fletcher suggested that the people were too poor to afford one. I took occasion to explain to Commissioner Russell the manner in which we handled the matter in the Philippines, where we had a general cadastral law, 30% of the cost of the survey being divided equally among the insular, provincial, and municipal governments, and 70% against the land owner to pay his taxes in five annual install-ments; and as the whole township was surveyed at the same time, the cost was so small that it did not trouble the land-owner. It is, however, questionable whether this plan would work here. General Russell hoped that the Haitians would have some cadas-tral law. He also proposed a modification of the constitution by which the number of legislators should be reduced to fif-teen. The idea that the Haitians should prepare their own con-stitution did not seem to be running in his mind; he had been doing the thing he thinks should be done for so long he cannot see it from any other point of view. His idea is to write a new constitution for them and make them take it. I several times checked this by asking how the people would feel about it and whether President Borno wanted such a measure.

9. See Chapter Six.

10. Johnson, *William Allen White's America*, pp. 419–420.

11. "Witnesses before the Commission," Box 5, National Archives Collection of material pertaining to the Forbes Commis-sion, Washington D.C. Hereafter cited as National Archives Collection.

Each night, after the hearings were completed, in addition to the material recorded by the official stenographers, Forbes would dictate to Redmayne his particular impressions of the day's efforts. Mr. Redmayne informed the present author that Forbes retained these dictations and that they were probably in the National Archives Collection. They are not there, how-ever. The only one found available is that one included by Forbes himself in the Haitian Journal, which is likely to be the most important one.

12. Forbes, Haitian Journal, pp. 29–30.

13. *Ibid.*, p. 35.

14. William Allen White, "Letter to Charles M. Vernon," *Selected Letters of William Allen White*, edited with an intro-duction by Walter Johnson, pp. 305–307. Forbes makes no mention in his Haitian Journal of the part played by White in the parade incident, although Johnson relates that Forbes observed to him, "There is no question but that Mr. White appealed great-ly to the emotional people of Haiti for whom he evinced such sympathetic attachment." (*William Allen White's America*, p. 421).

15. General John H. Russell, "Confidential Memorandum," March 6, 1930, in Forbes' personal collection of documents relative to the Haitian Commission of 1930, Appendix, Exhibit #1, Houghton Library, Harvard University.

Forbes spent his retirement years collecting materials relating to his career. Those pertaining to Haiti he collected into a leather-bound volume labeled "Personal Copy of the Report of the President's Commission on Conditions in Haiti." This is an ambiguous title, because contained therein is not only the official printed report issued by the State Department as *Report of the President's Commission for the Study and Review of Conditions in Haiti*, Latin American Series, No. 2, but masses of other material which have never been printed or reached the public eye, such as a confidential memorandum by Forbes on the political settlement, photographs, telegrams, letters, and confidential memoranda by Russell, Cotton, Dunn, and others. In order to avoid confusion with the official report, the present author hereafter refers to this personal copy as Forbes' Personal Haiti Papers.

16. Russell, "Confidential Memorandum," Mar. 7, 1930, Forbes' Personal Haiti Papers, Appendix, Exhibit #2.

Borno added that for psychological reasons he thought the proposal ought to be made to the Opposition. When Russell told him that this had in a general way already been done, he thought that there would be no difficulty in having a compromise candidate elected by the Council of State. Furthermore, if Emmanuel Ethéart could be induced to serve, he thought him to be an excellent choice, pointing out that Ethéart had kept out of politics, had friends on both sides, and now held the highest judicial post in the government. The advanced age and poor health of Ethéart would not permit him to take the office for longer than a very short period of time, and this was just what was desired in the Russell plan.

17. One may note that Forbes and the Commission held personal audience with Borno only four times during the stay in Haiti. Every communication with Borno came through Russell. This was in accordance with Forbes' idea that Russell, as head of the American civil government in Haiti, alone had the official right to act between the presidency and the American Commission, and that the Commission had no such official standing but was only a body empowered to investigate and make recommendations. See Forbes' "Confidential Memorandum: Steps taken to solve the acute political situation in Haiti," Forbes' Personal Haiti Papers, p. 6.

18. Forbes' "Confidential Memorandum," Forbes' Personal Haiti Papers, pp. 3–4.

19. *Ibid.*, p. 7.

20. *Ibid.*, Appendix, Exhibits #3 and 4.

21. *Ibid.*, p. 11.

22. *Ibid.*, Appendix, Exhibit #5.

23. *Ibid.*, p. 13.

24. Forbes, Haitian Journal, p. 45.

25. *Ibid.*, pp. 48–49.

26. See Forbes' Journal, Vol. III, Second Series, pp. 157–561. This is the first section of the Japanese Journal, covering the year and one-half that Forbes spent as ambassador to Japan.

27. Forbes' Personal Haiti Papers, Appendix, Exhibit #7.

28. *Ibid.*, pp. 16–17.

29. *Ibid.*, Appendix, Exhibit #10. "Have just consulted the President in regard to your radio received March 11 in which you state your intention to return to Port–au–Prince evening of the twelfth and sail for Florida about the 18th. He assumes that you will not sail until you have reached definite written agreement to which all parties will accede on your plan or some substitute therefore mentioned in your radio as it seems to him of first importance that some definite plan be arrived at before you leave the island and the situation which you report as to Borno that more important. (signed) Acting Secretary of State Cotton. March 11, 1930."

30. *Le Moniteur:* Journal officiel de la République d'Haiti paraissant le lundi et le jeudi, Directeur: Maurice C. Brun (Port–au–Prince: Mardi, 11 Mars 1930).

31. Forbes' Personal Haiti Papers, p. 21.

32. See the Forbes, Philippine Journals, 1909–1913, 4 vols., in Houghton Library, Harvard University. These deal with Forbes' administration as Governor–General of the Philippines during the presidency of William Howard Taft.

33. "Letter from Federated Committee of the Patriotic Groups of Haiti to the Commission of President Hoover," Mar. 15, 1930, Forbes' Personal Haiti Papers, Appendix, Exhibit #14.

34. *Ibid.*, "Memoir relative to the plan accepted by the Federated Committee of Patriotic Association," March 11, 1930, Appendix, Exhibit #13.

35. *Ibid.*, p. 23.

36. *Ibid.*, Appendix, Exhibit #16.

37. *Ibid.*, pp. 25-26.

38. Ernest Douyon was born Dec. 8, 1885. Educated at the College Chaptal in Paris and the École de Droit de Port-au-Prince, and the École de Droit des Cayes, he received his Bachelor of Laws in 1908. He served as a teacher in the lower schools from 1905-1914 and as a Professor at the École Libre de Droit des Cayes from 1916-1926, and was Secretary of Justice and Public Works at the time of the Forbes Commission. Later he became Secretary of Finance and Public Works, 1931-32, then President of the Court of Appeals in 1932.

Jean Price-Mars, a physician, is probably the most distinguished contemporary Haitian. Born at Grande Rivière du Nord October 15, 1876, he was educated at the Lycée Pétion, 1893-95, the École de Médecin, 1895-98, the Schools of Medicine and Letters at the University of Paris, 1898-1901. Entering political life, he became Secretary of the Haitian Legation at Berlin, 1901-03, served on the Haitian Government Commission to the St. Louis World's fair in 1904, was a National Deputy to the Legislature 1905-08, Legation Secretary and Charge d'Affaires at Washington, 1908-11, General Inspector of Public Education, 1912-15, Minister to France, 1915-16. At the time of the Forbes Commission, he served as Professor at the Lycée Pétion from 1918-30. Later he became a National Senator to the Legislature, 1930-35. The author of a number of celebrated books, previous to 1930 he had already published the significant *La Vocation de l'élite* (1919); *Ainsi parla l'oncle* (1928), a group of anthropological essays; and *Une étape de l'évolution haitienne* (1929).

Dr. Felix Armand was a practicing physician, respected in his profession, wealthy, and free from politics. The least known of the five candidates, this very fact made him desirable to the Commission.

Fouchard Martineau had been several times director of the

Customs, an Administrator of Finance, Delegate of Finance, and Deputy of the People. Honest and incorruptible, he had been a Senator at the time of the intervention of 1915.

Eugene Roy, aged seventy, was a former head of the Bureau of Syndicat, a form of government clearing house, and a broker. He was invariably consulted whenever disputes occurred within the government. American bankers and businessmen generally thought well of him.

39. General Russell, "Memorandum on the holding of national elections for deputies and senators," Forbes' Personal Haiti Papers, Appendix, Exhibit #20.

Russell's letter is, as follows:

"It appears that in accord with the customs and history of Haiti, a Council of State was formed as an advisory body in the early days of the American Intervention. On June 12, 1918, a new Constitution was voted on by the people. This Constitution ratified all acts of the American Intervention and the Haiti Government prior to that date and established a Council of State with legislative powers specifically stating that such Council of State would exercise legislative powers until the constitution of a legislative body at which time the Council of State would cease to exist.

"Article (c) of the transitory provisions states that the first election of the members of the legislative body after the adoption of the present constitution, shall take place on the 10th of January of an even year. The year will be fixed by decree of the President of the Republic published at least three months before the meeting of the primary assemblies.

"Last Spring the question of whether or not National Elections should be held on January 10, 1930, was carefully considered. It is well known that the installation of the normal legislative body with fifty-one members will materially slow up the development work now being so successfully conducted by the American Intervention in Haiti; in fact, it is very probable that it will seriously interfere with the carrying out of the provisions of the Treaty. On the other hand, the executive and judicial branches of the Government now in being are working, and with the time for the expiration of the Treaty approaching, it might well be said that the normal legislative branch of the Government should also be placed in operation under American guidance.

"After full consideration of the pros and cons of this question and having in view Article (c) of the transitory provisions of the Constitution of Haiti, as well as the fact of a presidential election in April, 1930, it was thought by the Haitian Government that it would be better not to hold National Elections until 1932. The Government of the United States, while very desirous of seeing National Elections held, decided that this was a question that should be passed upon by the President of Haiti in accordance with provision (c) of the Constitution.

"The time for calling elections was on or before October 10, 1929. When it was definitely understood that President Borno did not intend calling National Elections, the Opposition, at Port-au-Prince, began forming various political groups and spreading propaganda in towns throughout the country, principally in the port; and the work of the Opposition in inciting the people was greatly aided by a student strike and more recently by the advent of the President's Commission.

"The leaders of the Opposition have succeeded in joining their groups into a so-called Federation and have principally demanded National Elections, although withdrawal of the American Intervention is also one of the points raised by them. It is my belief that a fair estimate of the strength of the Opposition forces is not more than 25,000. The population of Haiti is two million. The people represented in this group, however, are those that in the past belonged to the controlling class and will, in all probability, be those who will run Haiti for a great many years until the mass of the people, if it is allowed to do so, becomes articulate.

"In accordance with the Constitution of Haiti, National Elections cannot be held until January 10, 1932. The people will not be more fit to hold National Elections in 1932 than they are today; character building and development of a middle class cannot be obtained overnight.

"In view of the demands on the part of the controlling class, which it is thought includes even some members of the present Government, that National Elections be held at the earliest possible date and considering the fact that the people of Haiti will be no better fitted to hold National Elections in 1932 than they are today, the question arises if it would not be possible to accede to the request of the groups to hold National Elections within the immediate future.

"Such action would be contrary to the Constitution and opposed to President Borno's views of upholding the Constitution. President Borno, however, would not be in power after May 15th, and would, therefore, not be in any way responsible. For the United States Government to recognize a violation of the Constitution and an illegally constituted assembly might establish a dangerous precedent, not only in Haiti, but throughout Latin-America.

"On the other hand, the point is apparently only a technical one and if the new duly constituted and constitutional Haitian administration which will go into effect May 15th next should request the holding of National Elections on popular demand, it would appear that the United States Government might well be justified in recognizing these elections and the new legislative body thus created.

"In view of the above the following is recommended:

1.   That if the President of Haiti, constitutionally elected by the Council of State of April 14th, next, after being installed in office on May 15th, 1930, requests in the name of his Government, the United States Government to recognize the holding of elections prior to January 10th, 1932, as well as the legality of the legislative body thus constituted, it would apear that the United States Government might well be justified in acceding to this request.

2.   In taking the above action, the United States Government might point out that it is taken with a view to speeding up the withdrawal from Haiti and that the constitution of the normal legislative body is considered as the first act in such withdrawal.

3.   It is not believed that the leaders of the Opposition groups should at the present time be given any information in this connection other than that the question in National Elections is one to be taken up by the new Haitian Government and the Government of the United States, after the new Government's installation; that at that time it would be discussed and that the United States is disposed to look favorably upon it, but will be guided to a large extent by conditions in Haiti between the present moment and that time."

40. *Ibid.*, Appendix, Exhibit #21.

41. Forbes' Personal Haiti Papers, pp. 32–33.

42. Millspaugh, *Haiti Under American Control*, pp. 191–192.

43. See Chapter VI, this study, for later developments in Haitian politics.

44. Forbes, Haitian Journal, pp. 84-87.

45. Two other letters are particularly significant in regard to Forbes' attempt to correct misconceptions in the American mind as to (a) the disregard of the Commission for constitutional legalities (b) the portrayal of Borno and Russell as evil demons or at least the villains in the play (c) the reluctance of the Council of State to act in accordance with the settlement (d) the use of American marines as an arm of aggression. The first letter is to White, the second to Cotton. The former is found on pp. 81-93 of the Haitian Journal, the latter on pp. 87-88.

Pertinent excerpts from the White letter are, as follows:

"...The situation had so many elements that were not new to me, after ten years of service in the Philippines during which I dealt constantly with people who had grievances, who were racially very touchy, and who spoke a different language, and had been brought up with different habits of thought, that our course was comparatively simple to me...The fact is that we are playing with such a strong hand of trumps that we have never had to show more than half of it. By withdrawing the Marines even temporarily and letting nature take its course, the Haitians would immediately have civil war or a dictatorship. They wanted the assurance that the Borno regime was to end and that they were going to be allowed to choose their president. And so we could start off by giving them their main contention, and it was merely a question of finding some way to give it to them with a minimum of disturbance to the legal aspects of the situation and with a minimum show of force. We always had as a last resort martial law, and we still have it; that can be declared at any time, and if necessary will be, and the elections then carried on under the directions of the Marines and the Garde. The obvious disadvantage of this course is the attitude that South and Central American nations would take toward it, particularly as the defeated Candidate or Candidates—and there would be many—would probably charge that the Marines had influenced the election unfavorably to their cause. And so it is better to have the thing run, insofar as it is possible, by the Haitians themselves, particularly this first election...

"Everyone seems to have been afraid that President Borno was playing the double game. I have been trying to put myself in his position and I have great sympathy for him...(A)fter eight years in which he has incurred great public odium on account of a policy of cooperation and doing his duty by his own people, an American Commission comes down and practically upsets everything that he has been doing, turns the whole situation over to his enemies avowedly determined to upset his policies, and does it with a very scant word of praise and appreciation to him...As you noticed, I arranged that we deal with Borno wholly through General Russell. This was in respect to General Russell's office and his contact with Borno, which had been cordial and protracted, and it seemed that he could handle it better. I did not arrange for any of us to be present when General Russell met President Borno on these occasions, but I wondered at the time and I have wondered since how well Borno was informed. If certain aspects of what was being done were withheld from him and he found them out later—and the ones to be withheld would have been the things to which he would be likely to object—he would be much more hostile than if he had been kept advised and persuaded as things went along. In other words, I have great sympathy with Borno's right to feel sore. I think that I should myself under similar circumstances.

"Coming to the Council of State, we were asking a practically impossible thing of them...The opposition was just as bitter against the continuation of the Council of State as it was against Borno and the leaders, whom we couldn't muzzle, when they rushed about claiming a victory, were proclaiming an early termination of the Council of State. We were asking the Council to sanction this by voting for the man who was going to abolish them. You can see the inherent difficulty of the situation. If there had been any chance at all that, by defeating the plan, they could have been kept in power, their adverse votes could be counted on with absolutely a certainty. The strength of the situation lay in the fact that they also were between the horns of a dilemma. The popular mind was so inflamed against them that if they failed to carry out the Commission's plan, they were in danger of bodily extinction; whereas if they carried out the plan, their extinction would be merely official. In other words, their lives would not have been safe, and are not safe today if they fail to carry out the plan which meets with such popular approval. This is the reason why it will probably go through."

Excerpts from the letter to Cotton are, as follows:

"I am disturbed at the nature of some of the publicity that I see going the rounds in regard to Haiti. The papers say that the Department is 'ordering' Borno to do thus and so, directing him to elect such and such a person, a candidate 'selected by the Commission,' just as though we were following the very course that makes all South and Central America angry, and adopting the dictatorial attitude which we are so often charged

111

with assuming. This is exactly the opposite of the attitude which our commission endeavored to assume...

"In their efforts to guess what the commission was going to decide, the newspapers have done General Russell a great injustice. They guessed that the commission was going to recommend his recall, announced that as its probable decision, and later distorted our recommendation that, when he does leave, he should be replaced by a non-military successor, into a justification of their announcement that he was to be recalled. It is now, I think, pretty generally and popularly supposed that General Russell's service there was unsatisfactory, that he is to be removed, and that that is the gist of our report. It was inevitable that this construction should be put upon it, but I feel very badly about the injustice it does to the reputation of an officer who has given the kind of service General Russell has given for such a long time. I cannot help wondering whether there is anything that can be done to palliate this unfortunate consequence of our activities.

"Another thing that troubles me is that President Borno is being held up as some sort of evil genius in the situation, that the commission is supposed to have put an end to his machinations and forced him to relinquish a grip which the papers are portraying in such a way as to make it appear sinister. This does great injustice to Borno. I should not blame him if he were very sore, after having incurred the odium of his people by reason of having adopted and maintained an unpopular policy of cooperation with the United States and the American forces, having supported their actions, and having as a result marvelously improved the condition of his people to a degree of which the youth of the country have no conception. They do not remember conditions before these reforms were brought about, as it was fifteen years ago and before many of them were old enough to take notice. Hence, as a result of the unfortunate form in which the publicity has been handled, President Borno, instead of being held up as a wise, capable and courteous administrator, is getting some such reputation in the United States as attached to the name of Castro in Venezuela, or other Central American dictators whose reputations were not creditable. While I do not rank Borno as anything like in the class with Porfirio Diaz, still I think he should be given credit for honest, courageous, and progressive administration, perhaps with its mistakes, but still vastly better than anything which had ever preceded it in Haiti.

"I don't know just how far to go about correcting these impressions. I think they have gone too far to be eradicated from the public mind...I think, however, that our compromise plan would never have gone through or been accepted by the opposition groups in Haiti if they had known how much of it emanated from the initiative of General Russell and President Borno..."

The reader may note, perhaps with surprise, Forbes' elevated view of Diaz. As late as the second decade of the 20th century, Diaz was still held in the minds of many responsible people to be the firm but benevolent ruler which Latin-Americans needed rather than as the corrupt oppressor of the Mexican Indian which in reality he was.

113

The Hoover Commissions to Haiti

Chapter 4

Other Aspects of the Report and the Long Range View

The first draft of the final report to the president was made aboard the *Rochester* steaming back to Miami. During the stay in Haiti each evening had been devoted to a discussion of the situation as it had manifested itself during the preceding day, and by the time the Commission was ready to leave Port-au-Prince, Forbes had some conception of the thinking of his associates. On the first night out, he composed a series of questions which he put to the men for their opinions, in an effort to resolve any differences in views, preparatory to distributing the specific assignments of the report. The only differences he found were in degree, not kind. White and Kerney wanted immediate withdrawal, considered American Occupation an affront to liberty-loving people, and did not see any purpose in remaining until the legal expiration date of the Treaty, 1936. Forbes and Fletcher chose a gradual withdrawal that would be completed by 1936. They were not convinced that the United States was doing the average Haitian very much good in leaving him to the mercies of the *élite* class but they adopted a "go to it and let's see" attitude.

Fletcher was assigned the sections on law and public order, the Garde d'Haiti, Marines, and Judiciary; Vezina took the relations of Church and State; Kerney took health, publicity, and education;[1] White dealt with race problems; and Forbes took the remainder--the historical background to the Occupation, the achievements of the Occupation, the appointment of the Forbes and Moton Commissions, the settlement of internal political affairs, public works, finance, the specific recommendations, and sequent steps.[2] There were to be sections on commerce, industry, and prisons, but these were omitted through error revolving about the elusive sixth member of the Commission, Willis Abbott of the *Christian Science Monitor*.

While in Delray Forbes had received a telephone message from Hoover's secretary telling him he wished to add the name of Willis Abbott to the Commission and asking if Forbes had any objection. Forbes did object; he felt five a better number than six and that "there was a disproportionate number of publicity members," although he had no objection on personal grounds. The President went ahead and named Abbott and this fact was given out to the newspapers. When Forbes telegraphed Hoover for information on the matter, he was told that "we needn't concern ourselves about him." Whatever the difficulty, Abbott never communicated with the Commission, never attended a meeting, although Forbes expected him any day on the weekly New York liner to Port-au-Prince. Forbes had been holding for him the commerce and industry assignment of the official report, but "when he seemed to be turning out to be an illusion, I got so engrossed in the business of electing a new President that I let the whole matter slide."[3]

Health

As indicated earlier, the only phase of the American occupation of which the Haitians unanimously approved was the Navy Health Service. They saw in the demobilization of the Army and establishment of an efficient Garde only a shrewd method of eliminating opposition to American dictatorial tyranny. They saw in the great edifices of public works an American attempt at self-glorification, and in the new highways which enabled produce to travel quickly to market the swift military transportation required to keep a people in subjection. For the *élite*, the technical education introduced meant an attempt to destroy the aristocratic rural life which had been their pride for generations. And the Marines were the arch-criminals who had introduced Dixieland racial discrimination for the first time since Dessalines had expelled the Whites. But the Health Service was different. Once the Haitians had conquered their original fears that the hypodermic needle was an instrument of black magic and the naval doctor a demon of torture, the gradual relief from the scourge of malaria, yaws, tuberculosis, and malnutrition proved to be one of the most attractive features

Other Aspects of the Report and the Long Range View

of the whole Wilsonian enterprise.[4]

Victor George Heiser[5] often referred to himself as a "veteran of foreign wars," but his wars were fought in Ethiopia, in Egypt, Ceylon, the Philippines, Hawaii, Polynesia, and the enemies were beri-beri, hookworm, cholera, pellagra, malaria, smallpox, and leprosy. He had been called the "private physician to the world." Although he had not as yet acquired the grass-roots fame that his *An American Doctor's Odyssey*[6] brought him after its publication in 1936, by 1930 he had already become a legend in the medical world for his exploits into the most rugged parts of the world. He had an amazing ability to get things done and a passionate devotion to medicine that would admit of no hypocrisy. Forbes could not have found a better man for the job ahead. Heiser was by training and nature well-equipped to pierce the veil of charlatanism. If the Public Health Service in Haiti were a failure, Heiser would perceive it.

Heiser was born in 1873 in Johnstown, Pennsylvania. He led a rather sedentary life which made him "ready for college but ill-equipped for life," until at the age of sixteen the Johnstown flood destroyed his home and the lives of his parents and forced him into the open world. The destruction and misery and hopelessness that he witnessed about him after the catastrophe unwittingly led him to the resolve to lessen misery wherever he could in the world. He became an assistant to a plumber, then to a carpenter, and did various odd jobs until the sale of his father's real estate enabled him to enter college. He took up engineering first, then decided to switch to medicine, receiving his Bachelor of Arts from the University of the State of New York in 1894 and his Medical degree (doing four years in three) from Jefferson Medical College in 1897.

While an intern at Lankenau Hospital, Heiser became interested in the Marine Hospital Service, took an examination for admittance, and was accepted although he had only gone half-way through his internship. In 1898 he was sent to care for returning disabled and wounded Spanish-American War veterans. Only twenty-five when his career started, he was to travel seventeen times around the earth before that career came to an end.

117

His first important task lay in the realm of immigration. Sent to Europe to examine and set standards for emigrants to the United States, then to Canada to help bring Canada's immigration laws in line with those of the United States, he developed conclusions and recommendations which were finally embodied in the United States Immigration Act of 1907. In the meantime, he had helped stem bubonic plague in Egypt and, as a result, been invited to the 1902 international Congress on Medicine at Cairo, where, he later insisted, he learned more from sitting on the veranda and chatting than he did from listening to learned papers at the regular sessions.

In 1903 he received the appointment which brought him into contact with Forbes, that of Chief Quarantine Officer for the Philippine Islands. He was also Director of Health for the area. Hundreds of men worked with him on a single campaign to bring an end to a cholera epidemic by eradicating rats and by sanitizing swamps. Leprosy, beri-beri, tuberculosis, malnutrition became common words for him, enemies to be destroyed. Despite the opposition of local Filipino politicians, peasants who felt that in sanitizing their fields and swamps he was encroaching upon their liberty, and the jealousy of fellow American doctors, he slowly constructed a Public Health Service. The Health Service vaccinated almost two million people in one year, attempted to disseminate medical knowledge among the people, and established hospitals and clinics throughout the islands. [7]

In 1915 Heiser became Associate Director of the International Health Division of the Rockefeller Foundation, the position he held at the time Forbes called him to Haiti. As a result he was not only closely aware of health conditions in Haiti, but he was also equipped to compare what he saw with what he knew of similar areas throughout the world, and he was not one to be easily impressed. His knowledge of tropical diseases, his wealth of personal experience in Latin-America as well as in other parts of the world, and his past close association with Forbes in the Philippines where both of them had worked together to solve similar health problems, made Heiser eminently capable of assessing the work being done in Haiti. [8]

118

Other Aspects of the Report and the Long Range View

Though Heiser was not technically a member of the President's Commission, he was actually an integral part of it. He sat in on all the nightly sessions, several of the Hearings, gave his advice, and travelled during the Commission's stay in Haiti more actively throughout the country than any other member of the Commission or its staff. He spent the first two days listening to the Hearings, then started his side-trips. He attended the Commission on its trip through the interior, and when the Commission's travel was cut short by Dunn's news of disturbance in Port-au-Prince, preferred not to return with the Commission, but to continue his leisurely study of towns and villages.

Apart from the Hearings and the brief trip made, the Commission had relatively little time in two and one-half weeks to become intimately acquainted with Haitian life. Accordingly, except for the question of internal politics, much of the Commission's information was often derived not so much from its own observations as from second-hand sources--the statements of Haitians, Russell's discussions, Russell's Annual Reports [9] to the Secretary of State (especially that of 1929), interviews with officials of the American Occupation Forces and the hierarchy of the Catholic Church, the Haitian Press, and so on. Heiser's information alone was not obtained second-hand. It would be well to trace briefly his precise activities on the Commission.[10]

On February 18, Heiser met with Dr. C. S. Butler, U.S.N., former Director of the Public Health in Haiti, who had been recently replaced by Dr. Kent C. Melhorn, U.S.N. Butler stated that the uprisings in December had been sparked by Freeman's[11] refusal to continue grants to students in Agriculture (the Service Technique), that the Haitians in agriculture had been taught by what were, in his opinion, American roughnecks who knew no French, and that the violence spread from the agricultural students to those in the medical school. He found that seventy per cent of Haitians had yaws, and that the two great enemies were malaria and tuberculosis. When Heiser asked about the ability of Haitians eventually to take over their own progressive medicine, he learned that they "are capable of acquiring knowledge and manual dexterity and can apply it to many practical problems but have no ability in administrative organization. [They] lack medical conscience. [It is] doubtful if medical ethics could be developed in spirit or practice. Devotion, sacrifice, human sympathy and moral obligation do not exist. [They] have no originality in research and are content to follow and do not question a rule laid down by others. [They] would not serve in rural areas unless controlled by whites."[12] Heiser was not content with this generalization; he had seen the opposite demonstrated too many times in other parts of the world, particularly in the Philippines and Southeast Asia, and in other parts of Latin-America itself.

In Port-au-Prince, on the 28th of February, he was met by the Head of the Medical Service of the Gendarmerie, who offered to prepare an itinerary for him in Haiti. Heiser consented, and thereafter found the way prepared for him through most of the valleys and towns of the country.

His first impression of Port-au-Prince was favorable. Local chlorination of the water provided a seventeen-day supply; the people appeared reasonably well-dressed; sidewalks and paved streets, though not general, were evident in large number; and he noted in his diary that soap consumption was greater here *per capita* in Haiti than elsewhere. Of course, since the *élite* used Port-au-Prince as their major residence, conditions were likely to be better than in other towns, but what Heiser saw impressed him as better than he had expected. At the end of a brief tour of the city, Heiser met Dr. Melhorn, who gave much the same information as had Butler in Florida on February 18th and put into his hands a copy of the 1929 High Commissioner's *Annual Report*, which gave a summary of medical progress to date.

March 1st and 2nd, Heiser remained at Port-au-Prince, studying the *Annual Report* and attending the Hearings in the hope of gleaning information from purely Haitian sources. He gained little information from the Hearings other than the previously noted information that the Navy medical service was the only phase of United States operations of which all classes of the people unanimously approved.

On March 3rd, he drove out to the Pont Beudet Isolation Camp for the Insane. This institution was twenty miles out of town in an old abandoned

Gendarmerie Barrack. A Dr. Ropp of the United States Navy was in charge. Primitive compared to United States standards, the camp held 193 patients, each of whom was fed for less than fifteen cents per day. In Haiti, people lived ordinarily on bananas, mangoes, corn, and beans, with meat perhaps once a week. Here at Pont Beudet, the patients enjoyed meat every day.

Attached to the Camp was a boys' reformatory, making the entire population 274. The cost per month was $2750.00, which was thirty-three cents per day per individual. The main trouble, Heiser found, with the institution was that no organized work had been provided for either boys or insane, but this was answered by the statement that the institution was relatively new and psychiatrists and social workers difficult to obtain. In any event this was the first institution of its type in Haiti. Formerly the insane had been chained or driven from village to village as possessed by demons, and delinquent boys had been pressed into army service or government construction work not much different from slave-labor.

March 4th, Heiser went to Dufort, thirty miles out of Port-au-Prince, accompanied by Kerney, to see a local clinic. He found the whole affair some-what crude. A charge of four cents was made for each patient, and more time was spent in collecting these few cents than in diagnosis. When he protested what he felt to be rather sloppy diagnoses, he was told that the diagnosis was usually correct, since most of the Haitian diseases were either yaws, malaria, tuberculosis, or syphilis. So many Haitians had yaws that the doctors felt that if they prescribed for this disease, they could not be far wrong.

The examinations were amusing. As Haitians proved to be unusually modest, each patient strutted behind a table which hid his lower parts. The examining physician made notes, asked questions about the patient's medical history, and answered just as many questions regarding the fee. The patient was told to dress, handed a prescription, and led out to argue with an orderly on the subject of payment. Generally, Heiser noted, the patients were not confident of the medical advice, usually seeking additional remedies prescribed by both Catholic priest and Vodun witch-doctor.[13]

This type of rural clinic was held weekly, ordinarily in connection with the market, when the
farmers in the valleys came to town to sell their
produce. The clinic had no building, only a structure
with a grass roof, for which the United States paid
the owner eight cents per day for rental. Heiser
asked twenty of the patients, as a matter of cur-
iosity, the name of the President of Haiti at the
present time, and none knew.

On March 5th, Heiser saw the Haitian General
Hospital at Port-au-Prince. The structure, started
in 1915, stretched over several city blocks and contained three hundred beds. The institution tried
to increase receipts by service to Americans and
Syrians (one of the foreign white groups living in
the country), who would not have gone to Haitian
doctors anyway, with the result that fees were higher
here than charged by local practitioners. Revenues
had increased from $5774.00 in 1924-25 to $19,132
in 1929-30. Much of this revenue had been used for
new buildings, quarters for sisters and priests (who
found employment in all medical centers in Haiti),
and a children's ward. Heiser was distressed--and
annoyed--because he could find no one who could give
exact figures as to disease incidence or treatment
results. This certainly seemed to be a weakness of
the Navy Medical Service. He jotted down the following figures which the finance office had given him:

Cost of each patient per day	$1.10
Haitian doctors	eleven
Haitian interns	five
Navy doctors	five
American Red Cross nurses	four
Haitian nurses	twenty
Haitian pupil nurses	twenty-eight
Large number of Sisters (exact number unre-corded)	

The Paris-trained Haitians made a particularly
good impression on him. He noticed that the urology,
skin, gynecology, and obstetrical departments had
Haitian heads, but that Americans operated the remainder of the Hospital. The Red Cross nurses were Americans paid by the Haitian Government.

Nurses' training was good. Only recently the
passing grade in all courses had been changed from

sixty to seventy per cent, and the nurses apeared
to have won the respect of Haitians. The main problems were dissatisfaction with Dr. Butler's ruling
that the nurses could have vacations with pay only
once in every three years, rapid turnovers (twenty-
two in the last ten years), color jealousy (not only
between white and Negro, but between light-skinned
Negroes and black-skinned), and occasional thieving.

To be certain that no disease might be prevalent
that had not been previously ascertained and treated,
and as a protection against the dreaded plague, autopsy was performed on everyone who died at the hospital. One of the things that startled Heiser was
the information that many Haitians would leave their
babies at the hospital, dead or alive (either for
autopsy or treatment), and never call for them again.

Unfortunately, even here Heiser found resentment
of Americans by Haitians, even among Haitians being
treated. Ernest Chauvet had reported in his newspaper
Le Nouvelliste, that the Hospital had discharged
12 Haitians to make room for one German. When confronted with the lie, he said not to worry, that
his readers demanded that sort of sensationalism.

From the Hospital, Heiser went to the École
National de Médicine et Pharmacie run by the
Rockefeller Foundation. Once a shack, it now consisted of two fine buildings, housing eighty students
in the medical school, fifteen in the School of Phar-
macy, and ten in the Dental School. Equipment was
not elaborate, but well-selected, and had been
donated by the Rockefeller Foundation along with
eleven fellowships. Furthermore, the Director, seemed
to be a man of unusual energy and conscientiousness
whose administration and planning of curriculum were
good, especially in the fields of anatomy, histology,
pathology, and obstetrics. Entrance requirements
demanded a Bachelor's degree.

That evening, Dr. Heiser addressed the Haitian
Medical Society on "World Happenings in Medicine"
at a meeting attended by 100 to 150 Haitian doctors.
A Dr. Hudicourt--President of the august body and
not the Hudicourt who had appeared at the Hearings
--read a paper which impressed Heiser as being more
concerned with that gentleman's recent visit to
Panama as a representative of Haitian medicine than

123

with medicine *per se*.

The next day, Heiser began a three-day provincial trip to study the medical aspects of the Navy Health Service as it presented itself in the more isolated areas of the country. At Petit-Goave he saw the barracks of the Garde (in charge of a Lieutenant André, "a fine physical mulatto"), the prison which the Garde maintained, and the hospital. The hospital, overlooking a lovely garden dotted with flowers and shrubs, held thirty-five beds, separate operating and dispensary buildings, a latrine, and a fine kitchen with modern stoves. The hospital was in charge of a "coal black" and lacked "that cleanliness found where whites were in charge." Before the Occupation, nothing had been here, and three days by horseback over a difficult trail had been necessary to get patients to Port-au-Prince.

An efficient Jamaican in charge of forty-five men handled sanitation. The problem with getting figures on sanitation needs lay in the lack of an adequate census in the provinces. Heiser thought that the local churches could be of inestimable value in this regard, but until that time absolutely no effort whatsoever toward obtaining adequate statistics had been made.

At Miragone he found an active dispensary and street-cleaning department. A Second-Lieutenant Kline of the Garde, who spoke with a German accent and who, for all his thoroughness, demonstrated a distinct Prussian arrogance to everything he was asked, supervised the medical administration. (A Lieutenant Blanchard administered a contingent of fifty marines in the area; typical of the American Occupation, he had been in Haiti two years and knew no French.)

On March 7, Heiser was in Cayes,[14] which had been the scene of recent riots, strikes, and confusion. He found malaria more serious here than in any other town in Haiti.

Although Cayes was called a town, its fifteen thousand population lay scattered over miles of territory, with twenty miles of intervening ditches, cesspools, and water-holes. In reality, Cayes was a great mass of tiny farms cluttered in hodge-podge fashion about irrigation-ditches and spots of arable soil. These ditches, mud-holes, and water-deposits, when added to the numerous distilleries left vacant by the recent alcohol tax,[15] were excellent breeding spots for mosquitoes. Drainage was essential, however, not only for ending the malaria, but because sugar cane, so important to the economy of the area, required a much drier soil.

Distressing was the lack of cleanliness in the market place. Meat, for example, was brought down from the hills without curing of any sort and dumped into large tubs covered by screens to await sale. A portion sold, the desired weight or part was cut from the whole with dirty knives, and the remainder dumped back into a tub well-occupied by dirt and insects.

At St. Louis de Sud Heiser noted the fine cement culverts, which were built with funds obtained from a lapsing appropriation which would have gone to build a Catholic Church.

The town hospital contained one hundred beds, but did not have the thoroughness found in Port-au-Prince. A Sister was in charge of each ward, but trained Haitians were in the operating room. These operating room Haitians trained their own assistants by a system of apprenticeship.

March 8th Heiser returned to Port-au-Prince to attend the confidential sessions of the Commission at the completion of the Hearings and listen to the plan of compromise which Forbes proposed. The next day, he was in Hinche on the tour into the interior taken by the Commission.

The Hinche area was particularly desolate and barren, having been virtually destroyed by Cacos during the years of revolution and turmoil. Deforestation, erosion, and lack of irrigation had run their course, with little attempt at all in the way of soil control.

Malaria was widely prevalent, with no systematic treatment, Heiser thought, although the large field swamp near the hospital had recently been drained, which gave some relief. Dousing the soggy earth and mud-pots with Paris green had also been done in increasing degree. Poor sanitation probably made its

contribution to the high malaria rate; street sweep-
ing, red rubbish tins, and house to house inspections
comprised all attempts at sanitation. Nor were latrines in evidence. Dr. Brinkley, in charge of the
120 bed hospital, complained that all repairs on
equipment had to be made by himself personally, as
Haitians could not do anything in that line, although
Jamaicans could. But he lacked sufficient numbers
of whites or Jamaicans. He did not think Haitian
nurses to be satisfactory, especially with the menial
tasks, which they considered to be beneath them.
He did like the plump vegetables which the ever-
present Sisters grew in Haitian gardens.

Heiser recounts that Forbes and Fletcher were
upset by the yaws cases they saw along the roads
of Mirebelais, Las Cahobas, Thomaside, and Hinche,
and the country paths in general. Forbes had seen
yaws before in the Philippines, but those had been
cases inherited from Spanish domination. The United
States Navy had been in Haiti fifteen years and still
yaws cripples were to be seen at the corners of virtually every village and hamlet through which the
Commission had passed.

At Cap-Haitien on the 10th Heiser saw the hospital which he called a monument to the Occupation.
Covering several city blocks in area and completely
new except for the center, the hospital possessed
excellent equipment, latrines, kitchens, proper facilities, and even a private-rooms building (which was
also used for nurses' quarters). Plans were being
made for an X-ray plant. Physicians, American and
Haitian, nurses, and Sisters seemed to be plentiful.
Shrubbery, flowers, and trees were in profusion.

Two Navy doctors, Lane and Shipley, were in
charge of the hospital. Oddly enough, both of them,
to Heiser's amusement, had originally been eye, ear,
nose, and throat men. They informed him that malaria
was uncommon, and that the city of Cap-Haitien suffered little disease. No diabetes case had come along
in two years. Seldom did they see gall stones, gastric or intestinal ulcers, kidney or bladder stones.
The incidence of cancer was not alarming. Cataracts
and typhoid were rare. They did see syphillis in
adults who had yaw markings. When mangoes were plentiful, cases increased in number. But, generally, the
disease rate was very low. "Even if (their) diet

(is) unbalanced, (they) seem to avoid many diseases. The centuries of neglect finally produced this apparently immune race, or does yaws protect--or does undernourishment--lead to avoidance of (sic.) many diseases?" mused Heiser in his diary.[16] He had one answer for it. He had been told that few people had grey hair; perhaps diseased persons died before getting to the hospital. Nonetheless the theory of an "immunity" tantalized him.

In the port of Gonaives, on the 12th, he found the chief problem to be that of dealing with foreign vessels. With no facilities for quarantining or handling infected ships, the town was vulnerable to plague, although Heiser had not been informed of any recent epidemics.

With the handling of the malaria problem, he was pleased. Here he found the best active effort in Haiti toward eradication. An excellent map in the health office--the first of its type in Haiti --[17]showed breeding areas together with those lowlands where draining and filling had either been completed or in progress. Surveys made of children living on the edge of the swamps showed 90 per cent infection, while those of other groups in or close to the middle of town showed reductions from three per cent to zero depending upon the distance from the breeding areas. The Director of the hospital at Gonaives, a Dr. Logue, had given the drainage activities his personal direction so that the work proceeded as quickly as time and money would permit. Heiser saw one main ditch of several miles in length stretching from the swampy areas into great cement drains that ran through the town into the sea. The street along the low swampy fields was known as the Avenue du Mort over which none but the dead passed; when Heiser saw it, it had become a street of residences, one of which was owned by Dr. Logue himself, and the former swamps were used for the production of crops. The ditches used as drains were regularly cleaned, and Heiser saw evidences that fish were entering. At the time of Heiser's visit, only a few cases of malaria had been reported.

The hospital at Gonaives had seventy-five beds, with cots on the veranda. In 1915 a dilapidated building, ultimately razed, stood on that same spot. The buildings of the hospital now covered a small block, and additions were being continually made from a gradual accumulation of savings, although the staff saw few private patients. Private patients were charged $2.00, and subsistence was $.11 per day. Rarely did a case of cancer, hookworm, or appendicitis occur; no intestinal ulcers or stones were in evidence. Hernia made a frequent appearance, however, and yaws, as in most of Haiti, predominated. The hospital staff consisted of two Haitian doctors, three trained Haitian nurses, and six Sisters.

Water in Gonaives had to be boiled, although Dr. Logue claimed that when drawn from a source in the hills, it was safe. Sanitation consisted of the usual street-cleaning employed in most Haitian towns, with latrines only half-dug. Dr. Logue stated that, as Gonaives was a port town, he had great difficulty keeping it clean for any length of time. Generally he used the large refuse and sweepings to fill in the low lands and swampy areas rather than follow the prescribed method of burning.

Heiser found St. Marc in charge of an Haitian, Dr. Louis Jourdan,[18] who concerned himself chiefly with the hospital. Although the hospital contained sixty beds, not all of them were filled, a condition which Heiser noted in most of the clinics, rural and urban, run solely by Haitian personnel. He also made the notation in his diary that he caught Dr. Jourdan in several false replies to his routine questions; Jourdan claimed that 100% of the latrines were in use, for example, but Heiser saw many evidences to the contrary. This tendency to falsify he found to be a characteristic trait among Haitian medical personnel.

Archaie had a dispensary and a sanitary inspector who limited his duties primarily to relief, although the authorities were attempting to have the sanitation force extend its activities as to mosquito control.

On March 13th, Heiser returned to Port-au-Prince where he rejoined the Commission. Dr. Melhorn spoke before the Commission on the question of how to guard the health of the Haitian people should American forces be withdrawn, since this matter was of the gravest concern to Forbes as well as to Dr. Heiser. Melhorn stated that (1) it was essential to obtain a proper functioning of the courts in the effort to maintain enforcement of sanitary regulations already established and yet to be established (2) it was essential to create a Civil Service to protect trained medical personnel from the encroachments of political favoritism or patronage (3) the Navy should continue a system of advisory personnel to the Haitians on a basis similar to the mission of the Navy in Peru and Brazil.

Except for yaws and malaria, he continued, Haiti experienced little epidemic disease during the American Occupation: no bacillary (he tried hard to show by records that they had had a serious outbreak in 1922, but it had resulted in only fourteen cases and no deaths at the hospital), no plague, no diphtheria, measles, pneumonia, diabetes, stones, gastric and intestinal ulcers. The tuberculosis problem, he admitted, was serious in the towns. Exact figures were not available because, although births and deaths were required by law to be registered under penalty for failure to do so, many Haitians still refused to do so because of the fee levied for registration.

Melhorn agreed with Heiser on the dire need for a census, if an accurate tabulation was to be made of precisely what the Occupation had done in matters of health. The Church census claimed 2,652,000 Haitians, but Melhorn could not vouch for its accuracy. For instance, in Port-au-Prince, the Church census claimed 123,000 persons, yet the Service d'Hygiene claimed 88,000 for Port-au-Prince.

Once again the phenomenally low disease rate for Haitians, considering the poverty, poor living conditions, malnutrition, lack of proteins, and universal yaws, amazed the investigators both in the Navy and on the Commission. Heiser suggested having the weights of school children in Haiti compared with those of Negro school children of the same age in the United States.

Was Melhorn confident that should American forces be entirely withdrawn, Haitians would be able to handle their medical needs? He was confident they would. Assuming 1936 as the withdrawal date, he said that if he could get the entire medical service Haitianized by 1934, with a two-year supervisory period to follow, all should be well.

On March 11th, Heiser went to the Central Penitentiary. He found 525 prisoners, many of whom--he was shocked to find--had been waiting two years for trial. Thirty-two were under sentence of death, but no executions had taken place, as President Borno refused to take the responsibility. The general health, so far as Heiser could ascertain, was excellent, with little tuberculosis and a noticeable absence of any other diseases. The prisoners experienced an average gain of weight of five pounds. Food, including meat, cost $.11 per day per prisoner. Although the men received little stimulation of mind and spirit, they were kept busily occupied in making furniture and uniforms. The Commandant, a certain Coyle, stated that it was impossible to teach Haitians the finer aspects of machine work. When the work demanded a greater accuracy than one sixteenth of an inch, they failed. Heiser suggested teaching them how to repair government vehicles.

The Garde d'Haiti had its own special hospital in Port-au-Prince, consisting of thirty beds. Those men requiring further treatment went to the General Hospital.

Heiser was surprised at the size, completeness, and organization of the Health Center in Port-au-Prince, occupying a two story building. Among its many activities, it had a special department for examining servants, food-handlers, the blind, the crippled, and so on. Photographs were taken of the trouble spots in the city, and Port-au-Prince was divided up into districts for quick action. Much was done to stimulate Haitians to complaints of hazardous health conditions, attendance at lectures and follow-up interviews. Students from the nurses' training school of the General Hospital were sent here frequently as a part of their curriculum. The Women's Volunteer Service at the Health Center had been started by Mrs. Melhorn herself, and helped to dissolve the social barrier and stigma attached to the *élite's* taking part in service efforts that required menial work. The colors, Heiser noted, were mixed.

When Heiser actually sat down to write his report, he demonstrated a gift for distinguishing the

important from the unimportant.[19] Where he felt that
the doctors of the country showed no willingness
to bring relief to remote places in Haiti, the United
States Medical Service had set up 153 rural clinics
with 1,341,596 visits made in 1929 alone, and 11
modern hospitals having a capacity of 11,000 beds
where before only a few hundred of the almshouse
type existed. Although the entire burden of medical
care lay on the government (private hospitals and
voluntary aid virtually lacking), Heiser could not
specifically state what benefits had accrued through
government aid since no decent census apart from
the inadequate Rockefeller Foundation Census of 1924
had been done. Port-au-Prince and the majority of
the towns were virtually free of malaria, while the
rural areas were gradually being brought under control. Economic conditions would have to improve,
however, before malaria could be completely
eliminated. Tuberculosis was highest in Port-au-
Prince. Typhoid and dysentery had been eliminated
by chlorinating the water supply, hookworm was not
serious, and diabetes, heart disease, pneumonia,
and stones of gall bladder, kidney, and urinary bladder were all rare. In regard to malnutrition, he
stated that "no one need go hungry in Haiti."
Mangoes, yams, rice, beans, were in abundance and
to be had with a minimum of effort; but the diet
was protein deficient through the lack of eggs, milk,
and meat. A major share of the difficulty lay in
the ignorance of the people in public health, which
the Health Center at Port-au-Prince was doing much
to counteract. Heiser seemed satisfied with the practical courses in nurses' training at Port-au-Prince,
the hospital corps-men trained by the medical officers of the Garde and the General Hospital, and very
pleased with the new medical school run under the
auspices of the Rockefeller Foundation, though no-
where in his report did he mention the Foundation
by name. He mentioned that one of the products of
the Haitian Nurses' Training Center was a graduate
nurse at Columbia University, who was soon to return
to open classes in her field at Port-au-Prince.

Four of the ten health districts were in charge
of Haitians. Of the 2,222 persons in the National
Health Service, 2,120 were Haitian, twenty medical
Navy officers, fourteen Navy hospital corpsmen, sixty-
three French nuns, two French priests, four American
Red Cross nurses, one French librarian, one Jamaican

131

plumber. Of the 159 Haitian doctors, forty were employed in the Government Service.

But the important thing was not making the President aware of facts which he could obtain from the
High Commissioner's Annual Reports. What was important was Heiser's verification of Russell's Reports
on the Medical Service, that much *had* been accomplished during the Intervention, and that much more remained to be done. What the Navy had tried to do, so
far as Heiser could determine, had been the result
of sincere efforts to benefit the Haitian people.

The report closed with the following comment
and recommendations:

> There is abundant evidence that great improvement has
> taken place in the health of the people since the Occupa-
> tion. The National Public Health Service enjoys the confi-
> dence and approval of the public to an unusual degree.
> The streets of the towns are well-swept; garbage and
> refuse are removed; slaughter houses are inspected; and
> an earnest effort made to control soil pollution and to
> provide safe drinking-water. The Gendarmerie had a good
> medical service. The jails are clean and sanitary, and
> the average health of the prisoners has been greatly im-
> proved. The hospitals are well-administered, and high-
> grade medical and surgical skill is provided. Machinery
> is available for the control of epidemics and to prevent
> the introduction of disease from abroad. Medical relief
> through the vast rural clinic system can be had by every-
> one, even in the most remote sections of the country.
> Diagnosis based upon laboratory findings is available
> for all necessary cases. The health and medical work has
> been directed and largely done by the United States Naval
> medical officers, ably assisted by Haitians and the French
> nuns.
>
> Steps have been taken to provide training to enable
> Haitians to take over the entire National Public Health
> Service. In view of the importance of building up the
> disease weakened Haitian people, it is recommended that
> it be made possible for the government of Haiti to avail
> itself of United States Naval medical officers to serve
> as adviser after the present treaty expires. It might
> also be desirable to employ a few American medical men
> other than naval officers to insure longer tenure and
> continuity of service. In the meantime the assignments
> of the United States Naval medical officers and hospital-

corps men should be lengthened, so that the experience gained in language, customs, and the conditions may be available to the people of Haiti for the greatest possible period.

Unless these steps are taken, it is feared that the Medical Service may deteriorate and that ground will be lost which has been won with so much sacrifice and effort. [20]

The Marines [21]

Fletcher reported that the marines, whose expense was borne solely by the American Government, were a stabilizing and supporting force in the preservation of order. He found little complaint as to the presence of the marines, except as they formed part of the American Occupation itself. As a matter of fact, he did not see many evidences of the marines at all while he was in Haiti, he said, since all of them, with the exception of 150, were at Port-au-Prince, and the rest stationed at Cap-Haitien. The Commission, he stated, had discussed the idea of removing them from the cities altogether to a barracks outside, where they would not be on public view at all, but this was found to be impractical and unwise. Although he recognized that the marines would be necessary to protect Americans and foreigners in cases of riot or public disturbance, he did recommend the gradual reduction of the Marine Brigade if (a) both United States and Haitian Governments concurred and (b) the situation warranted—although the Commandant of the Garde d'Haiti should be consulted prior to taking action. He cautioned that any withdawal of the spending money of 800 officers and men of the Marine Brigade would have a deleterious effect upon the economic life of the country, especially in the Depression days through which the country was presently passing.

Law and Order

The section on Law and Order really referred to the Garde alone.[22] Much of Fletcher's information on the subject came not only from Heiser's observations (whose travels gave him a good deal of opportunity to see the Garde in operation as well as the Health Service) but from interviews with Haitian and American Garde personnel and with Major General

133

Frank E. Evans, who commanded the Garde d'Haiti.
In an interview on March 13, 1930, much like the
one which Dr. Melhorn gave before the Commission
on the Health Service, Evans answered critics of the
Constabulary:

> The need for an efficient Haitian Garde is clear. The
> new Haitian Government will face conditions traditional
> in Haitian government from 1804 until the American Inter-
> vention in 1915. Those were: a desire on the part of un-
> scrupulous politicians to find a one-way road to the
> treasury; dishonesty and graft by some in office; the
> possible conversion of the government into a military
> despotism; exploitation of an illiterate and inarticulate
> peasantry. Like most Latin-American republics, Haiti was
> a republic in name only. Peasants were impressed into
> warring armies. To travel from one town to another a pass-
> port was necessary. The so-called Haitian army was incom-
> petent and parasitical, and the paymasters absorbed the
> bulk of the soldiers' pay. Under their favorite conception
> of a parliamentary government at whose head there was
> a military despot, control was centered in the hands of
> a few irresponsible leaders with little conception of
> high and disinterested national government.
>
> *Our Haitian officers want no return to such conditions.*
> [Italics inserted by present author.] In answer to a confi-
> dential memorandum issued to them a few weeks ago they
> expressed their desire for some form of legislation that
> would protect them from displacement by any political
> favorites. They have impressed this on me in personal
> talks for the past two years. They are desirous of a re-
> tirement law for officers and men, based on the American
> idea, that will further protect them in their chosen ca-
> reer; and of another providing for the creation of a re-
> serve of honorably discharged Gardes that will furnish
> troops for any national emergency.

Forbes suggested that this Garde, Haitianized,
might very well form, after Americans had left, an
élite in itself, a Praetorian Guard which, once corrupt, could bring through its very efficiency and
precision more terror and loss of freedom to Haiti
than the motley, over-generaled, over-officered Army
which had gone before. Evans thought that this did
not necessarily have to be so if a broader democratic
base could be simultaneously created in the country.

Returning to conditions that will face a Haitian government after American withdrawal, there seems to be one remedy that depends almost wholly on the stability and foresight of that government. Haitians of the requisite standard of patriotism will have to face the demands of a "lunatic fringe" of unscrupulous leaders, a growth of communistic tendencies fanned by unscrupulous agitators and a newborn strike consciousness. If the patriotic organizations will rally to the support of the government and exercise their influence to enforce discipline within their ranks, and keep the radical factions to the background, they will contribute much to the economic development that is necessary for a stable government.

Under the old regime the spoils system and over-centralization thrived. Legislative bodies were, in fact, simply appointed by a military despot. Free and honest elections were a fiction.

All these possible handicaps will require an efficient Garde, and the legislation needed to ensure its permanency and freedom from political influence should receive most serious consideration.

This last remark merely rephrased Dr. Melhorn's plea--a civil service for the employment of professionals on the basis of merit rather than political influence and favoritism.[23]

Fletcher and Forbes both considered Evans overly sanguine. Tempered as such, Fletcher's Report went as follows: Article 10 of the Treaty had obligated the Haitian Government to create a constabulary composed of native Haitians organized and officered by Americans for (1) the preservation of domestic peace (2) the security of individual rights (3) the full observance of the treaty. The American officers (Marine officers of second lieutenant and up) were supposed to be replaced gradually by Haitians after examinations conducted by a Board specially selected by the senior American officer of the Garde, such examinations to take place in the presence of representatives of the Haitian Government. Over the course of the fifteen years, other agreements had been made regarding the salaries of Garde personnel, conditions of living, uniforms, duties, general activities, and so on. At the present time (1930) the Garde performed not only police duties but acted as communal advisers on the disbursement of communal revenues, handled the Coast Guard, and was responsible for all lighthouses. The future significance of the Garde lay in its ability to maintain order after the withdrawal of United States Naval forces.

Fletcher declared the Garde to have performed conscientiously and well. Haitianization, however, had not proceeded as rapidly as had been expected, in the opinion of the Commission. No Haitian had been appointed above the rank of Captain, two Haitians were Captains out of twenty-three, seventeen Haitians First Lieutenants out of fifty-eight, nineteen Second Lieutenants out of fifty-seven. Out of all the cadet officers, twenty-eight of them were Haitian. The Garde had a 1930-1936 program prepared for total Haitianization, but this was only in the planning stages.

Fletcher thought that Haitianization could take place rapidly without changing the Gendarmerie Agreement in the Treaty, if the American authority would simply transfer American Marine officers back to the Marine Brigade, and let their places be taken by Haitians. If this could not be done through local authority, then Haitianization must lie with the Navy Department and Marine Corps Headquarters in Washington. Such reform, the report emphasized, was essential, even if discipline and efficiency temporarily suffer. The École Militaire, which had been closed at the end of 1929 because of the disturbances, Fletcher recommended be reopened for the training of Haitian officers, with support of the United States. Until the Garde was Haitianized, however, he suggested some provision be made for orderly promotion and for protection against promotion by political influence.

Judicial Procedure [24]

Friction had arisen between the Haitian courts and the American treaty officials. On one hand the courts refused to enforce (or preferred to obstruct) certain administrative measures, while, on the other hand, treaty officials refused to obey orders of the courts on the grounds that the treaty of 1915 was the real law of the land, superior to Haitian statute and case law, with none of its operations to be interfered with by the Haitian judiciary. Fletcher recommended that fuure conflicts be settled by direct and friendly negotiations between the two

136

Governments rather than through the strict use of the courts. In any event, he reported that although the administration of Haitian justice was unsatisfactory to the people (reforms were needed in the system itself i.e. the enactment of adequate salaries for judges), the Commission viewed the matter as out of its own particular jurisdiction and something primarily for Haitians to handle. Fletcher noted, though, that if a stable government were to be achieved after the withdrawal of the Occupation, the Judiciary had to receive careful consideration.

The Constitution [25]

The major complaints that Fletcher found were (1) in regard to the manner in which the Constitution of 1918 had been adopted (the plebiscite) and amended in 1928, (2) the manner in which the present Government (Borno's) had interpreted its provisions relating to powers of the Council of State (the refusal to call for legislative elections), (3) the granting to foreigners of the right to own Haitian land. Fletcher recommended that, since the Haitian people from 1804 to 1918 had prohibited foreigners from owning real estate, the United States should raise no objection if the Haitians wished to amend this particular provision of the 1918 Constitution. The United States would merely stipulate that the very few rights and titles acquired under the present constitution should be respected. The Commission, stated Fletcher, found no instance of undue advantage being taken by Americans as a result of the clause enabling them to acquire title to Haitian soil.

Race Prejudice [26]

White, writing rather emotionally, reported that racial antipathies lay behind many of the problems which the United States faced in Haiti. He recounted essentially what Hoover already knew; that the *élite* consisted of five per cent of the population, was urban, French cultured, educated, mulatto ("shading from octoroon to black"), wealthy ("careful to maintain its own caste, as in any other ruling class"); that the masses were poor and ignorant, black, of pure African descent, and generally because of their illiteracy politically inarticulate ("except in case of mobs or bandit gangs which formerly infested the countryside and furnished the forces of revolution"). Although the wild roaming bands had disappeared under American rule, the social forces that created them were still present, namely, poverty, ignorance, lack of a tradition of or desire for orderly free government. From what White could discover, the aim of Americans in Haiti had been to broaden the base of the articulate proletariat and in so doing, provide for future democracy. Such means as education, sanitation, roads, telephones, telegraph, regular mail routes, and generally improved means of communication had aided in this effort. The *élite* however, saw in these things a threat to its leadership, and here lay the heart of Haitian opposition to American rule. Where the Occupation failed, thought White in his report, was its failure to understand these social problems. Its "brusque attempt to plant democracy there by drill and harrow, its determination to set up a middle class—however wise and necessary it may seem to Americans—all these explain why, in part, the high hopes of our good works in this land have not been realized." [27]

White did not mention another source of discontent on the part of the *élite*. The Navy Department had been assigning marines from the southern states, with the result that the *élite*, who had for all practical purposes considered itself white and French and had drawn a color line between itself and the black mass, now found itself socially once again in the position it endured during colonial days. In this sense at least, so far as the *élite* was concerned, the Occupation had thrown Haiti back 150 years. The best night spots, cafes, restaurants were frequented by Americans whose white skins and jingling pockets became at one and the same time the envy and hatred of the mulatto aristocrat. The Cercle Bellevue, which had been one of the most celebrated restaurants in Port-au-Prince, frequented primarily by the wealthy *élite*, now became the scene of stormy quarrels among American officers who would not eat with Negroes, no matter how light the coloring, and mulattoes who filled their cups to overflowing with hatred. [28]

Financial Situation [29]

Forbes tried to shift this section of the Report to Kerney, but the attempt was not successful. Strictly speaking, finance should have been for Forbes

to handle anyway, but when the Financial Adviser
appeared to give the Commission his quota of information, Forbes was so busy that he asked Kerney to
handle the situation. "This came back to trouble
me," wrote Forbes later, "as he undertook to write
up our Report and it was a holy terror. He had taken
the few aspects of American work which had been done
badly or unwisely and then dressed them up to a distorted degree. He proceeded to light into them hard,
keeping all explanatory or favorable word back, so
that if adopted as written we should have given a
wholly wrong and wholly unjust picture."[30] Kerney
took the rejection of his financial report in stride
and with his usual good humor. In view of his bad
health and his lack of experience in this field (although he must have possessed a good deal of financial knowledge and talent in acquiring his newspaper
chain in Trenton), he really should never have been
called upon to handle finance in the first place.

Forbes reported the work of the Americans in
handling the revenues and expenditures of the
Haitians "so far noteworthy." A modern budgetary
system was established with preaudit, one of the
latest devices for "accurate, economical, and ex-
peditious management of accounts." Witnesses claimed
improprieties connected with this department, particularly that they were kept in ignorance of what
was being done, but no one, said Forbes, needed to
be in ignorance when the careful reports of the
Financial Adviser were readily available in both
English and French. Six auditors, moreover, from
the United States Comptroller's Office had made a
thorough analysis of all accounts for the Government,
and found these accounts correct except for very
minor errors and adjustments, since rectified.
Revenues had a conservative margin of surplus over
expenditures, which margin was used to pay off
several million dollars worth of the principal of
the public debt "in excess of the amount called for
by the amortization plan." Forbes questioned the
use of this money for reducing the public debt when
it could have been used to reduce taxation, expecial-
ly the export tax, and left the debt to work itself
out during its normal term, keeping more money in
the country where it was badly needed (and—though
Forbes did not say so—giving the wealthy *élite* palpable benefits which might have urged them to more
kindly views of the American achievements). Over

the course of the fifteen years, the Occupation had expanded its financial operations until 60% of the revenues were expended under American supervision, including the service of the public debt.

Forbes recommended that 5% maximum allowed out of Government revenues to cover the costs of the General Receivership should not be considered a flat allowance expected to be spent each year, but only a limit within which the Receiver must operate. He further recommended that appropriations disbursed by the treaty service in Haiti be budgeted with the same detail as "are the appropriations for the regular public services of the Haitian Government."

Stabilizing Haitian government revenues would be difficult so long as two major tax problems went unsolved. The first was the lack of diversified and increased production, agricultural and industrial --complicated all the more by the great hatred and suspicion that existed between country and city. The second was the neglect of direct taxation. The Haitian Government originally depended on customs revenue for income because where approximately 20% of the population consisted of ignorant peasants squatted on their land without benefit of deeds, registration offices, land survey maps, and an adequate system of settling title claims, direct taxation was difficult to enforce. Legislation would not solve this problem--or so Russell had felt in his 1929 *Annual Report*--but education might, with the result that efficient taxation in Haiti could only be achieved gradually over an indefinite period of time. [31]

Public Works

Forbes did not devote a special section to Public Works, but included his remarks in the general discussion of the achievements of the Occupation. [32] The major share of his information came from Russell's Reports, the remainder from his own observations and the testimony of Commander G. A. Duncan, USN, Engineer in Chief. [33]

He reported the construction of 800 miles of highway. "Before the intervention, the road between Port-au-Prince and Cap-Haitien, the two principal ports and cities of the Republic, was practically impassable except on horseback. The journey of 180 miles took three days. Now it is done in six hours by automobile."[34] A Coast Guard was organized, lighthouses built, and navigation rendered much safer, agriculture encouraged through irrigation projects, and hospitals, public buildings, and parks constructed. In seven years the registrations of automobiles had increased from 400 to 2,800, the linear feet of bridges multiplied by three, and a significant increase noted in the number of permits issued for private building construction. Gross trade enjoyed a wholesome increase as measured by the value of exports and imports.[35] Automatic lighthouses increased from four to fifteen; telephone subscribers from 400 to nearly 1,200, and the number of telephone calls from approximately 1,000,000 per year to over 5,000,000.[36]

Although Forbes failed to say so, this department of the Occupation with the possible exception of finance had been found to be the most unpopular of all. The Negro peasant needed no great highways to carry his tiny produce to the local market; the urban dweller had neither car nor horse to travel hundreds of miles, much less the desire; and the mulatto viewed the highways, buildings, and wharves as a further means of both subjugating the country and destroying the slow-paced cultured life he worshipped.

Relations between Church and State[37]

In his interview with the Archbishop of Port-au-Prince, Vezina had been told that the clergy welcomed the Commission to Haiti, but that it could have no part in the settling of affairs. Anticlericalism--especially under Calles in Revolutionary Mexico--had become too virulent in Latin-America to risk the chances of its spread to Haiti. "The fact that the clergy is foreign creates for it a delicate situation and one which at times is difficult. It must abstain from politics. It does, nevertheless, take a profound interest in everything which affects the well-being of the people, sharing the joys and sorrows of that people."[38]

Vezina restricted himself in his report, after a brief historical presentation, to statistics. He reported the organization of the Church to consist of an Archdiocese at Port-au-Prince, and four dioceses--at Cap-Haitien, Aux Cayes, Gonaives, and Port-de-Paix. Two hundred and five priests were resident in Haiti, 156 secular priests engaged in active missionary work and in charge of parishes,[39] while the others did educational work or were involved in labors connected with the dioceses. Of the 205 priests, only eight were Haitian.[40] There were 105 Brothers of Christian instruction, (eighty-three French, ten French-Canadian, nine Spanish, three Haitian), in addition to three congregations of Sisters: St. Joseph de Cluny, (with 146 Sisters), Les Filles de la Sagesse (198), and Les Filles de Marie (22). The priests, stated Vezina, not only spread religion but founded schools, parish churches, and mission chapels. The Brothers of Christian Instruction conducted seventeen boys' schools consisting of 6,731 pupils, half of the instructors Brothers and half laymen, each instructor paid by the Haitian Government less than forty dollars per month. The Brother Superintendent received a monthly salary of 100 dollars. The Sisters conducted thirty-six girls' secondary and boys' and girls' primary schools, in addition to one girls' industrial school conducted by Belgian Sisters and under the Service Technique of the Department of Agriculture. Furthermore, the Haitian Government authorized priests to establish rural schools (presbyterial schools), which now numbered 153 and employed women teachers paid by the Haitian Government at the rate of six dollars per month. These rural schools, comprising 10,623 pupils, Vezina felt, constituted the foundation of the educational system of Haiti. Four colleges existed with a total attendance of 2,500.

Vezina had done much more work, however, than his brief report indicated. He had made a splendid report on Church education in the country.[41] The main trouble with education as undertaken by the Church, he stated in this special report (which never saw publication) lay in the fact that the educational arm of the Church was bound up by contract with the Haitian Government, and could only act along channels permitted by and in accordance with that Government.

Dependent on the Department of Public Instruction were the three congregations of Sisters mentioned above, but only Les Filles de Marie had been able to obtain a contract and carry on public instruction.

142

Other Aspects of the Report and the Long Range View

The system of public instruction was centered in a National Council instituted by the law of August 4, 1920 (which he reported had been convened only once, on January 9, 1921). This National Council consisted of the Archbishop of Port-au-Prince, the Supreme Justice, the President of the central Medical Jury, an agricultural engineer, a delegate of the Protestant missions, a delegate of the Council of Administration of the School of Applied Sciences, two delegates of public superior education, two delegates of public secondary education, two delegates of congregational secondary education, delegates from free secondary education, normal, vocational, and primary education, and five members representing letters, arts, science, commerce, industry (to be named by decree of the President of the Republic upon nomination by the Secretary of Public Works). In addition, regional offices were to be established with regional councils in Cap-Haitien, Port-de-Paix, Gonaives, St. Marc, Petit-Goave, Anse-a-Veau, Jérémie, Cayes, Aquin, and Jacmel, these regional councils much like the National Council. The whole affair was to be under the auspices of the University of Haiti.

If anything suited the Gallic temperament, if anything satisfied the French appetite for detailed paper-apparatus, nothing suited better than this conglomeration of phrase and fancy. Here was constitutionalism applied to education, French culture applying an impractical mechanism to an impossible situation. So long as the matter seemed settled on parchment, the Government appeared at ease. Yet, the system had not worked. Almost pathetically, Vezina wrote that since the creation of the National Council of Public Instruction, only one meeting had taken place, that if this Council had been convened at least once a year, Dr. Freeman's repeated errors would not have occurred, the Haitian Treasury would have saved millions of dollars, and the Haitian people would have been given an educational system "more in accordance with their...powers of absorption..."

The Sequent Steps and the New United States Policy toward Haiti

Although White and Kerney strongly favored the immediate withdrawal of all American forces from

Haiti, Forbes thought that this would be too drastic
a change. He preferred we let the Treaty expire
naturally in five years, and then get out.[42] Forbes
had become convinced that to demand another extension
of the original treaty would be of no purpose, and
that to remain in Haiti at all after 1936 would be
a serious blunder of foreign policy. In conversations
with his brother Edward, Heiser, Dunn, Hoover and
Redmayne during or shortly after the working period
of the Commission, he seemed to come to the view
that, no matter what the United States did in Haiti,
it was becoming the scapegoat of every politician
who aspired to power. Its mere presence in the country
generated ill-feeling. Unquestionably, over the
course of their 125 years of independence Haitians
had known little stability, had turned the word
Republic into an empty term, and by 1915 had become
cannibals devouring themselves from an insatiable
hunger. Unquestionably, too, we had given them stability, tutored them in democracy, and brought a
nearly complete halt to corruption. Yet the change
was not genuine. The flower of democracy had been
grown elsewhere and planted in Haitian soil; it was
not a natural product of the Haitian climate. Democracy in Haiti stood without roots, without a national
will, without a tradition. If Haiti were ever to
find herself, it had to do it through its own disorder, and, though the path be difficult and spotted
with blood, by finding its own solutions to the ills
of the Haitian body-politic.

Forbes recommended, therefore, the following
steps for the United States:
(1) to effect over the course of the next six
years a rapid Haitianization of all services--
finance, medical, coast guard, Garde d'Haiti, public
works, education;
(2) to select American officers for the Occupation departments who were more liberal in their thinking and attitudes toward the colored race;
(3) to recognize the temporary president provided for by the internal settlement so that a legislative assembly might be readily gathered to elect
a permanent president and retake the reins of administration;
(4) to recognize the president elected by the
new National Assembly, provided that no fraud was
found to be involved in the election;
(5) to replace the High Commissioner with a

non-military minister;
(6) to insist that, loss in efficiency or not, this new non-military minister achieve Haitianization of the services without delay;
(7) to effect gradual withdrawal of the Marines;
(8) to modify the treaty when necessary to enable the United States to cut the strands of the Occupation by 1936.[43]

NOTES

1. Kerney had been ill, however, in Haiti, and was unable to bear the labors of a strenuous report. Vezina had done most of the work relating to education, and this was incorporated into Vezina's section on the relations between Church and State. Forbes eliminated publicity as superfluous, and Heiser, although not technically a member of the Commission, eventually wrote the entire section on Health. Forbes tried to give Kerney Finance, but as will be seen later in the chapter, he ultimately did it himself.

2. Heiser declared in private conversations with the author that the report was really Forbes'. He had a trenchant mind that seemed to dominate the situation. After each man had handed in his portion of the report, Forbes went over it with him, making suggestions, and assimilating data in an effort to make the finished report a cohesive unit.

3. Forbes, Haitian Journal, pp. 60–61.

4. National Archives Collection, "Witnesses before Commission," Box 5. This seems to have been the only aspect of the Hearings which was not criticized adversely by the witnesses.

5. The author is indebted to Dr. Heiser for much of this matter relating to Dr. Heiser's life. See also Maxine Block (ed.), *Current Biography*, pp. 360–362. Since 1912, Dr. Heiser has been included in each publication of *Who's Who in America*, with the exception of the 1960–61 edition (an error for which the editors apologized personally to him). Material pertaining to special aspects of Heiser's work is to be found in the *New York Times*, June 25, 1941, p. 23, and June 26, 1941, p. 25; the *New York Times Book Review*, May 11, 1941, p. 2; *Newsweek*, Aug. 29, 1936, pp. 29–32, and July 3, 1939, p. 30.

At the time of the interview (1960), Dr. Heiser was associated with the National Association of Manufacturers, and, although eighty-seven years of age, energetic, quick of mind and physical senses, and very much the living example of his medical theories of health and vitality. His memory of people, personalities, and events concerned in the Haitian venture was remarkably sharp and detailed.

6.   Heiser relates that *An American Doctor's Odyssey* originally consisted of two volumes, which included his work in Latin America, but the publishers felt that a two-volume work would never sell, and Heiser reluctantly condensed the manuscript. His efforts on the Haitian enterprise were not included, therefore, in the published work. Years later, when a new market developed, he was unable to find the unpublished portions of the manuscript, and to the present writing they have still not been discovered. When the book was published, it was criticized in some quarters as a masterpiece of egomania whose title might better have been *Alone in the Orient*.

7.   Forbes, *The Philippine Islands*, Vol. I, pp. 174, 332, 333, 332n, 335, 341n, 344, 345n, 358n, 360, 364; Vol. II, pp. 169n, 224n, 249, 250n.

8.   In the Philippines he had been Forbes' personal physician. A good many of the health problems of the Philippines had been discussed over games of chess, which both men loved and played frequently in their tents at night during their frequent travels through the islands.

9.   Russell's *Annual Reports*, especially the last one for the year 1929, were enormously valuable as a source of statistics and general information. The Commission found them reliable and candid in their pronouncements. Each consisted of a general statement by Russell of affairs during the particular year in question, followed by an appendix containing detailed summaries of the current work and achievement of the several departments of the Occupation.

10.   The following information on pp. 119–132 is taken from Heiser's private diary.

11.   George Fouché Freeman, despite the great criticism levelled at him during his administration of the Service Technique in Haiti, was a noted plant geneticist of no small ability. As a matter of fact, he had been chosen to head this phase of the Occupation because of his special knowledge. He had been educated at Alabama Polytechnic and Harvard University, where he received his Doctor of Science degree, then went into teaching at the Massachusetts College of Agriculture and the Kansas State Agricultural College. He later joined the Arizona Agricultural Experiment Station. He was chief of plant breeding

for the Société Sultanienne d'Agriculture, Cairo, Egypt, Chief of the Department of Cotton Breeding at the Texas Agricultural Experiment Station, and just before he accepted his position in Haiti, had been on special assignment as adviser in agriculture to the French Government in Indo-China.

12. Heiser, Diary, p. 5260.

13. See Leyburn, pp. 131-165, "Vodun"; pp. 166-174, "Religious Contributions." Vezina found Roman Catholicism to be stronger in certain areas of the country than in others. To a great extent, Roman Catholicism remained the religion of the upper class, French-cultured Haitians, a formalized religion that did not appear to strike deeply into the vitals of the black masses. At best, in the isolated rural valleys, it became permeated with the African spirit in varying degrees.

14. General John H. Russell, *High Commissioner's Annual Report* for 1929, Appendix IV, pp. 67-71. The strike of the students at the Medical school on Nov. 7, 1929, was in sympathy with that of the school of Agriculture. The medical school was closed until October, 1930. "Our students were more in sympathy with the strike movements than with the health interests of two million of their countrymen," states Russell on p. 70.

15. *Ibid.* Two thousand acres of swamp were reclaimed near Gonaives and Cayes at a cost of $1.78 per acre.

16. Heiser, Diary, pp. 5329-30.

17. At the Health Center at Port-au-Prince, infant, pre-natal, and post-natal care were also offered for the first time in Haiti. See Russell, *Annual Report* for 1929, Appendix IV.

18. *Ibid.* Four of the ten Sanitary Districts were run by Haitians: Port-de-Paix by Dr. S. Rey, St. Marc by Dr. L. Jourdan, Jérémie by Dr. L. Tarchon, and Petit-Goave by Dr. J. R. Jeanty.

19. *President's Commission for a Study and Review of Conditions in Haiti*, pp. 12-15.

20. *Ibid.*, p. 15. Heiser did not mention that a department of legal medicine had been established in the Haitian Government, under F. Jean-Louis. The purpose of this department was to make a revision of the Medical, Dental, Nursing, Midwifery Practice Act, modernize control of food and drugs, collect statistics, and enforce compliance with these and future acts thought essential to the maintenance of good health. In 1929,

there were convictions in 38.3% of 1,157 cases of infractions of the Sanitary Code. Russell felt strongly that before the Haitian Government could get its feet off the ground in matters of health, it must first be provided with adequate law enforcement of stringent codes.

Total cost of the health program for 1929 was $991,332; government allotments, $887,085; communal allotments, $29,029; reimbusements at hospitals, $25,971, and in sanitation, $2,418. Donations made by the Central Relief Commission, Rockefeller Foundation, and American Red Cross amounted to $26,829, $10,000, and $10,000 respectively.

Supplies had been transported 133,499 miles, 19,824 miles by horseback over difficult trails and through mountainous terrain in areas hitherto almost inaccessible.

The relationship of yaws and syphilis was being probed extensively during this period by aid of the Committee on Research in Syphilis, an American organization, and a special entomologist, Dr. R. L. Turner, had been brought into the country specifically for the control of malaria.

See National Archives Collection, Box #4, "Public Health Service: Testimony of K. C. Melhorn, Director General of the Public Health Service, before James Kerney, March 15, 1930," This is probably the testimony whch Dr. Heiser refers to in his diary, although this testimony took place on the 15th of the month rather than on the 13th. In this same folder is included a reprint of an article also by K. C. Melhorn, "Public Health in Haiti," *United States Naval Medical Bulletin*, Vol. 27, Nos. 3-4 (Washington D.C.: 1929).

21. *President's Commission for the Study and Review of Conditions in Haiti,* pp. 9-10. Col. Richard M. Cutts commanded the brigade as of June 25, 1929, relieving Col. John T. Myers. The *High Commissioner's Annual Report* for 1929 states the strength to be 600 men rather than the 800 that Fletcher reports.

22. *President's Commission for the Study and Review of Conditions in Haiti* , pp. 10-11.

23. National Archives Collection, Box #2, "Garde d'Haiti: Testimony of Major General Frank E. Evans, Mar. 13, 1930," 43 pp., pp. 2-4.

The Garde was in many ways the symbol of Occupation achievement so far as the Navy and Marine officials were concerned. The

Other Aspects of the Report and the Long Range View

Intervention had taken place originally to stabilize the country permanently, and the Garde represented this idea to the
military men who largely administered the nation in cooperation
with the Haitian Government.

The *Annual Report* for 1929, which Fletcher actively employed
for his statistical information, reported the following: Before
1915 the Haitian army consisted of 38 line and 4 artillery
regiments comprising 9,000 men; the Gendarmerie of 1,800 men;
four regiments of the President's Guard. Throughout this force
were 308 generals, 50 colonels, with pay averaging $20 per
month and an allowance of $80 per month for rations. Corrup-
tion was rampant, the prisons evil, with a system of recruit-
ment that amounted to impressment. Bribes of $2.00 usually
were sufficient to avoid service, but few of the black mass
could afford the money for so small a bribe as this. By 1929,
the Army had been dissolved and in its place was a Garde consisting of from 2,537 to 2,622 men, well-paid, literate, properly housed and equipped, with a special medical service of its
own, and performing all military and police functions the corrupt, over-generaled, over-staffed Haitian army did before,
and doing it efficiently. The ratio consisted of one Garde
to each 3.4 miles and 690 inhabitants. Navigation, the registration and licensing of motor-vehicles, the care of prisoners,
the insane, juvenile delinquents, had been added to the duties
of this new constabulary. For more efficient administration,
furthermore, the republic had been divided into twenty-one
districts, each approximately forty square miles. Each district
held generally one captain, five officers, 100 men, with two
sub-districts each under a lieutenant, and seven outposts.
A sanitary detachment was assigned to each district. Within
these districts, in addition to the duties above mentioned,
the Garde tended to construction, communications through rugged
country, fire, the maintenance of highways, the administration
of law and justice on the local or communal level. The officers
knew both French and Creole (at least the Haitian officers
did, if only a minority of the American). There were 309.5
miles of telephone lines, nine airplane fields, and all trails
were under the strict control of the Garde.

See also from the National Archives Collection, Box #2, "Compen-
dium of Information on the Garde d'Haiti," two folders; James
H. McCrocklin's *Garde d'Haiti*: Twenty Years of organization
and training by the United States Marine Corps 1915-1934.

So far as Haitianization of the Garde may be considered, with
which Forbes was so much concerned, in 1917 the number of
Haitian officers went from 5% to 19% in 1922 to 35% in 1928,
and to 36.42% in 1930. At the École Militaire, 75% of the

trainee officers were Haitian. Seventeen officers had been graduated, with thirteen left to go at the time of the Commission. Out of 198 officers in 1930, seventy-eight were Haitians. However, seventy-one of these, or 46.2%, held ranks below that of Major.

The Garde gave medical care to 45,711 prisoners and insane. For example, in one nine-month period in 1929, 9,160 prisoners were vaccinated against small-pox. Granted the merit of the medical services, the question still arises as to why the Garde was holding so many prisoners.

24. *President's Commission for the Study and Review of Conditions in Haiti*, pp. 17-18.

25. *Ibid.*, p. 18.

26. *Ibid.*, pp. 18-19.

27. *Ibid.*, p. 19.

28. The Cercle Bellevue became almost a symbol of *élite* humiliation, and in addition became a hotbed of opposition to American superiority and the American Occupation. After several incidents which proved embarrassing to the Haitian Administration, President Borno closed this "oldest social club in Port-au-Prince" on the charge of "political manifestations." See the New York *Times*, Feb. 4, 1928. When Eugene Roy became President, one of the first acts of his administration was to re-open the Cercle Bellevue (May 17, 1930).

29. *President's Commission for the Study and Review of Conditions in Haiti*, pp. 11-12.

30. Forbes, Haitian Journal, p. 61.

31. See pp. 19-20. In addition, the *Annual Report* gives the following pertinent figures: Total revenue receipts were $8,504,305.68, 15.66% less than 1927-28 (a record year), with total customs receipts $7,049,530, 21.81% less than 1927-28. Internal revenue receipts for 1928-29 were $1,207,052.96 compared with $848,324.02 in the previous year, making an increase of $358,728.93 or 42.28%. Excise taxes more than accounted for the increase, collections from other sources having declined 9.77%. Receipts from emigration declined 56.08%. Income from public land rentals, however, showed a slight increase. The first full year's operation of the new excise tax law produced $452,763.67 and "is a fiscal success." There was no difficulty in collecting the alcohol and cigarette and cigar taxes, al-

though opposition was evidenced to the requirement that smoking tobacco be wrapped in small packages and stamped.

Total expenditures from revenues received in 1928–29 amounted to $8,828,900.79 compared with $8,195,582.90 in the previous year, an increase of 7.66% Disbursements on account of the public debt increased 2.78%. There were smaller expenditures for the Garde, Foreign Relations, Justice, Agriculture, Labor. Those for Public Works, the Agricultural Service, Religion increased. Expenditures from revenue exceeded revenues for the year by $319,595.11 or 3.76%.

Total cash assets as of Sept. 31, 1929, were $6,538,672.38, making a decline of 4.29% from 1927–28. "The unobligated cash balance on Sept. 30, 1929, amounting to $4,072,291.65, was the largest on record, and the public treasury was in a better condition than ever before to meet the contingencies incident to an abrupt change in the trend of revenues such as that in prospect for 1929–30." (p. 55) The public debt was reduced during the year by $1,152,143.81 or 6.10%. It was reduced 5.28% in 1927–28. All amortization requirements were fulfilled well before the close of the year.

In personnel, by the end of 1929, there were twenty–six Americans in the Finance Department and 508 Haitians, compared with twenty–three Americans and 424 Haitians the previous year.

32. *President's Commission for the Study and Review of Conditions in Haiti,* pp. 6–8.

33. National Archives Collection, Box #4, "Public Works: Testimony of Commander G. A. Duncan, USN, Engineer-in-Chief." This testimony consists of two pieces: "A Brief Summary of Accomplishments of the Public Works Administration of Haiti under the Treaty with the United States of America 1916–1930" and "A Concise Statement of Accomplishments of the Public Works Administration of Haiti under the Treaty with the United States of America 1916–1930."

34. *President's Commission for the Study and Review of Conditions in Haiti* , p. 7.

35. The official report of the President's Commission contained no section devoted to commerce, but one should note that according to the *Annual Report* for 1929 Haiti experienced an unfavorable trade balance of $2,418,989. This was the result, undoubtedly, of the world–wide general depression rather than any particular fault of the commerce policies of the Occupation, since previous to this time the favorable trade balances

had been increasing each year. The tourist trade had also been poor, which deprived the country of needed dollars.

The prosperity of Haiti depended, as it still does, on coffee, forming 60–70% of the country's exports. The 1928–29 crop was lean due to unfavorable weather conditions. When, in October, 1929, the coffee valorization program of Brazil, which had been in operation since the close of World War I, collapsed, Haiti's economy was seriously affected. Russell had made attempts to switch the economy to sisal, pineapples, even corn, but with little success; coffee was the single crop that interested the masses of the growers, and this was chiefly wild coffee that needed only to be harvested. France purchased the majority of Haiti's exports (55.29%).

Airlines by Pan-American Airways at the time were in the process of being set up between Haiti, Cuba, Florida, and Puerto Rico, and Russell hoped that his latest development would have a salutary effect upon the depressed economy of the country.

36. Regarding the Public Works Department, the *Annual Report* for 1929 gave the following information: Before 1915 the motto had been in Haiti, "Never cross a bridge if you can go around it." The only telephone system in the country failed in 1911, automobiles were unheard of, and only a rudimentary telegraph system existed. By 1929 Haiti had 3,000 vehicles, 1,006 miles of roads, 210 bridges with a total span of 5,770 feet, a modern telephone system (automatic in Port-au-Prince and Cap-Haitien), paved streets in her major cities, public parks, twelve lighthouses built since 1915 (only four were in operation when the Americans arrived), nine wharves, a revival of irrigation that had been allowed to lapse since French colonial days, 100 miles of canals to serve a population of 62,000, and water supplies for sixty-four villages.

During 1929, the Public Works Department, according to the *Report*, had given employment to 8,933 people (where the previous year the number was a little over 7,000). $2,249,909 had been spent on public works—a Headquarters Building at Las Cahobas for the Garde, 250 student units for the Brothers' school at Port-de-Paix, twenty student units for the Sisters at Gonaives, ten standard rural dispensaries, public comfort stations at Port-au-Prince (at Place Louverture and under the Tribune, an old government building), a fishmarket at Fort St. Clair, post office building at Port-au-Prince for the Financial Adviser-General Receiver, a Public Works Administration office at Gonaives, and sixteen farm schools. In addition, the start of a 6,000 student industrial school for the Service Technique was made (day and evening classes) and a dormitory for thirty-two students at Plaisance started. Repairs had been made on the church at Hinche.

The Public Works Department was also reputedly responsible for many smaller routine tasks which ordinarily go unnoticed, but, neglected, are sorely missed, such as the installation of ten fire hydrants in Port-au-Prince and a chlorinator at the Bourdon Reservoir for the sterilization of the water supplies of Port-au-Prince and Pétionville, renewal of the entire Plaissance-Carisier aqueduct system at Port-au-Prince, improvements in the water supplies at Furcy, Pétionville, Miragoane, Petit-Goave, Gonaives, St. Marc, Cayes, Cap-Haitien, Jacmel (the city with the most abundant water supply), Jérémie (which had an inadequate supply), the paving of John Brown Avenue in Port-au-Prince with penetration asphalt, the enlargement of the Momance Dam, the rebuilding of the Pétionville Road, which was the Royal Road of Christophe, built in the early days of independence (a car could now go from Cap-Haitien to Milot in less than thirty minutes), the building of the Trouin-Jacmel Road, and a start made in the construction of the Pétionville-Kenskoff road.

37. *President's Commission for the Study and Review of Conditions in Haiti*, pp. 15–17.

38. National Archives Collection, Box #1, "Clergy: Statement of Clergy in Haiti." At another point: "The clergy...is almost wholly foreign and will be foreign probably for many years. In 1921 the Bishops founded the Apostolic School of Notre Dame for the training of Haitian priests. In spite of all that has been done, up to now the number of our students remains small. I sincerely am grateful to M. Vezina for having visited our Apostolic School the second day after his arrival in Port-au-Prince and I thank him for the kind words which he addressed to the students pointing out to them the important services which they will be in position to render to their country...

"The 1915 Treaty and the occupation in the beginning were not looked upon alike by all Haitians although they were all inspired by an equally great patriotism. It seemed..., therefore ... to be our duty to remain outside of the parties which resulted. The clergy remained independent of the opinions of them all.

"But the clergy will rejoice with all its heart when the present situation is ended and will joyfully chant a *Te Deum* in solemn Thanksgiving.

"Ministers as we are of a Church which teaches that the occupation by another country is an abnormal thing and sorrowful thing which everyone should seek to end as soon as possible; knowing moreover as we do now this beloved people suffers in its national dignity by being held in tutelage, with all our hearts we make our own their sufferings, their complaints and their hopes."

39. At the time of the Commission, there were 465 mission chapels and 112 parishes in the country.

40. The Haitian Government subsidized a seminary in France for the training of priests for Haiti, as well as a seminary at Port-au-Prince for the training of Haitian priests.

41. National Archives Collection, Box #1, "Education: Special Report on Education: Facts and Statistics collected by Mr. Elie Vezina from Brothers and Sisters having charge in some schools in Port-au-Prince," 6 pp.

Each regional council was to consist of the Prefect, the Chief of the Diocese or Pastor of the Parish, Dean of the Tribunal of First Instance, President of the Medical Jury, a delegate of the Protestants' Missions, representatives of the public superior schools, the public secondary schools (if they exist), the private superior schools, a delegate of the free secondary schools (if they exist), two representatives of primary education, three members chosen from the merchants, industrialists, engineers, men of science, artists, residing in the region.

42. *President's Commission for the Study and Review of Conditions in Haiti,* p. 9: "The Commission is of the opinion that the progressive steps looking toward the withdrawal of the assistance now being given by the American Occupation should be taken on the theory and understanding that the present treaty will remain in force until 1936, it being understood that such modifications as circumstances require and the two Governments agree upon may be made at any time. It is too early to suggest in what form the American Occupation should be liquidated upon the expiration of the treaty or in what form such further aid and assistance as the Haitian Government might desire from the United States should be provided. This can be more wisely decided in the light of the experience of the next few years."

43. The Sequent Steps were the practical stages by which the Commission's seven specific recommendations toward easing the frictions between the United States and Haiti might be implemented. These seven recommendations were, as follows:

"a) That the detail of Naval and Marine officers for all Haitian services be made for a minimum of four years and that an effort be made to secure Americans who will agree to continue employment in these services, so that upon the expiration of the treaty a force of American doctors, engineers, and police officers will be available for continued assistance to the Haitian Government, should it then desire it."

This recommendation was primarily made because of the following: Personnel for the Occupation was selected from the Navy and Marines. Officers chosen were usually detailed for three years in the country, and a good two years were necessary for these men to learn French and the native *patois*. Just when they generally approached maximum efficiency in their tasks, they were relieved of their duties in Haiti. If Americans could be chosen for a four-year tour, with the added chance that they might remain another term at least, the benefits to the Occupation would be considerable.

"b) That, if possible, some form of continuing appropriation for roads be urged for expenditure by the Haitian Government, with a policy that will provide enough funds to keep all existing roads in suitable repair before any new construction is undertaken; also, in regard to further construction, that only roads most urgently needed to develop regions now settled and under cultivation be undertaken until the present economic depression has passed;

c) That the United States interpose no objections to a moderate reduction of the customs duties, internal revenue taxes, especially those imposed upon alcohol and tobacco, or to a reduction or elimination of the export tax on coffee, if the condition of the Treasury warrants;

d) That it be suggested to the Haitian Government that it employ one American adviser in each administrative department of the Government to perform such work as the respective Cabinet Minister may delegate to him, these officers to give expert advice and assistance to the Haitian Government, similar to that given by American officers in China, Siam, and Nicaragua, for naval matters in Brazil, and for educational matters in Peru;

e) That, as an act of graciousness on the part of the United States, a moderate appropriation be made available during the continuance of the treaty to defray the cost of American civil officials in the Haitian Government service;

155

f) That an appointment of a military attaché be made to the Legation when the time shall have arrived for a Minister to replace the High Commissioner, as the first question of the preservation of order is of first importance and the Minister should have the advantage of his advice on military and police matters;

g) That an adequate Legation building be constructed immediately by the Government of the United States in the city of Port-au-Prince to provide a suitable residence for the American Minister and appropriate offices."

Forbes states on p. 61 of the Haitian Journal: "When we sat down to agree on our recommendations and devise and outline our 'sequent steps' the Commission found little trouble in agreeing upon both form and substance. Each one studied them over and had suggestions which were discussed in full committee, Fletcher, as usual, in the matter of preparation of our documents, taking a leading part. He is most accomplished and skillful."

Chapter 5

The Motion Commission on Education

> Had there been less of a disposition ·to deal with the island as a conquered territory and more to help a sister state in distress, less of a desire to demonstrate efficiency and more to help others to the efficient direction of their own affairs, less of enforced control and more of helpful cooperation, the United States might today have greater reason to be proud of her intervention in the affairs of a struggling neighbor.[1]

Robert Russa Moton enjoyed a close friendship with Herbert Hoover, probably more so than any other black, and in many ways more than many whites. Before Hoover became president and while Secretary of Commerce under Coolidge, he had appointed Moton to organize a committee of outstanding black people in the South to work with the Red Cross to help alleviate the miseries of the 1927 Mississippi River flood. Moton found Hoover to be just. On Moton's complaint, for example, Hoover discharged a woman government employee in Louisiana because of her notorious injustice to blacks. "In my judgment," wrote Moton to Mr. Sidney B. Thompson, "Secretary Hoover is a man who disregards differences in race, color, creed, and condition. He sees and serves humanity in terms of equality, justice, and absolute fairness. I have known him for many years, and rather intimately...and...this is the impression he has universally made on all who have come in intimate contact with him."[2]

Despite his prominence as President of Tuskegee, Moton never lost his essential humility and his sense of dedication to the elevation of black people. "I have to pray often for patience," he said once, --patience with whites who are satisfied with so little progress, patience with Negroes who are so slow in grasping opportunities, patience even with God who seems sometimes to move so slowly."[3] His dedication to the Negro had two aims--the elevation of black people as Americans and the elevation of blacks in terms of race everywhere in the world. Perhaps the best-known anecdote about Moton is that regarding the woman who, heedless of automobile signal lights at the corner of 5th Avenue and 42nd Street in New York, started to cross the street just as traffic moved against her. Thoughtless of self, Moton threw himself in front of the cars and rescued the jaywalker from almost certain death or serious injury. Asked his name by a newspaper reporter, he replied, "Just say a black man did it."

Much more recently removed from slave-fetters than the Haitian of 1930, Moton was born in Amelia County, Virginia, two years after the death of Lincoln.[4] Like many of the freed Negroes of the South after the War, his parents settled down to work in the same area in which they had spent most of their lives, obtaining employment on the plantation of Samuel Vaughan in Prince Edward County, where his father supervised the hands and his mother did the cooking. Elementary education was intermittent in those difficult years, despite the efforts of a de-voted mother and a more than solicitous employer, but Moton managed by alternating periods of work and study to complete his pre-college training.

At eighteen, he entered Hampton Institute, where he met Booker T. Washington, whose philosophy of vocational education for the Negro as a means toward advancing the American black along the proper path to his destiny gave him pride in himself and confidence in his race. Important for his later work was his conviction that the path of the Negro lay not so much in emulating the characteristics and absorbing the civilization of the white man as in developing his own special contributions to modern twentieth century life. The Negro, before he could make these contributions, must have pride in himself as a partner in civilization, not a hostile belligerent pride, but the quiet pride which comes from the awareness of his own capabilities. Even before graduation the enormously popular Moton was marked for a position on the faculty of Hampton Institute.

After the death of Washington, Moton was select-ed for the principalship of Tuskegee. His close association with the methods and ideas of Washington and the similarity between the administrative practices of Tuskegee and Hampton enabled the new administrator to assume his tasks with little confusion. The physical plant was enlarged, endowments increased, and a so-called "college department" established to train teachers and technicians.

What Clyde Barnett said of Booker T. Washington applied equally to Moton: "In politics he was the recognized leader of the Negro people. He was a Republican, although he rarely took part in open political combat. During the period when his influence had been established, there were few important appointments made to Negroes which he did not pass upon, and it would have amazed the white South of that day had they known how many important political posts went to white men in the South simply because he had pointed them out as capable, high class men with a sense of fairness as to race.[5] Moton was astute, a student of human nature, with a vast fund of common sense to temper his idealism, and was sought after by high government officials who had learned to trust his judgment.

Moton enjoyed familiarity with Taft, Wilson, Harding, Coolidge, and Franklin Delano Roosevelt, as well as Hoover. He knew Taft because of Taft's association with Hampton Institute as a trustee, and thus began his counsel at the White House, although he actually went there infrequently.

During World War I he asked Wilson to appoint Emmett Scott, a black, Assistant to the Secretary of War, that a camp be established for the training of black officers, and that a combat unit composed only of blacks be created--all three of which requests Wilson granted. Later he became Wilson's personal representative in France. It was at Moton's suggestion that Wilson issued his famous anti-lynching letter.

Very shortly after the First World War, Moton turned part of his attention to our foreign policy with regard to independent black nations. He wrote to Harding on February 14, 1921:

> As far as I have been able to ascertain, there has grown up in the countries south of us a feeling of distrust

of the motives of our country with respect to them. I also understand there has grown up in Haiti and Santo Domingo, not only distrust, but a bitterness against this country. I hope that you may find it possible to use, if necessary, an utmost of your authority to re-establish confidence in the minds of these sister countries. With respect to Haiti, San Domingo, and Liberia, I hope you may in your own wise and sympathetic way take a firm hand in the economic, educational, and sanitary rehabilitation of these countries and, especially, in the development of their wonderful natural resources. It is further hoped that whatever America does for these three Negro republics it will be done in the spirit of cooperation and not of domination, and that there will be no encroachment on their rights and prerogatives as individual nations.[6]

He suggested that a joint commission of American white and colored persons be appointed to report upon the pressing needs of these three nations and make pertinent recommendations. Although the suggestion met with little more than cordiality from Harding, and less from his successor, the suggestion was not lost on Hoover. Moton seemed to Hoover the logical black member of the Commission to Haiti. Besides, Borno had already indicated his high regard for Moton. In 1922 he had invited Moton to Haiti for the purpose of determining whether or not vocational schools on the Tuskegee model might be established. Although Moton was not able to go at the time, he did send William T. B. Williams in his place, which pleased Borno considerably.

Nonetheless, although the Senate and House were willing to include a black on the Commission, the objection came from the Haitians themselves,[7] with the result that Hoover decided to entrust to Moton and an all-black commission the field of education alone. Moton wrote to Forbes asking him when he should go to Haiti, and Forbes replied that to go sooner than the April 14th elections would be unwise, and that he should go in time for Roy's inauguration, May 15.[8] As matters developed, Moton got to Haiti a month later when he felt that the political broil had quieted sufficiently.

Although Forbes had not been able to choose his colleagues, Moton was permitted free rein. Accompanying him were Mordecai W. Johnson, 40, President of Howard; Benjamin F. Hubert, 46, President of

Georgia State College, Leo M. Favrot, 56, known for his work in the county training schools for Negroes in Louisiana, and W. T. B. Williams, 64.[9] As background reading in the history and development of Haitian education, Moton took along Rayford W. Logan's "Education in Haiti," which had been written only the year before, and which is probably still the best concise report on the course of Haitian education up to 1929.[10] The Commission remained in Haiti from June 10 to June 15, 1930, and the official report was printed in October of the same year.

The Commission found three major school systems in Haiti: the National Public free schools operating under the 1912 Compulsory Education Act, which all Haitian children were eligible to attend; the older Roman Catholic system in which some schools were free, while others charged fees, depending upon the circumstances of the students in the area of the school's location; and the Service Technique established by the Americans in 1922. In addition, a few Protestant denominational schools had been created.

As Elie Vezina had indicated in his probe of the Catholic educational system, all schools except the Service Technique were required by law to operate under the State Secretary for Public Instruction, which meant that the National Public Schools were the official schools of Haiti. The Government favored these schools and expected them eventually to become the sole educational system of the Nation, Moton found, which substantiated Vezina's findings that Catholic schools had difficulty getting permits to operate or expand. The National Schools, according to Moton's determinations, consisted of 217 urban primary, 384 rural primary, and six secondary (the lycées), equalling three fifths of all schools in Haiti. Teachers were chosen by the Secretary for Public Instruction, who had cabinet position and was usually close to the President of the Republic, and the entire mechanism was supposed to operate under this Secretary with the aid of the aforementioned Central Council of the University of Port-au-Prince and the various local councils of the nation. This National System did not demand strict uniformity, however, for within the system were the free communal schools, with teachers chosen by local communal commissions and paid out of communal treasuries rather than that of the National Government. There were ninety-six of this type (twenty-two urban, seventy-four rural), enough to give a flexibility to the entire pattern of the official educational matrix.

The Roman Catholic schools, apparently not very popular with the Government, despite their long tradition and their excellence, were, as indicated, both free and private, depending upon circumstances. The Congregational schools were in the towns and were taught by Brothers; the Presbyterial were on the farms and taught by priests. These schools, primarily under the administration of whites, had the taint of the foreigner in eyes of Haitian officials, and more than once were referred to as a relic of French colonialism in the country.

Generally, the primary level consisted of six years of training, the secondary level of six or seven years. Superior education was limited to law, medicine, and applied science (chiefly civil engineering). Law was most popular, as it offered the *élite* a path to civil service and political careers, medicine far less popular, and applied science a poor third. Few lower schools gave very much in the way of preparation in the physical sciences, which may have been why applied science did not attract many students. Haitian schools offered few vocational and commercial courses.

The Service Technique operated under the Department of Agriculture of the Haitian Government. Dr. Freeman, the Director, was appointed by the President of Haiti on nomination by the President of the United States, which made him for all practical purposes an American appointee. Though Moton did not make such a recommendation, Forbes privately held the opinion that a good deal of criticism might have been avoided had the Service Technique been under a well-known Haitian agricultural technician acting with the advice of a council of American and Haitian scientists. In any event, the emphasis at the Service Technique was upon agricultural and industrial education, with opportunities for practical learning offered in its operation of veterinary clinics, experimental stations, and special departments of forestry and markets.

Statistics were not readily available for the Commission, and those that were are probably not very reliable. The following figures give the general picture of urban and rural primary national and pres-byterial schools: With a population of 2,038,890, and a child population (ages 7-18) of 349,863, Haiti had 709 schools, an enrollment of 43,675 chlidren, and an attendance of 29,961. These statistics came from J. C. Dorsainvil's *Le Problème de L'Enseignement Primaire en Haiti*, published 1922, but, as Moton states, no figures of comparable reliability were available. [11]

Dorsainvil included only a few types of Catholic primary schools, and no private schools. Considering all of these, public and private, Moton assumed the school population of Haiti to be approximately 400,000 to 450,000, with a fourth of that enrolled in school and 80,000 attending. If these figures are incorrect, they illustrate the fundamental that a mere fraction of the school population received anything resembling elementary education.

Moton believed that the poor attendance was the result of rural weakness rather than urban. He found that the cities (with a gross population of 250,000 people and 54,000 children) had good enroll-ment, but the rural areas (with 1,750,000 people and almost 350,000 children of school age) had only 46,000 children enrolled in the schools. Haiti, of course, had a compulsory school law (Act 32, October 4, 1912), but if it operated at all, it certainly did not in the rural areas of the country. If they did anything, peasants in the rural areas made token enrollment of their children in order to comply with the written law, then withdrew them for needed work on the tiny farms, in the homes, and in getting goods to the central markets. In the cities, the children served few purposes *out* of school; in the rural dis-tricts, they served few purposes *in* school, at least in the minds of poor farmers whose only power-source lay in human hands and feet.

Moton totalled all primary schools at 1,067, with an enrollment of 86,284 (53,936 boys and 32,348 girls), and a total attendance of 67,458. [12] Secondary schools (including private schools for boys and girls, public schools for boys, normal schools for girls, and special schools) equalled 28, with a total enrollment of 5,527 and an attendance of 5,062. The one superior school in the country, the University of Port-au-Prince, had an enrollment and an attendance of 25. How many of these were women Moton did not state.

The Service Technique,[13] despite its brief period of existence, had sixty-nine schools, 311 teachers and employees, and a total enrollment of 11,430. This total enrollment included 9,274 day, 1,709 night, and 447 summer, which meant that the Service Technique had a year-round curriculum compared to the ten-month curriculum of the Haitian National and religious institutions (October through July). The Service Technique was composed of the École Centrale, École Elie Dubois, Maison Centrale, five Boys' Industrial Schools, one Girls' Industrial School, and 60 farm schools scattered throughout rural Haiti.

The Commission was particularly disappointed with the state of elementary education,[14] since this was the level at which democracy would either stand or fall. The salaries of teachers were low (especially in the rural areas, where teachers were paid 4-8 dollars per week); trained men teachers for boys were highly limited (the Commission suggested they be recruited from the boys' lycées in the cities); and the ratio of teachers to pupils was one to seventy (82,284 primary pupils were taught by 1,196 teachers). This ratio did not apply to the Service Technique, however, where the ratio was more acceptable.

The Commission considered the National Schools to be the weakest in Haiti, with most of them located in rented buildings, short on equipment, and with low certification requirements or none for teachers. The Roman Catholic, on the other hand, had suitable buildings, were better equipped both with physical apparatus as well as trained teachers, and appeared to set the standards for both elementary and secondary education in Haiti.

The curriculum at both National and Roman Catholic schools, determined by the Secretary for State Instruction, was essentially the same—French, reading and writing, moral and civil instruction, religious instruction, history and geography, manual work, arithmetic, elementary geometry, algebra, elementary science, hygiene, drawing, games and songs.

Primary education at the Service Technique gave greater emphasis to the vocational aspect, less time to the literary branches which had been the mainstay of Haitian education for the past 125 years. While in the cities industrial education was stressed, and in the rural areas agricultural education, fundamentally the curriculum was identical throughout the nation. During the last three years of the course of study, which was eight years in length instead of six as required in the National and Catholic schools, students were expected to specialize in trades or occupations of their choice.[15]

The Service Technique differed from traditional Haitian education in purpose and in method. The purpose of Haitian education still lay along lines set by a caste philosophy, which asked education not so much to enlighten the people as to teach each class its traditional function. The purpose was not to break with the past but to strengthen the past, not to advance but to remain secure. As to method. where Haitian education sought to adjust the child to the school, the Service Technique attempted to adjust the school to the child and provide for individual differences. The latter method tended to destroy the social order upon which the *élite* had based its way of life.

The buildings of the Service Technique were excellent, well-equipped, and generally new. Seventy-three new structures had been completed since 1922. As a matter of fact, the only new buildings constructed for educational purpose since 1922 had been built for the Service Technique.

Public secondary education[16] was established for boys only (the lycée). The most important lycée, and the biggest, was at Port-au-Prince, but the nation had five others. As with the public primary schools, buildings were poor, libraries and laboratories were either non-existent or in exceedingly poor condition, and the individual schoolrooms lacked blackboards, desks, lighting, and lunchroom facilities in many cases. Physical education and opportunities for sports were entirely lacking, nor was space provided for school assemblies. The Catholic schools again seemed better housed and equipped.

Both National and Catholic secondary levels had a six-year program which started approximately where the seventh grade in the American schools begins, and which consisted generally of reading, French, Latin, mathematics, history and geography (including the history of Haiti), Greek, Spanish, and the sciences. Hygiene was taken in the first year, botany and second, zoology and third, physics and chemistry the fourth and fifth, physics, chemistry, physiology, the sixth. With laboratories and libraries so inadequate, the sciences could not have been very effectively taught. Civics and moral instruction, together with drawing, completed the course.

An additional seventh year was offered to students with promise, adding courses in hygiene, cosmography, philosophy and the history of philosophy, common law, and political economy. Students planning to advance to Law and careers in government service, theology, and journalism, ordinarily took this seventh year.

The Commission reported that Haiti had a total of 6,609 students above what would be the eighth grade in the United States, and 5,567 in the secondary schols generally. Out of every 1,000 persons in Haiti 2.8 were in the secondary schools, compared with 9.8 per thousand Negroes in the United States. Despite the longer period of secondary education in Haiti, the ratio of enrollment of students in the Haitian secondary schools to the enrollment of students in all Haitian schools was smaller than that of the United States.

The lycées were taught by Haitians, the Catholic secondary schools by brothers and priests. Salaries in the National schools at this level amounted to thirty to sixty dollars per month for a twelve month period; in the Catholic, professors received fifty dollars, directors sixty.

Once again, Moton felt that the great defect in the secondary system was the overwhelming emphasis upon literary education rather than vocational, especially since the Service Technique as yet extended only to primary education.

Higher education[17] trained only in four major categories: Medicine, Law, Applied Science, Teacher Training. As of June, 1930, the School of `Medicine had sixty-nine students (fifty-one in Medicine, nine each in Pharmacy and Dentistry); the School of Nursing, thirty-eight (thirty-six in Nursing, two in Midwifery); Law, 271; Applied Science, twenty-five; the École Centrale (the Service Technique school for the training of agricultural and industrial teachers, the only official teacher-training institution in Haiti), 654. One hundred and fifty more had to be added for the seventh year of secondary schools, which corresponded roughly to the first and second years of college, making a grand total of 1,207 students above the twelve years of primary and secondary education, or one out of every three thousand in the population.

Moton's chief objection in this scheme was the total lack of teacher training, with especial reference to the scientific fields upon which modern strong stable nations are constructed. "The consequence," he said, "is that there is almost entire absence of objectively gathered and scientifically organized information regarding human problems in Haiti. There is no training in social work, and there is no organized activity which corresponds to the social service so prevalent in the cities of the United States or in the leading countries of Europe."[18]

The School of Medicine was organized under the State Department of the Interior in the Public Health Service, with clinical advantages at the Haitian General Hospital at Port-au-Prince, "its out-patient service...in daily touch with the far-reaching public-health work of this department."[19] As with the School of Nursing, the main trouble seemed to have been that students received poor preparation in the National and Catholic schools for the training demanded at the higher level. Medical graduates seemed to be good and generally respected, nevertheless. Since 1920, seventy-eight had been graduated, giving the entire nation 159 physicians, 42% of which made their livings in the Public Health clinics.

Law was administered by the Department of Justice, but the legal requirements demanded in terms of student preparation were not enforced, Moton found. The faculty consisted of twelve professors and a director.

The School of Applied Science had been founded in 1902, and had since graduated eighty-five engineers (civil primarily, with a few mechanical, electrical, chemical, and architectural). Occupying three ancient buildings, one of which was more than a hundred years old while the other two had originally been foundries, few aspects of the training were little better than archaic. The last-received equipment had arrived twenty to twenty-five years before, only a handful of books were in the library, and the twelve professors (seven of whom were former students) were paid at the miserable rate of two dollars per hour.

The École Centrale at Damien, the teacher training institution of the Service Technique, marked a contrast to the rather sombre picture of higher education under traditional sponsorship. Housed in a beautiful new building, the school possessed completely new equipment, modern shops, experimental farms, gardens, and so on. Because of the strike of 1929-30, the school had difficulty obtaining students with the certificate of graduation from philosophy or rhetoric in the secondary classical course. Freeman accordingly admitted students with lesser qualifications, which resulted in complaints from the Departments of Agriculture and Public Instruction.

Regardless of its achievements within the relatively brief period of its existence, the American-sponsored Service Technique had not been a success in Haitian eyes. "Notwithstanding the evidence of good faith and good work set forth in the program of the Service Technique, the intelligent Haitians, with the exception of a few immediately connected with the service, are practically unanimous in their opinions that the Service Technique is not a success," said Moton, although he noted that the critics generally approved the underlying idea.[20]

What were the major objections?[21] First, the Service was on too large, too costly a scale; it should have been initiated on a small scale and gradually been extended. How would the Haitian Government with its meager revenues support so huge an enterprise when the United States withdrew its financial support at the end of the Occupation? The weakness of this objection lay in the fact that the United States most likely was willing to continue financial aid, after American troops were withdrawn, until the Haitian Government became capable of supporting the Service. Had the Service begun on a small level in 1922, and evolved slowly, what could it have achieved in the mere fourteen years remaining to the Occupation authorities? Working on a large scale, the Service was subject to Conservative attack on the basis of its threat to financial stability; on a smaller scale, it would have been equally subject to attack from the liberal elements on the basis of insincerity and inaction. With this first objection went the complaint that the peasants were taught the use of machinery before they were taught the use of the hoe, which appears equally invalid when one realizes that machinery makes the hoe obsolete.

Second, too many American specialists in the Service were paid high salaries from the Haitian treasury, intimating that American imperialists were exploiting the nation's reserves. To the average Haitian accustomed to a low standard of living these salaries might have appeared high, but they were not high when one considered American standards and the difficulty of getting specialists from the United States.

Third, some specialists were so lacking in tropical knowledge as to be of little assistance. Some were accused of not being properly equipped for the work they had to do.

Fourth, the Service operated extravagantly, with too much duplication of effort, too much overhead; the misuse of funds was a frequent charge. Moton felt that this was only partially correct, since the Service was something new to Haitian experience and judgment.

Fifth, American heads of department did not speak French, nor did they make any effort to learn. Moton agreed with this, as had Forbes in regard to the remainder of the Occupation machinery.

Sixth, young Haitians were used as interpreters in the classrooms. Not only was this a deleterious factor in the teaching-learning situation, but fre-

quently American instructors did not even bother
to come to class, leaving imcompetent young Haitian
interpreters to carry on classroom instruction.
Freeman had investigated this objection, and found
that it applied only to a few instructors, who had
been reprimanded.

Seventh, the Service Technique intended to supplant the *élite's* traditional goals of Haitian education. This was correct. Here lay a difficult philosophical problem, which Moton did not resolve. Was
the United States to reconstitute the Haitian educational machinery along lines of its own traditions,
or on the basis of needs determined by the Haitian
ruling class? If the former, then the United States
must suffer accusations of dictatorship; if the
latter, then the United States must foster and support the same sort of education that originally led
to the Occupation. In either case, the occupying
power is on the horns of a dilemma. The Occupation,
of course, ended too soon for the United States to
take a stand on this issue, but had it continued,
two paths would have been open. Assuming technical
education to be indispensable to a nation in a world
where scientific and industrial progress mean stability, mass production, high standards of living,
and military strength, the United States could have
either imposed technical education on the country
despite outcries of dictatorship, or through a wide-
spread system of publicity tried to re-orient the
élite to an acceptance of technical education. The
latter path is undoubtedly better--though slower.
Certainly, judging matters from world events in the
many years which have elapsed since the Haitian
Commissions of 1930, a country either accepts indus-
trialization as a way of life or that pattern of
life is forced upon it by extreme radical movements
within and without.

Eighth, the design to build twelve industrial
schools at Port-au-Prince reached toward an excessive
number, disregarded the people in the Port-au-Prince
area, and would tend to impoverish them.

Ninth, Service Technique officials were high-
handed in that they failed very often to consult
with the Haitian Government and in many ways considered themselves representatives of a superior philosophy. The Commission thought this charge justified.

170

Setting up separate primary schools in town and country, said Moton, was a mistake. Haitian school law
had been violated. Moton contended that the United
States, by establishing an entirely new set of
schools, retarded rather than hastened the solution
of the educational problem. The Service Technique
had better buildings, equipment, and teachers than
other schools because it had greater funds available,[22] which promoted jealousy and envy from the
competing National and Catholic schools. Had the
United States poured its funds and assistance into
improving the National free schools, it would have
gone a long way toward obtaining for Haiti the well-
equipped, well-housed, well-staffed educational
system which the American Occupation desired for
her.

Tenth, no increase in agricultural production
or in the improvement of standards of living among
the peasants had occurred. This was hardly fair,
since eight years were required to complete the primary curriculum, and relatively few teachers had
as yet been graduated from the École Centrale. This
objection was somewhat inconsistent with the first.

Eleventh, instead of increasing opportunities
for industrial enterprise, the Service had destroyed
enterprise by competition with Haitians, putting
many of them out of business. Products made in its
industrial shops were sold at low prices in the
cities and towns, the revenue used for the improvement of the physical plants. In the United States,
this was standard procedure, but in Haiti, where
manufacturing existed only on a small scale, the
better finished, cheaper products were a threat to
urban enterprise. For example, the Service
Technique's printing plant with modern equipment
ruined the business of local Port-au-Prince printing
establishments.

Twelfth, the Government used revenue from sales
of these industrial products to supplement its allotment, encouraging further extravagance and mis-use
of funds. In reality, Freeman hoped, through the
sales of these products, to help the Service
Technique to be self-supporting. Theoretically, the
Service in time might have become a self-operating
mechanism independent of government allotment.

Thirteenth, financial reports were not sufficiently detailed to enable the Haitian Government to see just where its money was being spent. The American Financial Adviser accepted these reports, leaving the Haitian Government helpless in its demands.

Fourteenth, the lowering of admittance standards after the strike of October, 1929, endangered the entire Haitian educational system.

Fifteenth, in the haste to supply teachers, the Service Technique sent many poorly trained graduates out to rural areas. The major difficulty seemed to be that a good number of teachers with an urban industrial background were going to agricultural rural areas.

Sixteenth, American employees who had come to Haiti with preconceived notions regarding the colored races practiced racial discrimination. Moton, as did Forbes, agreed with this objection.

Clearly, when all was said and done, the conclusion was inescapable that the number of schools in Haiti was insufficient to provide education for the total child population at any level--primary, secondary, superior--particularly at the two upper levels. But what was to be was another question? And the problem was further complicated by the uncertainty attendant upon whether the United States would remain in Haiti or not.

Moton's recommendations were extensive and were aimed at four major objectives which Moton set up for the Haitian people: (1) the raising of the standards of living for all the people, (2) the increase of agricultural and industrial effectiveness among the people, (3) the preparation of the masses for intelligent participation in the government, and (4) the training of leaders for the nation.[23] Unless the educational system worked toward these particular objectives, it was not working in the best interests of the Haitian community.

Clearly, this was the philosophy which Booker T. Washington applied to the former black slave of the South, and the philosophy which Moton himself had been furthering at Tuskegee. Yet he realized --perhaps more than did Forbes, and, because of his race, with more sympathy—how much opposition these objectives would engender among the cultivated *élite*, whose position, thus threatened, was not far removed from that of the white southern planter in the years immediately preceding the American Civil War.[24]

The major recommendations[25] were that the Service Technique come under the Secretary of State for Public Instruction; that the National and local councils be made operative; that the Service Technique stop expanding and begin adapting itself to the limits, expense-wise, of the Haitian Government; that a National University be established which would be the focal point of Haitian education and which would, through the advice of the most brilliant men and women of Haiti, set the standards for public and private instruction throughout the primary and secondary levels, in both literary, industrial, and agricultural education; that the "traditional" education of the *élite* be recognized by the formation of a National University composed of both technical and liberal arts colleges; that sufficient teachers of high standards be produced to supply the demands of a great revitalized Haitian educational system through the establishment in the National University of a school of education; that the Service Technique, now comprising only primary education of eight grades, once absorbed into the National schools, be extended to include secondary and superior levels of instruction; that girls' education be extended into the secondary and superior levels; and that throughout the warp and woof of the Haitian educational fabric be infused the philosophy of individual differences and preferences.

Moton certainly was not an imperialist. Nor was he interested in exploiting an under-developed people. If anyone had dedicated his life to the uplifting of blacks, Moton was that man. The success of his venture in Haiti meant enrichment of his own work at Tuskegee, and its failure meant the opposite. Surely, Moton could have been accused of nothing except the deepest sincerity in his efforts to solve the Haitian educational enigma. But the fact remains that over two generations after Moton's approximately sixty recommendations, the Haitian educational system still produced a nation 90% illiterate.

Where, then, did Moton fail? Or did he? Or did

the United States fail in helping Haiti follow through on Moton's proposals? There are those who say that Nationalization of the schools was the answer. But was it? For all practical purposes, once the Service Technique came under the Secretary for Public Instruction, the Haitian schools *were* nationalized. What has been wrong with the Haitian educational system since Moton's time is a question found buried in the larger question of what has been wrong with our general policy in Haiti since Forbes' time. Moton set up a blueprint that from its inception was ignored.

NOTES

1. *Report of the United States Commission on Education in Haiti*, p. 73, hereinafter referred to as the *Moton Commission Report*.

2. W. H. Hughes and F. D. Patterson (eds.), *Robert Russa Moton* of Hampton and Tuskegee, pp. 201–202.

3. *Ibid.*, p. 228.

4. Robert Russa Moton, *Finding a Way Out: An Autobiography* is probably the best source of the social philosophy of the great Negro educator. Dr. Moton died May 31, 1940. See also "Progress of Negro Education in the South," *Proceedings of the National Education Association*, 1916, pp. 106–11.

5. Hughes and Patterson (eds.), *Robert Russa Moton of Hampton and Tuskegee*, pp. 188–189.

6. *Ibid.*, p. 193.

7. See Chapter Two, this study.

8. "Dear Dr. Moton:

"Your cordial letter has come and I am hoping that we can meet and talk things over very thoroughly at Hampton. The situation in Haiti is very mixed and tragic.

"Our commission immediately established contacts with the opposition to the government, which was vocal and much more numerous than the friends of the government. The Americans, by the manner in which they seized control and carried it on, had made their activities very unpopular except in the matter of sanitation. For example, they had the Church strongly against them, partly by reason of their incursion into the educational field. I am writing to the State Department, requesting that all the material which we received applicable to education be turned over to you. You will have noticed in our report we touched very lightly on the educational aspect of things, and we have as a reason that this was a field to be developed later by your group.

"I should advise your going to Washington and reading over the testimony submitted to our commission. We had relays of stenographers take down in shorthand everything that was said, and while much of it is worthless and not worth reading in detail, yet I think it would be wise for you to have a knowledge of about what was put before us. The testimony of Mr. Leger was most important. That should be read with care. In that he charged the Americans with having for the first time introduced a color consciousness among the Haitians. He was about the most intelligent and straight man with whom we dealt, and was the leader of the opposition group through whom I conducted most of my negotiations with the opposition.

"The whole situation to me is a tragedy—a tragedy because I don't see any good ending to it. I cannot feel happy over what we have done because it will inevitably for a while inure to the disadvantage of the great mass of the population. We have acted in a fair way to wreck a working organization that was doing a great good for the people. Unfortunately this structure was built on unsound and insecure foundations. It had not got popular support and so it could not endure. Hence I feel that the action of our commission was the best way out of a very bad situation. In fact, when we got there it looked as if there were no way out. And it was only by dint of a lot of manipulation and negotiation, using persuasion here and pressure there, that we managed, to reach any kind of conclusion. The details of all this I will give you when we meet.

"Some of the things the United States has done in Haiti have been done admirably, and some, on the other hand very badly. It is very hard to apportion the proper amount of praise and blame. Where really intelligent work has been done by really intelligent men, it is heart-breaking to have to criticize and there is a great deal that we left unsaid and that had to be left unsaid. If, for example, we had put our critical comments in our report, the Haitian newspapers and the hostile press in the United States would have culled those items, left out the words of praise, and, using our own words and our findings as their sanction, painted a wholly black picture which would have been utterly unjust. That is a very easy thing to

do if one wants to be mean. None of the good achievements would
have been noted.

"My experience in administration of dependencies is extensive
enough so that I have absolute familiarity with many of the
fundamental problems with which General Russell and his cohorts
were confronted, and I had met and solved many of the problems
which he had to meet. This in one sense equips me for such
a job as I had to do in Haiti, and in another sense disquali-
fied me because of my being wedded to a certain line of policy.
Hence, I had to be very self-distrustful in criticizing what
General Russell was doing, fearing lest I should be unfair
and too much inclined to my own preconceived ideas.

"I come now to the important part of my letter; namely, answer-
ing your question as to when you had better go to Haiti. Under
no circumstances would it have been wise for you to go prior
to the elections which take place on April 14. Conditions are
extremely tense and highly critical. President Borno retires
from office on the 15th of May. If the Council of State fails
to act Monday, April 14, and to elect Mr. Roy, the compromise
candidate, according to the compromise plan which we worked
out and which was agreed to by both sides, it will have been
due to the unwise action of the opposition leaders in rushing
about and claiming too much and setting the administration
against them. That is to say, these foolish opposition leaders
will have announced the immediate abolition of the Council
of State and will then expect the Council of State to sign
its own death warrant by electing the man who is to abolish
the Council. All the opposition leaders had to do was to keep
quiet and the whole situation would have worked itself out.
But the leaders down there impressed me as a very poor set,
not well-grounded in morals and not men abounding in good
sense. I think you will be convinced of this if you read the
testimony submitted to us. I don't doubt they were not in the
group of agitators that appeared before us.

"Now, in case the Council of State fails to elect the compromise candidate agreed upon, there will be precipitated into
the situation a new problem which will immediately and vitally
affect the question of when you should go. And until the next
steps have been decided upon, both in Washington and in Haiti,
and the new president selected, I think it would be highly
inopportune for your commission, or any commission, to expect
to accomplish anything there. In fact, my recommendation would
be that, probably under any circumstances, the 10th of May
would be the earliest date on which it would be wise for you
to arrive. Upon the point, however, if the election of Mr.
Roy goes through smoothly, General Russell would have a perfect-

ly good opinion, and I should ask his advice if you want to be there before the 10th of May. The reason I say the 10th of May is because the inauguration of the new president will take place on the 15th and I think it might be a good thing to have your commission there to attend the inauguration and that that would be a favorable time to conduct your investigation...I am afraid we are going to have some rather trying problems at the Hampton meeting." (Forbes, Haitian Journal, pp. 74–76).

9. Johnson was born in Paris, Tennessee, January 12, 1890, studied at Morehouse College in Atlanta, the University of Chicago, the Rochester Theological Seminary, where he received a Bachelor of Divinity degree in 1919, and at Harvard, where he obtained his Doctor of Divinity in 1923. Professor of economics and history at Morehouse from 1911 to 1913, he also served with the YMCA, was pastor of the First Baptist Church at Charleston, West Virginia, and became in 1926 President of Howard University. As the first black president of Howard, he had a major hand in securing the passage in 1928 of a Congressional act which gave the university federal status and made possible the granting of federal funds for its support and operation. Howard was therefore the first university of any description to receive annual direct support from the Federal Government.

Hubert was born in Mayfield, Georgia, Dec. 25, 1884, and was also educated at Morehouse. Further study brought him to the Massachusetts State College at Amherst, the University of Wisconsin, Allen University, University of Minnesota, and Harvard. From 1912 until 1919 he was director of Agriculture and the Agricultural Extension Service at South Carolina State College, and from 1920 and 1926 Professor of Agriculture and Superintendent of Agricultural Instruction at the University of Georgia State College (later called Savannah State).

Williams, the oldest member of the Commission, was born at Stone Bridge, Virginia, June 3, 1866. A student at Hampton from 1886 to 1888, he continued his education at Phillips Academy, Andover, Massachusetts, 1889 to 1893, and then went to Harvard. He was a public school principal in the Indianapolis schools from 1897 to 1902, then field agent for Hampton. His close contact with Moton came with his appointment to Tuskegee. In 1922, as indicated in the text above, Moton chose him to go to Haiti to do the vocational schools survey which Borno desired. See *Bulletin of Pan-American Union*, Vol. 56, p. 93.

Favrot, born 1874, was known chiefly for his work in the county training schools for Negroes in Louisiana. See his *Some pro-blems in the Education of the Negro in the South and How We Are Trying to Meet Them in Louisiana* and his *A Study of County Training Schools for Negroes in the South.*

10. Rayford W. Logan, "Education in Haiti," *Journal of Negro History,* Oct. 1930.

11. *Moton Commission Report,* pp. 5-6. Dorsainvil's complete table from which Moton obtained his figures is, as follows:

Department	Schools	Population of Haiti	Child Pop. of Haiti (ages 7-18)	Enroll-ment	Attend-ance
West	221	744,220	126,508	12,179	8,143
South	159	511,740	89,272	11,110	7,989
North	201	353,600	60,092	13,513	9,648
Artibonite	92	331,330	56,311	4,889	3,007
Northwest	36	981,000	17,680	1,984	1,174
	709	2,038,890	349,863	43,675	29,961

12. *Moton Commission Report,* p. 8.

13. *Ibid.,* p. 9.

14. *Moton Commission Report,* pp. 15-18.

15. For girls, the specialization gave the following choices: embroidery, lace-making, dressmaking, millinery, cloth-weaving, basket-weaving, cooking, domestic science, housekeeping, book-keeping, shorthand, typewriting. For boys, the choices were shoemaking, saddle-making, basket-making, tailoring, forging, sheetmetal work, plumbing, automobile mechanics, carpentry, cabinet-making, cement work, bricklaying, masonry, bookkeeping, shorthand, typewriting.

16. *Moton Commission Report,* pp. 19-22.

17. *Ibid.,* pp. 23-29.

18. *Ibid.,* p. 24.

19. *Ibid.,* p. 25.

20. *Ibid.,* p. 57. Also see *Annual Report of the Technical Service of the Department of Agriculture and Professional Education,* 1928-29, Bulletin No. 17, Republic of Haiti.

21. *Moton Commission Report*, pp. 57-61.

22. Sixty-five per cent of United States educational appropriations to Haiti went to the Service Technique, while the National Schools were neglected. Moton felt that the educational apparatus in Haiti which had proved its worth was that of the National Public Schools, and that only in these National schools was the salvation of the nation to be found.

23. *Moton Commission Report*, pp. 62-64.

24. *Ibid.*, p. 65, Moton states: "To understand the Haitian people one must bear in mind constantly something of their history and traditions. It must be remembered first that they emerged from slavery and that they threw off the yoke of the French completely in 1804. Few nations have thrown off the yoke of slavery and survived as an independent nation over so long a period. They have a right to be proud of this achievement and to honor the heroes who led their fight for freedom... Any gesture on the part of a foreign nation that might be interpreted as a desire to infringe upon or limit this freedom in any way arouses instant suspicion and opposition.

"The Haitians are basically members of the Negro race. They are proud of their achievements as black people. They know full well that the white race is dominant in the world today and resent bitterly the air of superiority on the part of any member of the white race that this dominant position may sometimes cause him to assume. They are proud of their noteworthy contributions in the fields of history, literature, and poetry; of the sculptors and musicians they have produced...Any intimation that any race regards them as inferior is a source of keen resentment...They do not care to come to America because here they detect signs of racial discrimination. They enjoy travel in France because in that country their race and color cause them no embarrassment. They call themselves the oldest child of the French Revolution..."

On p. 51, he states: "Whatever shortcoming of Haiti's present school system, evidence is not lacking that the Haitian people have an abiding faith in education. The school laws framed under the direction of her rulers and statesmen during past years show a clear grasp of many of her educational needs and a completeness of detail in the wording of the regulations to make these laws effective. There is found outlined in a law of 1864, for example, a special three-year secondary course differing from the early courses of the lycees and providing for agricultural and manual arts. In 1890, the establishment of a school for practical agriculture for boys was similarly

authorized at Port-au-Prince, and Ecole Elie Dubois with practical courses for girls was established the same year. An appreciation of the value of normal training for all types of
teachers is likewise reflected in the certification laws. The
general plan for the organization and administration of her
school system, while perhaps not fully adapted to the needs
of a democratic society, is a workable plan, and, in the hands
of a well-qualified personnel, could be made to produce results. On reading the school laws of Haiti, one is forced to
the conclusion that Haiti has not lacked the capacity to con-
ceive and the will to provide a school system, but she has
unfortunately lacked the trained personnel and the money to
execute the ideals. It is the belief of the Commission that
with certain modifications and additions her exacting educational program can be made to meet fully the demands of a democratic society."

At still another point, he states: "The approach to a practical
idea must be made with full regard for the people's national
ideals, and with the objective of preserving what is fine and
noble in their present system, while supplementing this with
such practical training as will produce a complete and well-
rounded educational program." (p. 66).

25. See Appendix, this volume, for the recommendations made
by the Moton Commission.

Chapter 6

A Time for Assessment

In any assessment of the Forbes Commission, certain questions must be answered: (1) Were the methods employed by Forbes in gathering information adequate to the situation's demands? (2) What were the immediate and long-range results of the internal political settlement? (3) Did the later history of Haiti, after withdrawal had been made complete, justify Forbes' personal apprehensions? (4) What is the place of the Forbes Commission in the formulation of the new attitude? (5) What were the results of the Commission's recommendations for a new foreign policy with regard to Haiti and the other nations of the Americas south of the Rio Grande? (6) And finally, what have been the flaws in this new foreign policy as they have appeared in Latin America during the intervening years from the end of Hoover's administration to the present.

Before these questions may be answered, however, a clarification of the nature of our Occupation of Haiti is altogether proper. Did we enter Haiti for reasons of morality or self-interest?

The moral or idealistic versus the realistic or self-interest schools of thought have debated our methods of establishing American foreign policy since the Revolution.[1] The problem has never been adequately settled. Should this nation, trusting in the goodness of man, and believing that the evils of society are the result of lack of education, obsolete patterns of life, and poverty, follow a foreign policy based not upon its own self-interest at any particular time but upon abstract principles of justice, fairness, and charity as set down by the Judeo-Christian tradition? Or should it recognize that, noble and desirable as such abstract principles are, they are goals only to strive for, unattainable in

181

this life, and that, therefore, if we are to survive, our prime consideration in all questions of foreign policy must be the benefit of our own American democracy? For those on the moral side of the fence, the world is envisioned as a network of coordinate states working together in a trusting union much like the states of the American Union, the cantons of the Swiss Confederation, or the British Commonwealth of Nations. Those on the realistic side think of the world as a constantly seething mass of rising and falling powers, those dominant at any given moment or time checked by the traditional "balance of power" technique.

Which method dominated the American scene from the struggle for independence until the Occupation of Haiti in 1915? The realists see an amazingly successful foreign policy guided by the star of self-interest. Our alliance with France in 1778 brought us the aid we needed for a successful revolt, and the treaty of 1800 freed us from this same alliance when we no longer needed it. The wars with the Barbary states ended the threat to our trade in the Mediterranean, and the War of 1812 (in which we sided with Napoleon) strengthened our rights upon the sea, eliminated Britain from the Northwest Territory, and completed our domination of the Mississippi. The acquisition of Louisiana, the Floridas, most of Oregon, the whole area formerly owned by Mexico north and west of the Rio Grande, the Mesilla River Valley, Alaska, the Philippines and Puerto Rico were achievements made at the expense of either weak nations or strong ones too much involved in troubles elsewhere. As Bemis puts it, "America's advantage from Europe's distress."[2] The Civil War from the realist's view point could be judged not as a struggle to free the slaves but one to free American northern industrial enterprise from the shackles of southern legislative domination. If John Quincy Adams, Polk, and Hay were realistic statesmen, their philosophy of foreign policy could not have been more richly rewarded by material success.

Even Jefferson, whom we view as the progenitor of the moralistic conception, shifted to the realistic when the needs of the nation demanded. Few played the "balance of power" game as carefully as he. While Britain held the ascendancy until the rise of Napoleon, he was pro-French; when Napoleon raised his shadow over Europe, he favored British sea supremacy despite his previously avowed predilection for French liberalism. He was willing to "marry" the United States to the British fleet and nation if Napoleon were to supplant Spain on the Mississippi, but after the battle of Trafalgar, he was back again on the side of the French. The year 1812 saw him again hoping that a return to political balance in Europe might restore the peace, in 1814 he was against Napoleon, in 1815, he was wavering again. "It was only when, after 1815, the danger to the balance of power seemed to have passed that Jefferson allowed himself again to indulge in the cultivation of moral principles divorced from the political exigencies of the hour." [3]

Looking at this same period (1776-1915) from the idealistic viewpoint, one might say that, after all, democracy and liberalism are the real interests of the United States. Surely the era following the Mexican War saw a surging influx of moral conceptions into our national attitude. The Civil War was fought to free men, not for economic reasons; the Pan-American Union was established as an indication of our good-will toward our sister states to the south; we liberated Cuba at the expense of our own blood and treasure; we undertook the social and economic regeneration of the Philippines, Central America, and the Caribbean.

But one rather thinks that American foreign policy cannot be divided on such lines. Morgenthau has some justification for his belief (1) that our nation started out with a realistic policy which was enormously successful; (2) that after the Mexican War we spoke of moral principles but acted still along realistic lines; and (3) that moral considerations, which entered with the McKinley administration triumphed with that of Wilson, and have continued to plague us ever since.[4] Yet these lines are too pat. Moral considerations have always been with us. We have tried during the course of our history to do what any self-respecting individual tries to do --live a life which is at one and the same time both materially successful and reasonably compatible with high spiritual values. The United States has never pursued deliberately either a long-term self-interest policy or a long-term moral policy; it has pursued a foreign policy into whose fibers have been woven the stuff of both.

When Forbes accused Wilson of "woolly idealism,"
he erred.[5] A study of Wilson's administration shows
very clearly that his moral actions were rarely divorced from the self-interest of the nation. Somehow,
the interests of the United States coincided with
the high moral concepts of his philosophy. We intervened in Haiti because Wilson desired to end the
century and a quarter of bloodshed and internal disorder, to teach the Negro Haitian in a day, so to
speak, what the Anglo-Saxon had learned in fifteen
hundred years of history,[6] because he honestly wished
to use the might and treasure of the United States
to lift the Haitian masses out of their ignorance,
poverty, and degradation. At the same time, he wished
to protect the investments of American citizens from
confiscation (one aspect of dollar diplomacy) and
to prevent European powers, particularly Germany,
from using injury to their nationals as a pretext
for getting a foothold in the Caribbean (strategy
diplomacy).[7] Wilson's Occupation of Haiti became
vulnerable only after the First World War ended and
we continued to remain in Haiti. Only then did the
Nation start the attacks which led ten years later
to the Forbes Commission. The Occupation became vulnerable because the defensible strategic self-
interest aspect evaporated leaving only the ugly
dollar interest aspect and the high moral purpose
of democratic tutelage. And much of the liberal press
doubted that very much of the democratic tutelage
purpose survived Wilson. We remained in Haiti because
Haiti offered us a grand experiment: we had the
chance to test in our own little laboratory the
"civilizing" doctrines which western European expan-
sionist philosophy was trying out on a vast scale
in Africa and Asia. And our Occupation failed for
the same reasons that those of Britain, France, and
Germany failed--because the American Government was
accused of having only one purpose in Haiti, exploitation. Of the three reasons why Wilson entered Haiti
--dollar diplomacy, strategy diplomacy, and democratic tutelage--all that remained in the eyes of the
world by 1930 was dollar diplomacy. William Allen
White, listening to a particularly horrid story at
the hearings in Port-au-Prince, wrote:

> In that twilight zone wherein the desire to help one's
> fellow-men passes from fraternal association to paternal

control, despotism begins to rot the heart of benevolence.
And here is a curious thing: I am satisfied by talking
for hours with many Americans here, that they are honest
--as men go in politics--and are sincerely imbued with
a desire to help the Haitians. They feel that we who op-
pose them are undoing a great work. Yet so inexorably
does the possession of power disintegrate the spirit that
benevolence is destroyed by tyranny. There can never be
a benevolent despot.[8]

Franklin D. Roosevelt is given credit for the Good
Neighbor Policy, but if he is to be given credit
it must be neither for originating the idea, nor
for initiating the policy, but rather for inheriting
it from the Coolidge-Hoover administrations and prose-
cuting it with vigor. During the 1920 presidential
campaign, in which he ran with Cox on the Democratic
ticket, he ridiculed the Republican argument against
the League of Nations (that Great Britain would have
six votes in the Assembly while the United States
had only one) by the declaration (referring apparently to the political advantages of the protectorate
system) that the United States would have on her
side the eleven tiny republics of the Caribbean.
He went on to boast that he himself had written the
Haitian Constitution of 1918 and that it was pretty
good.[9]

Only when criticism of our Caribbean policy
had become so blatant two campaigns later, and the
Democrats needed fighting issues against the apparent-
ly impregnable Republican administration, did
Roosevelt make an about-face. In an article entitled
"Our Foreign Policy," he stated:

In 1909 began four years which counted as a definite set-
back in our liberal leadership. "Dollar Dipolmacy" as
adopted by President Taft and Secretary Knox placed money
leadership ahead of moral leadership in the Far East...
Honduras...Nicaragua...

The Wilson Administration started splendidly by eliminating "Dollar Diplomacy"...but intervention as we practiced
it in Santo Domingo and Haiti was not another forward
step. It is not that assistance of some sort was not
necessary; it was the method which was wrong...It is true
...that...in Haiti we seem to have paid too little attention to making the citizens of (that state) more capable
of reassuming the control of (their) own (government).

But we have done a fine piece of material work and the world ought to thank us.

But does it?..The other republics of the Americas do not thank us; on the contrary they disapprove our intervention almost unanimously. By what right, they say, other than the right of main force, does the United States arrogate unto itself the privilege of intervening alone in the internal affairs of another Sovereign Republic?[10]

Yet what did words matter? Had the period of the 1920's continued prosperous for American business at large, the question of the protectorates might never have been injected into the presidential political arena as the decade ended. Harding in 1920 had taken advantage of Roosevelt's revelation that he thought we controlled eleven Caribbean votes by stating that if he were elected he would not use his office to "cover with a veil of secrecy repeated acts of unwarranted interference in domestic affairs of the little republics of the Western Hemisphere." But, as Rippy says of Harding, "Any anti-imperialist who ever hoped to find a kindred spirit in him was doomed to disappointment." The remark was made purely for purposes for the campaign and nothing more.[11]

What is important is not so much what men say when they are anxious for power but what they actually do once that power is conferred upon them. Despite Harding's statement, the Harding and Coolidge administrations were a period of indecision between those of Wilson and Hoover. Our withdrawal from the Dominican Republic was not Coolidge's work. The liquidation of our naval control of the Dominican Republic in 1924 had been determined by Secretary of State Hughes in 1921, and preparations had progressed much too far to be stopped by Coolidge anyway.[12] Our active intervention continued in Honduras and in Nicaragua; in addition we were seriously embroiled in Cuban and Mexican internal politics.[13] If the Harding administration followed some direction in terms of a Latin-American policy, that direction was the result of Charles Evans Hughes' work and not Harding's; when Calvin Coolidge took over and dismissed Hughes for Frank B. Kellogg, Sumner Welles "labelled the period after Hughes' departure from the Department of State the 'unhappy four years' in which inter-American relations deteriorated."[14]

Hoover came to the presidency of the United States with an enormous background in Latin-American affairs.[15]During Harding's and Coolidge's administrations he held the chairmanship of the Inter-American High Commission which, along with his post as Secretary of Commerce, gave him well-rounded experience with and insight into Latin-American problems. He had been concerned with our continued interference in the affairs of other nations of the Hemisphere, particularly in the last days of the Coolidge administration when the United States was awakening to the deterioration of our relations with the countries south of the Rio Grande. Yet the answers were not easily apparent. Many of the Latin-American countries were not ready for democracy. Were we to permit dictators to tyrannize and pillage their peoples while we stood silently by? What type of government were we to recognize? Was it fair to permit Latin-American governments to renounce their obligations both to our own citizens and those of trusting foreign states? If we were neither to intervene in the affairs of any nation in this Hemisphere nor to permit any other to intervene, then far from helping our southern neighbors we were only increasing their irresponsibility. If we withdrew completely from the protectorates, were we not merely retreating from our own responsibilities? Could a substitute be found for military intervention; and, if so, what might be its character? Hoover was not sure of the answers, but he knew that the old ones had not worked. [16] He wanted to try a new foreign policy in Latin-America; Forbes was to help him shape it.

Breaching the constitutional wall and arranging to have the return of a Haitian national legislature had the immediate value of ending the rioting, boycotts, and strikes, which had been engineered by the Opposition parties, and the long-range value of preparing Haitians to administer their government when the Occupation ended in 1936. Withdrawing our Occupation had the immediate value of ending in both the United States and Latin-America the adverse criticism which our stay in Haiti had produced, and the long-range value of setting a new American foreign policy of non-interference toward our neighbors to the south.

But as has been indicated previously in this study, Forbes himself was not altogether happy with what he did. He could not see any real good in the solution. As a result of the pressures upon him, those of the American liberal press, the Haitian Opposition press, opinion in Europe and Asia, he was to a large degree only an instrument of historical forces stronger than he or his Commission. He knew that Borno was an enlightened member of the *élite* honestly working with the Americans to instruct Haitians in the arts of Anglo-Saxon democracy, and that without the continued assistance of Americans the progress made in the past fifteen years would disintegrate. He felt that once the Occupation was withdrawn, chaos would prevail once again, and the black mass would sink silently into the ignorance from which it was slowly being lifted, while the cultured *élite*, apathetic to the misery of his dark brother, climbed once more into the driver's seat. He saw the revived legislature, in which the blacks would have little or no representation, as just a genteel means by which the *élite* would control the nation. Nor was his apprehension unjustified. In the generations since the withdrawal of American forces, Haiti's *élite* has not demonstrated a sincere desire to regenerate the nation. Poverty, illiteracy, and the degradation of the black mass of the people through economic and social exploitation are still the stigmata of almost 90% of all Haitians. What depressed Forbes was the knowledge that the mulatto was not sincere. The mulatto hated the Service Technique because it threatened his claim to leadership, the general receivership because it deprived him of graft, the Occupation because it drew an even stronger color-line than he drew himself against his own darker-skinned brother, and he hated Borno because he considered him a traitor to his class.[17]

Still, what was Forbes to do? To maintain Borno in power, or someone else amenable to the Occupation, or to extend the treaty another twenty or thirty years in the hope that with enough time the United States might produce tangible evidence that she intended nothing but good-will toward Haiti, might be dangerous. Regardless of good intentions, the Occupation appeared like imperialism to Latin-America. And even if tangible results were obtained, could the United States occupy every Latin-American nation which it viewed as unstable politically and economically? It might just as well annex every country south of the Rio Grande. In addition, nothing that had been done had been particularly appreciated.

He knew that to set up a mulatto-dominated legislature, to topple Borno, and to remove Russell would
be mistakes; but he also knew that to remain would
be a greater mistake. So he took the only path which
seemed to him to be sensible--to ride a course
between that of Vezina, who did not have any faith
in the ability of the Haitians to govern themselves,
and that of Kerney and White, who wished to abrogate
the treaty and withdraw immediately. He decided that
the wiser path would be to speed up Haitianization
of all services, establish a legislature, and begin
a gradual withdrawal, so that by 1936, with the end
of the treaty of Occupation, the nation would see
the Americans off in a spirit of amity and be prepared to administer itself without bloodshed or
disorder.

The over-all policy which Forbes aimed at in
Haiti--and which, as we know, became Roosevelt's
"Good Neighbor Policy" toward Latin-America--was
that of withdrawing from the country all military
and civilian forces which were not requested by the
recognized government, but of letting Haiti understand at the same time that the United States Government was prepared to aid her. At her request such
aid could be obtained in any reasonable venture which
would help to establish an orderly, democratic, economically and politically stable nation with a sense
of international responsibility. Theodore Roosevelt's
corollary to the Monroe Doctrine was to be scrapped,
and in its place to be put another type of interven-
tion--that of non-military financial, technical,
and diplomatic assistance. This might mean that
foreign investors would have to trust solely to the
trustworthiness of the Haitian Government, or that
the National Debt might not be adequately serviced,
or that perhaps foreign nationals might occasionally
suffer; but Forbes' final determination that the
destiny of Haiti lay for better or for worse in
Haitian hands has a sagacity that cannot be questioned. Britain went through a thousand years of
turmoil before she had her Glorious Revolution; 125
years of Haitian independence was not really too
great a span. The British Constitution became what
it is because of the anguish which produced it. Only
by lifting themselves would the blacks of Haiti gain
the intellectual capacities necessary to win control
of their nation; by their will alone, and not by
that of a foreigner, no matter how well-meaning,

would the black Haitians attain the strength to win equality with the mulatto. Ultimately, the problems of Haiti would need to be solved by Haitians if they were to be genuine solutions. All that the United States could do was to stand by waiting for the call for help, to give that help when it was asked, and to withdraw that help when no longer desired. Forbes' thinking had flaws, as the next fifty years were to prove, but the thinking was far superior to that of the fifty years which had preceded.

In effect, Forbes said, the tutelage system pronounced by the French and English in the late 19th Century and which we adopted for Latin-America is a failure. It could only be successful in a country such as the Philippines where nationalism had not yet assumed sufficient momentum. Once nationalism entered, tutelage had to depart. It was not successful in Haiti because that country had known independence for too long; it was successful in the Philippines because those islands had never known what it was to be free, and Americans (at least temporarily) were a welcome substitute for the Spanish landlord.

Captain John H. Craige, Head of the Marine Police, had nothing but contempt for the Commission:

> It remained for President Hoover to write the last act to the drama, more preposterous, inconsistent and unintelligible than any that had gone before. The intelligent mulattoes of the Port-au-Prince *élite* still snicker discreetly behind the hand when they refer to this performance. They speak of the incident as the "Hoover Revolution." [18]

He complained that Hoover had no more right to send an American Commission to Haiti "to try President Borno than Mr. Stalin would have had to send a Bolshevik Commission to Washington to try him, Hoover." [19] He complained that after we had approved a constitution, protested for fifteen years that Haiti was a free and sovereign state, and repeatedly announced our non-intervention in Haitian affairs except as we were authorized by the 1915 treaty, we could not justify sending an entirely extra-legal commission into the country to inquire into its president's methods of governing his own land.

The fallacy in this thinking lies in the double assumption that the 1915 treaty and 1918 constitution were Haitian documents. They were American creations foisted upon the little country whether we thought them to be for her own good or not. If Hoover's Commission were illegal, its illegality arose out of the supposed legality of our Intervention to begin with.

The weaknesses of the Forbes Commission were not in its legality or illegality, or its ultimate conclusions. Any weaknesses it possessed were rooted in its methods of operation. What were several of these weaknesses?

First, Forbes stayed too short a time in Haiti. He was a man of experience, acquainted with colored races--at least the Malay and Indian--but neither he nor any of the members of the Commission had been in Haiti previously, nor had any close association with the type of black they were to find in that Republic, nor with the exception of Elie Vezina had any previous acquaintance with the peculiar forces at work in the country whose problems they were to try to settle. They remained in the country a mere two weeks, and it was rumored that Forbes shortened his stay in order to get back to his home in Thomasville for the polo season. They were led on a fast pace through the countryside, and even this brief trip abridged by the news of riots in Port-au-Prince, while what they saw came either through the windows of a limousine or along the paths of guided tours.

Forbes knew the Philippines because he lived there for ten years. He knew the Filipino people through observation. He studied and became proficient in their language, travelled throughout the islands and lived for lengthy periods in the towns, the villages, and the jungle habitations of even the yet uncivilized tribes. His knowledge of Haiti was a knowledge of books, of hearsay, and inadequate personal observation. In order truly to gain the understandings essential to effectuate a settlement of the complicated, internal disorder, one needed to live among the people for at least a year or two, speak the language (not merely the elegant French of *élite* society but the *patois* of the ignorant black mass), travel the virtually inaccessible valleys

191

of the mountainous north, and partake heart and soul
of the Haitian spirit. The Forbes Commission consisted of five well-meaning elderly men who wanted
to clear up the mess they found but who really had
anticipated little more than a vacation in a tropical
country. True, a quick solution was necessary in
view of the turbulence aroused by Borno's refusal
to call for legislative elections, but the emergency
does not change the fact that no man can possibly
be equipped to solve so complicated a problem in
two weeks' time.

Second, the type of fact-gathering employed
was not of the sort to establish a reliable view
of the situation. The Hearings were held in a resplen-
dent atmosphere which was far removed from the poor
huts of the peasants. The witnesses, judging from
the stenographic reports deposited in the National
Archives in Washington, were primarily of the very
classes which the Occupation had displaced or at
least thwarted and who could be expected to be little
other than opposed to a continuation of American
intervention. Did they speak for the Haitian people?
Did they speak for the great, laboring, silent
millions of farm and town? The answer is, of course,
that they did not. To what purpose, then, were the
hearings apart from airing the antagonisms of the
innumerable parties which pretended to speak for
Haiti? The voice of Haiti was no more to be found
at these elegant hearings than the voice of France
was to be heard in the palaces of Versailles or the
voice of Russia in the Kremlin of the Romanoffs.

Yet, one might ask, even if the silent voice
of the black mass could be made to speak, would it
have added very much of significance to that which
had already been spoken? Could it have revealed the
answers any more clearly than did the voice of the
educated and cultured? Perhaps not, but it would
have at least revealed the Haitian soul in either
its blissful contentment or anger, its dullness or
sensitivity, its submission or its fury. The Hearings
at Port-au-Prince should have been merely the first
stage; they should have been continued in the slums
of the towns and the hidden farms of the rural areas.

Third, too much reliance was placed upon docu-
ments--those of the High Commissioner, the Financial
Adviser-General Receiver, statistics of the Secretary

for Public Instruction, reports of the Service Technique. The Commission had gone to Haiti to observe for itself, and in writing its report it had weighted itself with the comments of other parties. Had Hoover wished the collection of factual material, he could have done it by other means; the Forbes Commission, if it were to serve a genuine purpose, had to be less an information bureau and more a direct observer. This was, as well, the great defect of the Moton Commission; it spent a few days in fact-gathering and not enough time in actually walking through the physical plants of the educational system. Again, had the members of both commissions been younger men on a recognized task of strenuous physical effort, their reports might have possessed greater usefulness.

Fourth, the Forbes Commission consisted of men in later middle age whose physical capacities did not match the agility of their minds. Forbes was suffering from heart trouble--he accepted both the Haiti chairmanship and the immediately following ambassadorial post to Japan with reluctance--Kerney suffered from heart disease, and the other three members, Vezina, Fletcher, and White, were unable to sleep or eat properly on the trip. They were unable to do the travelling, speaking, and first-hand observation which was required because such things were beyond their physical capacities.[20]

Fifth, too much publicity was given to the enterprise. No commission which is publicized by presidential announcements, debated in both houses of Congress, discussed in the leading newspapers of the United States and Haiti, dispatched on a cruiser, and received by military units, the high-echelon Haitian officials, and batteries of journalists could hope to discover very much that was not already known. It resembled the opera bouffé of Haitian political history. Could one wonder that the Opposition parties had their stage-machinery at every strategic point, that Russell and Borno both were prepared to put forth their best appearance, that the members of the Commission worked in an artificial atmosphere that smacked more of playhouse than pure sunlight? Wherever the Commission went, with whomever it talked, the results were rehearsed performances and anxious, guarded words.

Sixth, the Commission was not properly balanced. Forbes was an administrator, Fletcher a career diplomat, but White, Vezina, and Kerney were editors, acquainted more with the gathering and reporting of facts than the use of them. Apart from Forbes, all of them earned their livings through writing. All were well-to-do men financially, and Forbes and Kerney were very wealthy. Whatever their political affiliations, all, with the possible exception of White, were of a conservative turn of mind. Forbes objected to the similarity of backgrounds in the members of the Commission, but, as his journal reveals, he had no hand in the selection.[21] The Commission would have been better balanced if Forbes as an experienced administrator had been given an engineer, an educator, an editor, a scientist, a physician, and a lawyer as his five colleagues. Heiser, who was not really a member of the Commission and who was asked to come along by Forbes only as a member of the advisory staff, was the only man with a strong training in objective reasoning. Heiser, who did more travelling, more direct observation, more calm probing for the truth than any member of the Commission, might as well have been officially marked as one of them.

Seventh, the Commission was surrounded by too many influences which it could not escape--the depression at home calling for reduced foreign expenditures, the recriminations of a domestic liberal press (particularly the *Nation*), the fear of effecting a solution incompatible with the 1918 Constitution, the obligations of Haitian debtors to American, French, and British creditors, and the indirect influences of the concurrent London Disarmament Conference. Craige, somewhat bitterly, goes so far as to say that the Forbes Commission ousted its own men, Russell and Borno, after loyal service, simply to mollify the so-called liberal opinion in the United States.[22]

Finally, haste was the common denominator.[23] Whether one agrees or not with the precariousness of the situation, the essential thing to remember is that Forbes did believe that a general uprising was imminent unless a solution were immediately found. That a bloody uprising would have resulted is doubtful; Haitian history is marked with caco and army revolts, but mass risings are unknown. But why speculate on that which might have happened but did not? The historian has business enough attempting to discover the truths behind what *does* happen. Haste prevented the members of the Commission from making the important intellectual preparation for the job; haste shortened the trip to a remarkable two weeks; haste prevented Borno and Russell from adequately presenting their case; haste dictated the Official Report. The major weaknesses of the Commission, in short, seem to have arisen out of the haste with which the Commission worked. (1) A longer stay in the Haitian Republic, (2) a knowledge of the Creole and French tongues, (3) fact-finding based upon personal observations and hearings that offered genuine opportunities for all classes of society to express themselves, (4) extensive travel throughout the country, (5) younger men whose physical capacities matched the agility of their minds, (6) a minimum of publicity, (7) a greater balance in the occupational composition of the Commission, (8) a reasonable freedom from domestic influences, and (9) sufficient leisure for the members to judge their accumulated knowledge in its relation to the purposes of the Commission, would have gone a great distance toward improving the final report.

In line with Forbes' view that our military occupation of the country should be terminated and that in the meantime our relations with Haiti should be conducted by civilians, General Russell resigned and his place taken by Dr. Dana G. Munro. Munro, at the time of his appointment chief of the Latin-American Division of the State Department, took over the duties of High Commissioner and acted at the same time as diplomatic representative from the United States. His knowledge of Latin-American affairs together with his sympathy for the Haitians made him more popular than Russell had ever been. Yet one must remember that Russell's task had been more difficult. How Munro would have worked out as High Commissioner during the 1920's is left to speculation. The forces at work would have made any man in that position a natural target for ambitious Haitian politicians, American and Haitian editors looking for good copy, United States Congressmen searching for issues, and travelling authors. Forbes' conclusion that Russell had done the best job possible in a difficult situation was probably more than justified.

In any case, Munro started the Haitianization of the treaty services—the Garde, Public Health, Public Works, Service Technique, Finance. [24] The new Haitian Government, comprised of a National Legislature elected in October, 1930, and Stenio Vincent, chosen by the National Assembly that same month for the Presidency, insisted upon the withdrawal of all aspects of the Occupation even before the scheduled 1936 date. Hoover refused to withdraw immediately but made the Haitianization Agreement of August 5, 1931, for the complete withdrawal of the Public Works, the Public Health Service, and the Service Technique by October 1, 1931. [25] The service of payments on the public debt and auditing of expenditures were still to be under the control of the American Financial Adviser-General Receiver. This was only logical in Hoover's mind because, where the Public Works and Health Services and Service Technique affected only Haiti, the financial department affected American and foreign bondholders whom Hoover did not wish to see suffer in the event that Haitians were unwilling or unable to service the debts. Simultaneously martial law was discontinued and the American military occupation came technically to an end.

Once control of the country passed to Haitians, the question for the United States was just how fast American elements could be withdrawn. On September 3, 1932, a treaty was signed in which all American officers were to be withdrawn from the Garde by December 31, 1934, while the marines were to begin withdrawal not later than that date. [26] A fiscal representative appointed by the president of Haiti on nomination by the president of the United States, as a replacement for the Financial Adviser-General Receiver, beginning December 31, 1934, caused a great deal of consternation in the Haitian legislature. Although this fiscal representative was supposed to employ only Haitian personnel in his department, the legislature felt that Haiti would not become truly independent until she regained control of her finances. As a result of this issue, the legislature rejected the treaty. Even though the treaty had gone so far as to grant complete withdrawal of all American elements of the Occupation by December 31, 1934, two years ahead of schedule, the legislature refused to backtrack on principle. Nonetheless, Hoover continued the rapid Haitianization of the services on the basis of the August 5th agreement.

196

No further progress was made between the two governments until the administration of Roosevelt.[27] Norman Armour[28] replaced Munro, and an Executive Agreement was arranged on August 7, 1933.[29] Roosevelt preferred this instead of a treaty because it obviated the necessity for approval by the legislatures of both countries and left both presidents free to work out solutions more efficiently and quickly. The Haitianization of the Garde was advanced to October 1, 1934, and the date of the appointment of the fiscal representative changed to January 1, 1934. The remainder of Hoover's agreement of August 5, 1931, remained substantially untouched.

In April, 1934, Vincent visited Washington to confer with Roosevelt. They had met each other years before and were able to confer on a basis of warm understanding.[30] A Pan-American Conference had just taken place (1933) at Montevideo at which the Latin-American nations had drafted a proposal prohibiting intervention by any state in the internal or external affairs of any other state. Cordell Hull, Secretary of State, had said that, though he agreed with this principle, the United States needed time in which to make its withdrawal; but the other delegates demanded acceptance of the proposal without reservations of any kind.[31] The United States had rejected such a proposal in 1928, but now Roosevelt was too busy at home to quibble over the point, and Hull for all practical purposes accepted. With this factor in mind, Vincent asked an end to the financial remnants of the Occupation.

Since, Roosevelt, like Hoover, wished not to anger the many American bondholders who might unjustly suffer were the United States to relax its grip on Haitian finances, Roosevelt and Vincent issued a joint statement in which they declared that the August 7, 1933, agreement was to be carried out, but with new commercial and financial agreements to be negotiated.[32] In other words, modifications of the financial status were to be made that would insure the safety of American investors and at the same time give more freedom to the Haitian Government. To demonstrate his good intentions, Roosevelt ordered a number of the buildings and mechanical equipment owned by the United States Occupation authorities surrendered to Haiti.

In July of the same year, Roosevelt visited
Vincent at Port-au-Prince. He scheduled the marines
to leave by August 15; they started leaving the end
of July, and true to his word, the last marine left
Haitian soil by the scheduled date.

Still, the Haitian legislature was not satisfied. It demanded that the United States withdraw
all financial control. Roosevelt finally effected
this by two steps. (1) We proposed that the National
City Bank of New York sell its controlling interest
in the National Bank of Haiti to the Haitian Government. Vincent agreed to this heartily, as did the
majority of the members of the legislature. When
eleven senators objected, Vincent submitted the proposal to a National Referendum, which approved. The
plan was accordingly carried out. (2) On September
13, 1941, after many conferences, an agreement re-
placing that of 1933 was made, eliminating the fiscal
representative and transferring all funds from his
hands to the National Bank in Haiti. In short, although the Occupation in all other respects ended
in 1934, these financial controls were maintained
until their final liquidation seven years later.[33]

How did the subsequent history of Haiti justify
the internal political settlement and new American
foreign policy engineered by the Forbes Commission?
Vincent remained at the head of the nation until
1941. Once one of the bitterest opponents of the
American Occupation, he came by the close of his
administration to recognize Haiti's political, economic, and geographic dependence on the United States.
Like Dartiguenave and Borno, he was a member of the
élite, who spent his entire life in the Haitian
Government. While still a law student he worked as
a school inspector, then went to Europe as a diplomatic attaché. On his return he became in quick
succession a government commissioner, judge, senator,
and president of the Senate. Intellectual, sensitive,
of enormous physical vitality into his late fifties,
he liked to think of himself as the "Second
Liberator." School children were taught to sing the
happy little tune "Merci, Papa Vincent" before school
and during lunch. He compared himself and his work
to that of Franklin Delano Roosevelt and could not
see why Roosevelt continued in power while he,
equally capable, and his job equally undone, had
to surrender his office.[34]

His first task after obtaining close control
of the Garde d'Haiti, which was now the only armed
force in the country and upon whose good wishes depended his continued security, was the traditional
altering of the constitution. Haiti still had not
learned that a constitution is a framework within
which all parties work, a basic set of principles
that may only be altered with due consideration,
not an *ex post facto* set of laws by which the victor
consolidates his winnings. The power of the executive
was enormously increased to the point where he held
the whip-hand over that much-desired legislature
which the Opposition parties had informed Forbes
was so essential to a democratic Haiti. The president
could name ten of the twenty-one senators and had
the right to submit the names of the remaining eleven
to the Chamber of Deputies for its rubber-stamped
approval. By a later amendment, the president was
given the power to remove senators. The Chamber of
Deputies and local officials were chosen by the populace at large, but the Senate and the president were
chosen indirectly. As the reader notes, the president
really selected the members of the Senate, and the
president was selected by the Senate and Chamber
of Deputies, who were largely highly influenced by
the Senate, with the result that the selection of
a chief executive was not very much more democratic
than the selection of Borno by his own self-appointed
Council of State. Although the Chamber of Deputies
was supposed to be representative of the nation,
one must remember that 90% of the population was
virtually illiterate, and that the Chamber represented the *élite* primarily. In 1935, a new constitution
was adopted extending Vincent's term until 1941 and
granting the people the right to choose the chief
executive and revise the constitution directly. "Both
the constitution and its special clause were submitted to a popular plebiscite. The government counted the votes and announced that an overwhelming
majority had given approval." [35] In 1939, also by
plebiscite, the people renounced their right to
choose directly the chief executive and revise the
constitution. The old pattern had not yet been
changed; government in Haiti was not a trust but
remained personal property.

During President Vincent's ten years in office he proved
himself a capable administrator, improving Haiti's domestic conditions and world position. Many times he went

out into the fields and talked with the peasants, urging
them to rotate their crops and adopt other modern farming
methods. But he permitted no interference with his plans.
He kept the legislative branch in the subordinate position
that it had occupied during most of the nation's history.
He showed scant respect for civil liberties. And he maintained himself in power through a close alliance with
the Haitian Guard.[36]

Vincent paid close attention to public works,
commerce, and finance, but he failed to set the precedent which might have brought Haiti into the modern
era. In the period before the Occupation, the mulatto
claimed that he had to control the legislature in
order to offset the black president installed by
a black Army. But in the Haiti immediately following
the Occupation, the legislature, the Garde, and the
executive power were all in the hands of the mulatto.
Had Vincent then demonstrated the faith and trust
of a Jefferson or a Pétion, the mulatto would have
proved his sincerity when he spoke of his patriotism.
And it was not long before the blacks realized that
the *élite* was under no great passion, as the educated
class, to lead Haiti out of the morass of ignorance
and poverty. At best it had only a half-hearted will.
If Vincent's administration did anything, it demonstrated that Haiti's destiny did *not* lie with the
élite; it lay with the vast black and, as yet, ignorant mass. Only when the president, the judiciary,
the legislature were in the hands of trained, educated men of the black populace would Haiti take
the first long step toward modern, orderly democracy
and a high standard of living. The question by the
end of Vincent's term was whether the black mass
would come into its own by a gradual weakening of
the mulatto hold or by a violent social revolution
such as had occurred in Mexico in the first decade
of the present century.

Vincent wanted to remain president in 1941,
but even the 1935 constitution prevented his running
for a third time unless approved by special
plebiscite, for on March 10 the Chamber of Deputies
actually voted to extend his term. But his term was
already longer than that held by Borno, and there
were grumblings in the Garde. A month later he made
up his mind that he would not run again, naming
another mulatto, Dr. Élie Lescot, then minister to
Washington, his successor. Ten days after his

announcement to this effect, Lescot was elected president by the legislature.

Lescot,[37] whose administration ran from 1941 until 1946, carried the authoritarian regime of Vincent to extremes. He declared war on the Axis, December 3, 1941, and then proceeded to use the so-called "emergency" to maintain himself in power by prohibiting all elections for the duration of the emergency. Béllègarde states that in 1944 the United States, with millions of men fighting all over the world, found no reason to limit its normally freely contested presidential election.[38] Other attacks on Lescot came as the result of rising prices, dropping wages, and the activities of the Haitian-American Company, whose experiments in the growth of a rubber substitute weed known as *criptostegia* the peasants complained were destroying the best land in the country. A students' strike set the nation's capital aflame with hatred, and mobs attacked the homes of cabinet ministers. No longer supported by the Garde, Lescot fled with his family to Canada, January 11, 1946. A junta was formed consisting of Colonel Frank Lavaud, commander of the Garde, Major Antoine Levelt, director of the Military Academy, and Major Paul Magloire, who headed the Palace Guard.

The junta recognized that the sixteen years following the Forbes Commission had not fulfilled the promises so grandly proclaimed by the Opposition groups in 1930. Not only in Haiti, not only among the liberals of the United States, but throughout the world, the evidence was clear that the black Haitian was to receive little justice from the light-skinned politician who controlled the government. Yet the world of 1946 was a new-born world that demanded justice. Fascism had been beaten, the Atlantic and United Nations Charters had proclaimed in bold print the principle of human rights, and Red influence was making itself felt. The junta accordingly wrote a new constitution; then, in an attempt to whitewash the *élite* class before the world, it looked beyond itself to a black for the next president. It chose Dumarsais Estimé, a forty-six year old lawyer, former farmer and rural schoolteacher, who, although black and not of the *élite*, was nonetheless cultured, educated, well-to-do, and familiar with political office in Haiti.[39]

Though the junta which selected Estimé believed
him "safe," it could not have been more mistaken.
Estimé believed that social revolution could not
come slowly, that the future of Haiti lay with the
black working class, that the *élite* standards could
no longer serve Haiti, and that the moneyed groups
stood in the way of genuine progress toward lifting
the people out of their illiteracy and poverty. "His
announced goal--was to improve the desperate living
conditions of the impoverished masses." [40] That he
was Communist is doubtful, but that he was Socialist
in his political and economic philosophy is unques-
tionable.

Hated as few presidents before him, he produced
during his administration genuinely worthwhile results. He discharged the American debt; cleared the
filthy slums of the Port-au-Prince waterfront and
beautified the area; publicized Haiti as a vacation-
spot with the result that the tourist trade became
Haiti's second largest source of revenue; constructed
an experimental modern city at Belladere complete
with plumbing, electricity, and paved streets; fought
hookworm by requiring by law that peasants wear
shoes; encouraged the development of unions; formed
an agreement with the Export-Import Bank of the
United States for the financing of a $6,000,000 irri-
gation and land-reclamation project in the Artibonite
Valley; and tried, though without too much success,
to collectivize the peasants by offering those who
cooperated sixteen acres of land, seed, tools, and
advice. A United Nations investigatory commission,
however, reported that the basic problem of Haiti
came from the "relentless pressure of a steadily
growing, insufficiently educated population upon
limited, vulnerable, and--so far as agricultural
land is concerned--alarmingly shrinking natural
resources." [41]

Even with Estimé's advanced thinking, the forces
were too great for his efforts. The *élite* proved
too strongly opposed to Estimé's program for swift
education of the black mass, while the Church opposed
birth control. Haiti has been, to a high degree,
burdened with the same problem as Ireland and Italy,
overpopulation. Yet Ireland's and Italy's surplus
populations were able to find their way to the United
States, to the Spanish and Portuguese-speaking
nations of Latin-America. No one would take the sur-

plus population of Haiti. When during Vincent's administration (October, 1937) Haitians crossed the frontier into the Dominican Republic looking for work in the sugar-cane fields, Trujillo had them rounded up by the thousands and massacred with bullet and knife. Batista's hostility prevented their entering Cuba for the same type of work. Nor were they welcome in any other country that had any color consciousness. The result was that Haiti became in the 1940's a nation bursting with an exploding population --and no solution in sight.

By 1950, despite Estimé's dissolution of radical parties and newspapers, the *élite*, business communities, and Garde were anxious to rid themselves of what they considered to be the greatest radical of all, Estimé himself. Yet he had really proposed very little that Franklin D. Roosevelt had not proposed in the 1930's. The trouble was that if the New Deal was a strong departure from American economic philosophy, how much more a departure, how much more shocking, was Estimé's proposals to the cultured groups of Haiti. When Estimé attempted to amend the Constitution to permit himself to be reelected in 1950 (the 1946 Constitution forbade immediate reelection, but retained a six-year presidential term), the Senate refused such amendment. When a mob sacked the Senate chamber, Estimé praised the action in a newspaper article.

The Garde finally acted. On May 10, 1950, it turned the government over to the military junta, now controlled by Brigadier General Paul Magloire, and five months later Magloire was elected president of the nation. Estimé received a pension and exile.

Magloire won the election without opposition, the people voting directly after dissolution of the Senate and Chamber of Deputies. Although also a black and not a member of the *élite*, he had certain advantages over Estimé. He was a military leader, firmly entrenched in the Garde, the final arbiter of national politics. He had a winning personality of a type which gave him wide influence with the leaders of the nation. Moderate in his economic and social view, he obtained the trust of the *élite* and the business community. He advocated non-discrimination on the basis of skin-color in his choice of government offices. He remained on friendly terms with the Church; and he accepted the principle of a slow evolvement of the black mass into its role of democratic action.[42]

In 1950, at a Constitutional Convention held in Gonaives and superintended by Dantès Béllègarde, a new constitution was drafted. The usual liberties of man were enumerated, primarily those included in the American "Bill of Rights" and the French Revolution's "Declaration of the Rights of Man." But too easy amendment, the fatal defect which in the past served as the poison shaft to destroy past constitutions, remained. Amendments could be proposed by either the president, the Senate, or the Chamber of Deputies; both houses had to meet in joint session to consider the matter; two thirds of the total membership was necessary for a quorum, and two thirds of this quorum was necessary for passage of the proposed amendment.

Election of the president continued to be by direct vote (that is, communal electors were chosen by direct, secret vote) as well as the Chamber of Deputies, but the Senate was selected by the provincial (Department) assemblies. The president was elected for six years, with no eligibility for immediate reelection, senators (twenty-one in number) for six years, and deputies (thirty-seven) for four years. Suffrage was granted to all Haitians twenty-one years of age without regard to sex, creed, or color, but women, though they could hold office and vote on the local level, were not permitted to vote on the national executive level. The president, be it noted, in addition to being empowered to select all cabinet ministers, judges, army officers, and diplomats, was granted the right to dissolve the Senate and the Chamber of Deputies at will--a clear road to despotism, for, unlike the separation of the executive, judicial, and legislative powers in the American Constitution, ultimately all legislative, judicial, and executive powers vest in one and the same body. Nor did the National Assembly have any control over the president's appointments. In only two major ways did the Constitution restrict the Chief Executive: (1) the National Assembly had to approve all treaties and declarations of war (2) judges could not be removed by presidential whim. The president alone might introduce appropriation measures, adjourn the National Assembly, convene the National Assembly in special session to consider only the proposals which he desired to place before it. Why the Convention permitted the National Assembly the right to pass a law over the president's objections by a two-thirds vote of each house is not clear when one realizes that legislation by decree in Haiti is the rule rather than the exception. "Some of the most important reforms in Haitian history have been made by presidential order."[43]

The cabinet, in short, became a cross between the British system and the American. Like the British, each cabinet member supposedly took absolute responsibility for the acts to which he gave his consent, yet like the Americans, he did not represent a particular party in the National Assembly but remained merely a head of department. The simple fact is that the president became so all-important, so all-controlling, that the cabinet members were little better than clerks performing routine duties.

Direct vote of the people, though provided for by the Convention, really meant little when one realizes that the vast majority could neither read nor write. Of what use was a provision for secret balloting when few persons could read the newpapers, understand the issues involved in any election, or make their voices heard? In practice, the rural "bosses" of the political machines "usually collect the registration cards of their unlettered followers --paying a small sum for this privilege--and then vote these cards in batches. This system has been used for so many years that no one thinks to challenge it."[44]

Six years after Magloire came to power, he was in serious trouble; the problems seemed unconquerable, and as discouragement set in, the administration gradually lost its drive. In the midst of growing graft and cynicism, Magloire made known that he would probably not complete his term of office, and yet he still continued to remain in power. But he was losing the support of the army, and in December 1956, a general strike forced him into exile. From December 5, 1956 until May 25, 1957, Haiti was again in the throes of conflict, with four governments rapidly succeeding one another in the space of 170 days of chaos, rioting, and confusion.

The presidential election of September 1957 under army supervision in which 900,000 of the 1,600,000 registered voters (including women for the first time) took part, brought Dr. Francois Duvalier to power. "The official tally gave Duvalier 679,884 votes and Senator Louis Dejoie, the only opponent who was able to remain in the race to the finish received 266,993. Twenty-three of Duvalier's thirty-seven followers seeking seats in the Chamber of Deputies were elected."[45] A quiet-spoken physician and a graduate of the University of Michigan, Duvalier had the support of the American government in his bid to eliminate Magloire-styled arbitrary control and bring about badly needed social reform and civil liberties. But Duvalier did not fulfill expectations. He purged Dejoie's *L'Alliance Démocratique d'Haiti* and other political parties in the country with the exception of his own, banned strikes, censored newspapers and imprisoned unyielding editors, intimidated judges, and stripped the army of officers suspected of not being entirely loyal to him. "By mid-1958, night-time raids, arbitrary imprisonment, torture, and mysterious disappearance and death had become commonplace, and the National Assembly had been rendered sufficiently subservient to declare a state of siege and vote the president extraordinary powers."[46] And at the center of this web of terror lay the dreaded *tonton macoute* (Creole for bogeymen or bagmen), comparable to Hitler's brown-shirts during the early 1930's, and the *Police Secrete,* a veritable Gestapo. By 1964, it became apparent that civil liberties and social reforms were not to be attempted, and in their place Duvalier substituted a new constitution that made him president for life and enabled him to rule by decree. In January 1971, the president persuaded the National Assembly to amend the Constitution so that the age qualifications for the presidency were lowered from forty to eighteen, and when Duvalier died three months later, his nineteen-year-old son Jean-Claude also became president-for-life. Were Haiti under a succession of responsible executives, or under a succession of alternating responsible-irresponsible rulers in the vein of English political development--a wise monarch remedying the evils of the one preceding--we might expect more in the way of constitutional progress. Haiti's tragedy has been her seemingly interminable line of poor executives.

A little more than thirty-five years after the Hoover Commissions, Haiti found herself far from democracy or a reasonably advanced standard of living. Despite $45,000,000 in Point Four assistance during the 1950-60 decade plus $32,000,000 in loans from the Export-Import Bank and Development Loan Fund (in 1961 the United States made $13,500,000 available for Haiti, or one-half the national budget), the average per capita income in the early 1960's was sixty dollars. Although between 1968 and 1972, Haiti's economy continued to grow after over two decades of stagnation, according to reports by the United Nations, data has proved to be sketchy, while in terms of per capita income, Haiti continues to be the poorest country in the Western Hemisphere. If investments have increased, they have done so because of growing tourism and because of the dubious stability that strong dictatorship brings, not because of an advancing society. Two generations or so after Forbes and Moton, Haiti is suffocating in an educational, political, and economic quagmire, where one out of seven children attends school and a 90% illiteracy rate is deemed normal. So many years after Forbes and Moton, cruise-ships stopping at Port-au-Prince sterilize Haitian goods brought back to their decks by souvenir-hunting tourists, the telephone system is maddeningly inoperative, the wharves and buildings constructed by the Occupation forces are in disrepair, and the only major highway in Haiti is the road leading to Cap-Haitien. The Opposition in 1930 promised Forbes that liquidation of the Borno administration and the removal of American marines would restore political freedom, economic progress, and racial equality to Haiti. But that promise has not been fulfilled, and the years since have seen increasing graft, lack of genuine patriotism, and a restriction of civil rights.

When Forbes wrote to Moton that the "whole situation to me is a tragedy--a tragedy because I don't see any good ending to it," he meant that the United States, in eliminating the Occupation, was wrecking a practical organization without really substituting anything better. Occupation was a poor policy, but, as events were to demonstrate, the policy we followed after our withdrawal was worse. Hoover never intended the "Good Neighbor" policy to become the "Forgotten Neighbor" policy, but this is what happened. Before 1930, we applied our aid to Haiti with continual watching, scolding, chastising, until the little nation chafed beneath the iron hand like a small child in the grip of a puritanical, if well-meaning parent. Then we went to the other extreme. Like the indulgent father too busy to look personally into the affairs of a difficult son, we believed that we could solve Haiti's problems by the writing of checks. But this technique worked no better. Occupying Haiti lost favor because it appeared to smack of oppression; while grants of large sums of money to be spent free of adequate supervision only served to pad the pockets of those already rich and powerful.

What should we have done once the Occupation was liquidated? First, we should have refused to recognize or to aid any leader who did not come to power as the result of free elections. There is a contradiction in claiming, as we do, to represent democracy, and yet support flagrantly undemocratic political elements. That political leaders claim to be anti-Communist should be of no concern. The easiest way we may take to lose the confidence of reform-hungry peoples is to ally ourselves with totalitarian elements because they claim to be anti-Communist. It is a gross miscalculation to believe that an enemy of the Communists is necessarily an ally of the United States. The history of the last two centuries has demonstrated that the revolution that began at Lexington did not end in 1783, but continues still. Second, not only should we have refused to aid any leader who came to power by means other than free elections, but we should have actively assisted sincere Haitian revolutionists in his overthrow. By not accepting this principle, we found ourselves often backing the wrong side, not the side of order and good government but the *status quo* against salutary change. To be on the side of law and order is not enough; the United States must be on the side of a law and order that looks to human rights. We support the dictator Marcos in the Philippines despite the fact that he has destroyed the democracy that men like Forbes and his successors struggled to construct, solely, it seems, because Marcos is an avowed anti-Communist. We support the brutal government in Chile and equally brutal regimes in El Salvador and in Haiti today for the same reasons. Were the United States with the revolutionaries in those countries, there would be no need for such revolutionaries to turn to the Soviet Union for aid.

Third, we should have kept American private
ownership out of Haiti. Haitian resources needed
American investment, not American ownership. No
matter how beneficial, nothing proved more irritating
to the proud Haitian than to know that many of the
imposing structures in Haiti were foreign-owned.
Fourth, we should have abandoned in so far as possible any system of aid that did not include supervision of the spending. Large sums of money stimulated graft, were rarely used efficiently, and were
all too often directed to the military needs of the
men in power. We would have done better to determine
in any particular year the schools, bridges, highways, public buildings, dams, warehouses that Haiti
needed, then gone in and built them. This would have
been especially beneficial in regard to the schools.
Instead of pouring financial power into the hands
of the Haitian government in the hopes that schools
would be built, teachers trained, equipment purchased
and operated, we would have accomplished more to
construct the school plants ourselves and equip them,
and train Haitian teachers and administrators. Fifth,
aid should have been ear-marked for specific purposes
that contributed directly to the economic, social,
and political well-being of the Haitian masses. The
most poorly run business firm would not do a day's
business without knowing how and where and why its
funds were being spent, yet we did this sort of thing
as a matter of course.

Undoubtedly, the Forbes Commission would appear
today to be more significant had Haiti thereafter
followed a road leading to the democratic nation
the United States hoped she would become. But this
does not diminish what Forbes actually accomplished.
To attribute too little to him is as dangerous as
attributing too much. Forbes achieved in Haiti what
he was sent to do. He settled the immediate internal
situation, and did it without bloodshed; he assessed
the Occupation; he advised against its continuation
and recommended steps for its liquidation. Further
than this his Report did not go.

He did not establish United States policy toward
Haiti in the years following the withdrawal of our
marines, nor help in its formulation, nor give any
indication of what sort of policy the United States
should follow. Forbes' significance is that he represents a termination of one stage of our thinking

in reference to Haiti and Latin-America, and the beginning of another. Perhaps this stage would have terminated without him. But that is not the point. The Forbes Commission was, so to speak, the inscription on the tomb of the Roosevelt Corollary.

The United States, as Forbes saw it, had two choices in Haiti: (1) either to remain there and do the job of rearing a new democratically oriented people, whether that job took one generation or two or three or more, regardless of adverse criticism (2) to withdraw from Haiti, but maintain from outside the pressures necessary to keep Haiti on the path toward responsible democracy. He chose the latter. And perhaps he was correct. But unfortunately, in the years that followed, the American people ignored both choices. We tossed out the first choice by withdrawing, and then ignored the second choice by forgetting Haiti entirely, after which we piled deliberate injury upon failure by supporting the Duvalier dictatorship in the name of anti-Communism. The Forbes Commission need not have been a tragedy but it was transformed into such by the same type of politics that permitted Hitlerism in Europe.

NOTES

1. See generally Dexter Perkins, *The American Approach to Foreign Policy*; C. A. Beard, *The Idea of National Interest*; S. F. Bemis, *A Diplomatic History of the United States*; George Kennan, *American Diplomacy, 1900-1950*; H. J. Morgenthau; *In Defense of the National Interest*; R. W. Tucker, "Professor Morgenthau's Theory of Political Realism," *American Political Science Review*, March, 1952.

2. S. F. Bemis, *Pinckney's Treaty: America's Advantage from Europe's Distress*, 1783-1800.

3. Hans J. Morgenthau, "The Mainsprings of American Foreign Policy: The National Interest vs. Moral Abstractions," *American Political Science Review*, Dec. 1950, p. 8.

4. *Ibid.*

5. See p. 60, this study: "The United States is lousy with great kind-hearted woolly-headed enthusiasts..."

6. Wilson never wandered very far from the thought that he was the school-master in the presidential chair, and it was

this attitude that particularly antagonized Forbes both in the Philippines and in Haiti. See generally Ray Stannard Baker, *Woodrow Wilson; Life and Letters*, Vols. IV and V.

7.   J. F. Rippy, *The Caribbean Danger Zone*, pp. 182–193.

8.   Helen Hill Weed, "Victory in Haiti," *Nation*, Mar. 26, 1930, p. 378.

9.   *New York Times*, Aug. 19 and 23, 1920.

10. Franklin D. Roosevelt, "Our Foreign Policy," *Foreign Affairs*, July, 1928, pp. 573–586.

11. Rippy, *The Caribbean Danger Zone*, p. 247.

12. *Ibid.*, p. 248.

13. See generally Bemis, *The Latin American Policy of the United States*; Graham H. Stuart, *Latin America and the United States*; Rippy, *Latin America in World Politics*.

14. Alexander DeConde, *Herbert Hoover's Latin-American Policy*, p. 7.

15. *Ibid.*, pp. 13–33.

16. *Ibid.*, pp. 79–89.

17. In *Cannibal Cousins*, pp. 265–266, John H. Craige remarks of Ernest Chauvet, who was probably typical of the *élite* class:

"I always had a feeling that perhaps Chauvet did a good deal of his laughing so that he would not weep. From his point of view, his situation was tragic. He was young, eloquent, able. Yet he was separated from a state job and had no chance to make his fortune in the traditional manner of his race. Naturally, he hated President Borno and the Government. Under a Haitian regime he might have been certain that a few months, a few years, would bring a change. But the Americans had ended sudden changes. Meanwhile, the years were rolling by and his health was none too good. Of course he hated the Americans."

18. *Ibid.*, pp. 293–294.

19. *Ibid.*, p. 295.

20. These observations are based upon conversations with Dr. Heiser.

21. See p. 59, this study.

22. Craige, *Cannibal Cousins*, p. 294.

23. Forbes, Haitian Journal. In reading the account written by Forbes, one gets the impression that only the swiftest solution would avert bloodshed.

24. De Conde, pp. 88–89.

25. James W. Gantenbein (ed), *The Evolution of Our Latin American Policy: A Documentary Record*, pp. 919–922.

26. *Ibid.*, pp. 923–930.

27. Edward O. Guerrant, *Roosevelt's Good Neighbor Policy*.

28. Norman Armour was a career diplomat. Born in Brighton, England, Oct. 14, 1887, he received his education at Princeton and Harvard (LL.B., 1913). He was admitted to the New Jersey Bar in 1914, but decided to spend his life in the diplomatic service. Before his appointment as minister to Haiti, he had seen service in Paris, Petrograd, Brussels, the Hague, Montevideo, Rome, and Tokyo.

29. Gantenbein, pp. 930–936.

30. John Gunther, *Inside Latin-America*, on pp. 450–451, relates: "Vincent and Roosevelt met at Cap–Haitien in 1917 when Roosevelt was Secretary of the Navy and Vincent was Secretary of Interior in Haiti. Both were momentarily disgusted with politics: both swore they would never take public office again. But––Vincent chuckled––it was in the cards for Roosevelt to be President of the United States three times and himself President twice." (written by Gunther in 1941)

31. See generally *Report of the Delegates of the United States of America to the Seventh International Conference of American States: First, Second and Eighth Committees*, Montevideo, 1933.

32. Samuel I. Rosenman (ed.), *The Public Papers and Addresses of Franklin Delano Roosevelt*, Vol. III, pp. 184–186.

33. Guerrant, pp. 9–10; Gantenbein, pp. 937–942.

34. Gunther, pp. 450–452.

35. Austin F. MacDonald, *Latin American Politics and Government*, p. 593.

36. *Ibid.*

37. Rodman, pp. 27–29.

38. *Ibid.*, p. 28.

39. *Ibid.*, pp. 29–30; MacDonald, p. 594; Herring, p. 422.

40. MacDonald, *Ibid.*

41. Quoted in Lewis Hanke, *Mexico and the Caribbean*, p. 38.

42. Rodman, pp. 30–31.

43. MacDonald, p. 596.

44. *Ibid.*, pp. 595–596.

45. Thomas E. Weil, *et al*, *Area Handbook for Haiti* (Washington, D.C., 1973), p. 114.

46. *Ibid.*, p. 115. Also see Hanke, p. 39; Herring, p. 423; Rippy, *Latin America: A Modern History*, p. 410. At his inauguration, Dr. Duvalier stated: "My government will guarantee the exercise of liberty to all Haitians." This was Oct. 22, 1957. On May 2, 1958, after a series of explosions in the Capital, the National Assembly declared a state of siege and suspended the Constitution. July 31, 1958, Duvalier was given the power to govern by decree (technically for a six-month period). For an interesting and informative presentation of life during the last years of Dr. Duvalier's administration from the point of view of a celebrated artist, see Katherine Dunham, *Island Possessed.*

APPENDIX

(A)

The following document was prepared apparently by an Haitian committee unfamiliar with the English language, and is filled with spelling, grammatical and stylistic errors. For purposes of authenticity and to spare the reader annoyance, the present author reproduces the document just as it came off the press and without the repeated use of (sic).

COPY OF DOCUMENT PROTESTING THE UNITED STATES OCCUPATION OF HAITI, PRESENTED TO THE FORBES COMMISSION BY THE OPPOSITION PARTIES

THE NATIONAL LEAGUE OF CONSTITUTIONAL ACTION

Created with a view to protect the Haitian National rights, interpreting the aspirations of the Haitian people.

Does hereby expose to Mr. President of the United States the following facts:

1.   The troubles that have lately occurred in Haiti producing such a deep repercussion in the world, specially in Latin-America, have attracted the universal attention on a situation that the Honorable Secretary of State, Mr. Stimson, has qualified as "causing acute anguish."

2.   The existing conditions in Haiti "cause acute anguish" because, since the American intervention on July 28th, 1915, a military Occupation, implicating a permanent Martial Law, has been established, absorbing gradually all the governmental and administrative activities of the Haitian Republic.

3.   This absorption reached its climax with the dissolution twice, in 1916 and 1917, of the Legislative Assemblies emanated from the popular vote, and with their substitution by a Council of State, a body of politicians appointed by the President of Haiti and removable at his fancy.

4.   By virtue of a "transitory" provision of the Constitution of 1918, the Legislative Power is vested in the Council of State until the constitution of the Legislative Body.

The Legislative Body has not been constituted because another provision of that same Constitution of 1918 equally "transitory" prescribes that "The first election of the members of the Legislative Body shall take place on the 10th of January of an even year", and that such year shall be determined by a Presidential decree within three months previous to the meeting of the primary Assemblies. Five even years have elapsed since, and still the President, — taking the prescription, in its dealings with the convocation of electors, as a privilege and not as an obligation, — has been refraining himself from fulfilling that formality.

The forbearance of the President of Haiti has produced as consequence that the democratic, republican and representative constitution of the Haitian Government has been converted into a dictatorship.

5. The present Government of Haiti is a dictatorship:
    1.) because the elective franchise is refused to the Haitian citizens,
    2.) because the Nation, who is represented by the universality of those citizens possessing their political rights, does not participate directly to the management of public affairs.
    3.) because the Nation has to obey to laws and to pay taxes which have not been voted by its elected representatives,
    4.) because it does not control the collection of taxes, nor the expenditure made in his behalf by foreign irresponsible employees.

6. This dictatorship is of a military character because it is backed by armed forces of the United States who enforce and maintain that dictatorial Government.

In fact, the actual Government of Haiti is in hand of the American High Commissioner who totally enslaves the native Government. This fact has been established without any possible contention by Dr. MILLSPAUGH, former Financial Adviser in Haiti, and by many American observers whose disinterestedness and impartiality in the matter are beyond all doubt.

7. The military dictatorship established in Haiti has proven to be a total failure.

ECONOMICAL FAILURE. Nothing in an efficient way has been done in order to increase the Haitian production; and while our export is decreasing, many legislative measures discouraging agriculturists and industrials have been adopted; commerce also is at bay.

SOCIAL FAILURE. Many attempts have been put in action to sour the peasant's temper against the townpeople by making them belief that the rural masses were systematically abused by the Haitian elite; but in fact no serious measures have ever been adopted to protect them and to increase their standard of living. On the contrary, they have been illtreated physically by means of "corvee" (forced labor), a vestige of the colonial system, wronged in their properties through certain laws put forth with the scope of depriving them of their lands, and not being protected by the police force nor judges they were compelled to use violent revendications which have led to the hecatombs of 1918–1919 and those of the 6th December last.

POLITICAL FAILURE. The Haitian Nation has gone back rather than advanced in the path of democratic progress and self-government; even the Municipal autonomy – basis of our political organization – has been abolished as it is proved by the underdealings employed in order to bar the elections of 1930. The judicial power whose authority lays on the competency, integrity and independence of the Judges has been weakened and demoralized with the suppression of the inmovability of the Judges.

MORAL FAILURE. Never before, the defiance of law had reached such an extent as nowadays, for law is not considered as emanation of the National will but merely as instrument of tyranny and arbitraries; never before, stoop of character and corruption were as common as today, –– nepotism and favoritism being the inflexible rule followed in the recruiting of the high officials of the Republic.

All these facts –– which could be easily established by an impartial investigation –– have produced unrest, insecurity and a general agitation which endanger public peace.

Order prevails in Haiti, but a material and factitious order imposed and maintained by means of machine guns. The real peace, the lasting and fertile peace, that which rests on liberty, justice and respect of the National institutions and on popular sympathy, does not exist.

8. Aware of this lamentable condition, the President of the United States has expressed his willingness to bring about those changes claimed for by the Haitian opinion and by the American conscience, stating that it should be observed a more human attitude towards Haiti, an attitude of more respect for the dignity and independence of the Haitian people and more in accordance with the democratic principles of the Government of the United States, a measure that will contribute to calm the natural apprehensions of Latin-America that that should be employed in the policy of good understanding and unselfish

friendship that Mr. HOOVER is willing to practice towards our sisters Republics.

Therefore, in his Message of 3th December last to Congress, Mr. President of the United States did assert his intention of sending to Haiti a Commission to inquire into the situation and to submit to his approval the necessary solution. But, some days afterwards, as a consequence of the troubles occurred in Haiti during the students' strike, Mr. President of the United States recommended that immediate steps should be taken by Congress.

These troubles were magnified in official reports in order to justify the expedition of more armed forces to Haiti with the hope, by doing so, that the Haitian revendications would be drowned in a bloodshed and the reparative measures promised by Mr. President HOOVER indefinitely postponed.

Although the importance assigned to those troubles were exaggerated, it is a matter of fact that they have revealed the discontent and the deep excitement among the people as a result of the unjustified and vexatious tyranny whereupon the present system is based.

The excitement which upsets the whole Nation is a drawback to the development of its pacific achievements, entangles consequently the economical development of the country, and shall not come to an end unless the dictatorship is suppressed. And that cannot be obtained unless the Government of the United States' formal promise made in 1915 to the Haitian people be an actual fact, by assisting Haiti in the establishing of a stable government elected by itself.

9. Hence, as a result of the armed forces employed by the American Occupation in 1916 and 1917 to dissolve the Legislative Chambers, in 1920 1922–1924–1926 and 1928 to suppress the legislative elections, — that, in opposition with the Constitution of 1918 imposed by the United States, — *no government by the people for the people could ever be established in Haiti.*

On 12th of August 1915, Mr. Dartiguenave had been elected President of the Republic by the *National Assembly* composed of the *Senate and the Chamber of Deputies.*

The National Assembly alone, in its Constitutional privilege, is empowered to elect a President of the Republic.

The Constitution of 1918, "which was forced down the

217

throat of Haitian people with American bayonets", according to the historical words of President HARDING -- does not differ on that point from the previous Constitution. Its Section III, Chapter I, title III refering to the National Assembly reads as follows:

"Art. 40. -- The two Chambers shall meet as a National Assembly in such cases as statutable by the Constitution.

"The powers of the National Assembly are limited and cannot be exercised on any other subject but those specially assigned by the Constitution.

"Art. 41. -- The President of the Senate presides the National Assembly whereof the President of the Chamber of Deputies is the Vice-President, while the Secretaries of the Senate and of the Chamber of Deputies are Secretaries of the National Assembly.

"Art. 42. -- The attributes of the National Assembly are:
1) to elect the President of the Republic and to receive his oath;
2) Etc...

"Art. 48. -- No resolutions can be adopted if the presence of a majority of the two Houses has not been ascertained."

Hence, in the Haitian Constitutional system the National Assembly constitutes a special organization whose attributes are restrictively determined and its composition immutably fixed by the Constitution; it is the joining of the two Legislative Chambers into one single assembly. Its attributes are different from those of the Legislative Body composed of a House of Deputies and a Senate exercising separately "legislative power" according to the condition established by the Constitution in its Chapter II (articles 49-70).

10. Article D of the "transitory" provisions of the Constitution of 1918 prescribes that the Council of State shall exercise the Legislative Power *until the Legislative Body is elected*. According to article 55, legislative power consist in the "making of laws on all matters of public interests."

The practice of this "legislative power", conferred provisionally and temporary upon the Council of State, does not entitle it to exercise the attributes of the National Assembly, namely to elect the President of the Republic.

Consequently, it is without any right nor title that the

Council of State — an *unique* Assembly of employees appointed by the President of the Republic — has elected Mr. LOUIS BORNO president of the Republic in 1922, adding a constitutional violation to another one, Mr. Borno not being eligible to the presidency as born of an alien father (article 73, 1st alinea).

It is equally without any right nor title that the Council of State, composed of employees appointed by Mr. BORNO, has reelected Mr. BORNO in 1926 as President of the Republic, notwithstanding the evident proof of his ineligibility established by a letter which he wrote and signed, and wherein he admits himself that his father was still a Frenchman at the time of his birth.

11. The Council of State, composed as it is of parents, relations and partisans of Mr. BORNO and blindly subdued to the latter, has — publicly and in writings — declared that they will not receive any watch-word but from Mr. BORNO. It is a fact that the Council of State has no constitutional attributes, neither moral authority nor necessary independence to elect the President of the Republic in 1930. If Mr. BORNO, or any one else *publicly* or *secretly* designated by himself, should be nominated President of the Republic in April 14th, 1930, by the Council of State, the discontent and the general agitation will be extreme and certainly the cause of disorders that the Americans only will be able to check by a huge and heartless bloodshed.

12. United States have promised their assistance to the Haitian people in the establishment of a stable Government. Time has come for Washington to keep to its promises.

The Haitian people ask the assistance of the United States in the establishment of such a government, whose stability rests on the free suffrage of the National Chambers, and the election of the President of the Republic by the National Assembly which consists, according to the Constitution, of the meeting of the Senate and the Chamber of Deputies melted into one single assembly.

13. Art. 27. of the Constitution reads as follows: "The National Sovereignty resides in the universality of the citizens."

On behalf of that "national Sovereignty" the Haitian citizens ask for an honest and free election who will restore the Legislative and the Executive Powers, — two principal elements of the Government of the Republic, which is essentially civil, democratic and representative according to the expression of the Constitution of 1918 (Article 28).

As the legislative elections are to take place at an early date, the intervention of the U. S. Government is deemed necessary by the Haitian citizens.

This intervention is asked for because Mr. BORNO, notwithstanding his formal promise of a reconstruction of the Legislative Chambers contained in his message of April 1928 to the Council of State, retracted under the pretenses that a state of excitement prevails in Haiti while the High Commissioner as well as the Chief of the Garde d'Haiti in their official reports have made at that very time a quite different statement.

The present agitation is due at the contrary to a large extent to that violation of his formal engagement, to that disregard of the most sacred right of citizens: the right to vote.

The Government of the United States cannot invoke, to reject this demand of intervention, that the treaty of 1915 does not confer upon it the right to impose on the President of Haiti the respect of the constitutional prescriptions dealing with the constitution of the Legislative Body.

General WALLER, Chief of the American forces of Occupation, without taking notice of the treaty of 1915, had caused in 1916 the doors of the Haitian Parliament to be closed.

Colonel ELI K. COLE, Chief of the armed forces of Occupation in 1917, forced the President of Haiti to decree, despite the Haitian Constitution, the dissolution of the Haitian Legislative Body, while General Smedley BUTLER, chief of the Gendarmerie d'Haiti, threw both Senators and Deputies from their benches.

The United States Government is in the obligation to restore what the American forces have destroyed in Haiti. Its honor and the responsibility it has taken towards Haiti in face of the civilized World call for such a measure of supreme reparation.

If Mr. LOUIS BORNO, notwithstanding the intervention of the American Government, declines to convene the electors, it should be up to the American Occupation to take care of same, for the sake of the Haitian people and the safeguard of public peace. This act shall not be taxed as being more arbitrary than the recent actuation of the Occupation Forces, who, by virtue of the martial law, had placed under their order the Garde d'Haiti, — a national force under the authority of the President of Haiti who is the Chief Commander of all the armed forces of the Republic. (Article 75 of the Constitution).

14. The Haitian citizens ask for free and fair legislative elections in order that the Legislative Chambers once restored may be the faithful representation of the interests and aspirations of the Haitian Nation.

Liberty and fairness are not secured at present because the electoral process, adulterated intentionally by means of a law voted by the Council of State, is beyond all control of the electors, and only the Executive's agents are clothed with the power of judging of the validity of such elections.

The Haitian citizens ask for a new regulation to be adopted or that the old electoral law, offering more guarantee of honesty, be in force. Many homage has been paid to the U. S. Government in 1927 when Honorable Mr. Stimson was commissioned to study and to recommend the way to put an end to the internal troubles in NICARAGUA.

Mr. Stimson was commissioned to study a way to give a free and honest Presidential elections to the Nicaraguans. General Franck McCoy was appointed to carry out the program of Colonel Stimson and peace ever since has been restored in Nicaragua. As a matter of fact United States had assumed less obligation towards Nicaragua than those it has contracted with Haiti.

Haitian citizens ask that the American Government should work out a similar plan for Haiti by sending here a man of conscience — whose impartiality and spirit of justice might inspire confidence to the Haitian people — to organize and supervise the coming legislative elections.

15. Our detractors assert that the Haitian people is not ripe yet for universal suffrage. This assertion is a falsehood. History of Haiti shows at the contrary that the legislative elections, *whenever they were carried on freely and honestly,* have always brought the most clever and honest men in the Chambers.

Illiteracy is still great in Haiti, but it does not reach beyond that of certain democratic countries of Europe and America.

There is a huge percentage of Haitian agriculturits, industrials, merchants, handicrafsmen, skill workmen, engi-

221

neers, physicians, teachers, lawyers, artists, writers, etc. who form a numerous elite entitled to share the management and direction of their own public affairs. Through their efforts, within the space of a century, the most backward of masses sprung from the most abject slavery, to a well organized society, which, undoubtedly -- like any other -- has gone through a series of troubles, but has, nevertheless, accomplish a moral and material achievement that cannot be denied. Those who perfidiously detract the Haitian people as not being sufficiently intelligent to choose their representatives are the same though who admitted in 1918 and 1928 that the Haitian people deserved to utter their opinion by means of a plebiscite on the most delicate matters of Constitutional Law.

No material prosperity is to be obtained without peace, and a real peace never will be reached unless popular elections are ordered and carried out honestly for the benefit of the reconstruction of a National Government.

Only such a Government enjoying of people's confidence shall have the necessary authority to facilitate the work of the Commission and to cooperate with it in the task of reconstruction and reparation longed for by Mr. President Hoover.

The National League of Constitutional Action, interpreting the legitimate aspirations of the Haitian citizens, demands:

1. That the Government of the United States, appreciating the obligations it has assumed towards the Haitian people in the treaty of 1915, and considering the maintainance of a lasting peace in Haiti as the most primordial and indispensable condition of any economical and moral advancement of the country, should take immediately the necessary measures to guarantee that peace.

2. That an actual peace, being incompatible with the existing military dictatorship, the Government of the United States should put an end to such a dictatorship by re-establishing the civil, democratic and representative Government abolished by its Agents in Haiti since 1915 by dissolving the Legislative Body.

3. That, owing to the proximity of the Presidential election, -- to which the Department of State, according to his recent declaration in a communique, cannot remain indifferent -- the Government of the United States should use all possible means to see that the Haitian electors be convened at an earliest date with the view to elect members to both Senate and House of Deputies, say for instance on the 15th day of March 1930

in compliance with articles 35, 2nd alinea, and 39, 2nd alinea, of the Constitution.

4. That, owing to the fact that no Legislative nor Presidential elections shall meet the approval of the Haitian people unless they were conducted on all liberty and fairness, the Government of the United States should cause to be adopted a new regulation of the electoral operations, and that such elections be watched by non-suspectable Agents and not by those who, in some way or another, have been mixed up in the Haitian administration since 1915.

Considering the nearness of presidencial vacancy and the constitutional impossibility for the Council of State to elect the President of Haiti on the 14th of April 1930, the *National League of Constitutional Action* respectfully does hereby ask Mr. President of the United States to take as soon as possible a decision in the way indicated above as a preliminary measure while the bill concerning the sending off of a Commission of Inquiry and Reparation is laying before the Federal Senate.

The signers of this appeal do not obey in these revendications to any personal prejudice. They do hereby take the engagement to give their support -- with the greatest disinterestedness -- to the citizen that the Haitian people may freely elect to the Presidency and to assist him in the practice of a policy of peace and improvement tending to lift up the moral level and to better life's conditions of all classes of the Haitian society. They are equally aware that only a close policy of friendship and interamerican good-understanding is necessary, and first of all that such a policy should rest on the respect of the equality and independence of the 21 States of AMERICA. Nothing in their opinion is better fitted to help this policy expressed with such a high persuasion by Mr. President HOOVER than the restoration of the National Haitian Government.

Full of confidence in the loyalty and the spirit of justice of Mr. President HOOVER, they beg to offer him hereby the anticipated expression of their most respectful thankfulness.

by

SEYMOUR PRADEL

President

PIERRE HUDICOURT

General Secretary

The Hoover Commissions to Haiti

The Members of the Committee
R. T. AUGUSTE, DANTES BELLEGARDE, PLACIDE DAVID, Dr. J. C.
DORSAINVIL, ERNEST CHAUVET, A. FAUBERT, CH. MORAVIA, G. N.
LEGER, C. MAYNARD, H. PAULEUS SANNON, STENIO VINCENT, T. LALEAU

(B)

RECOMMENDATIONS MADE BY THE
MOTON COMMISSION ON
EDUCATION

I. Administration

In pursuance of the foregoing presentation of the present
status of education in Haiti and discussion of her social and
economic needs, the Commission makes the following recommendations:

(National Schools)

1. That a unified educational program in Haiti be restored, whereby all types of educational institutions shall
be under the direction of the Secretary of State for Public
Instruction.

2. That the State educational council authorized under
the laws of Haiti be restored and made to function; its membership to be representative of the five political departments
of the Republic, of education at its three levels—primary,
secondary, and superior—and also of vocational education;
the number to be limited to constitute a working body; that
the council by legislative enactment be clothed with authority
to adopt regulations for the general administration of all
schools, to recommend the educational budget to the legislative
assembly, and to operate in the administration of schools;
the chairman and executive officer to be the Secretary of State
for Public Instruction.

3. That the Secretary of State for Public Instruction
be provided with an adequate staff of assistants to include
trained directors, one each in the fields of primary, secondary, and superior education, and one in the field of agricultural and industrial education; each of these to be charged
with the general direction of his particular field of education; these directors to be selected for their superior training and fitness for the task, their tenure of office to be
made reasonably secure.

4. That the district inspectors and their assistants be appointed by the state educational council on the nomination of the Secretary of State for Public Instruction; qualifications of inspectors to include minimum requirements of academic and normal-school training; in addition to the inspectors, supervisors be provided in the fields of agricultural and industrial education and other special supervisors as may be needed.

5. That local school boards be created either in the several districts or in the communes for the encouragement of local interest in, and responsibility for, the educational program in their section.

6. That funds from the National Treasury be budgeted and distributed for education in accordance with a more equitable plan as regards number, residence, and classification of pupils and other considerations involved.

7. That a schedule of teachers' salaries be adopted, giving payment on a basis of their preparation, type of service rendered, and success in their work, as well as on their fitness in other respects as provided in the laws of Haiti.

8. That immediate steps be taken for the increase of teachers' salaries, on the lower levels especially, on such a scale as will permit all teachers to devote the full amount of time to the work called for in the schedules of the department, thereby adding to the dignity of the profession and increasing its attractions for qualified persons.

(Service Technique)

9. That there be an immediate cessation of capital outlay for farm schools until those already built can be adequately staffed and efficiently operated.

10. That there be an immediate reduction in the scale of operations in all branches of the Service Technique, so as to provide a more equitable allocation of the budgetary funds for education between the schools operated by the Service Technique and those operated by the National Government.

11. That a clearly defined separation be made in administration and in the budget, between the experimental and extension work in agriculture and the strictly educational work of training teachers and technicians.

12. That the operation of farm schools and the extension

service be conducted within the limits of the number of teachers and agents with standard qualifications for the work.

13. That measures be taken to coordinate more closely the activities of demonstration agents and the teachers of farm schools.

14. That teachers in farm schools be encouraged to live near the schools and that model teacherages be built for their use as part of the farm school equipment.

15. That a differentiation of courses be made at the Ecole Centrale to give (a) advanced training in agriculture and in-dustrial arts for technicians, demonstration agents, supervi-sors, and secondary teachers, and (b) for teachers in farm and industrial schools for primary grades.

16. That a careful articulation be made of primary school courses in farm and industrial schools with the work of the lycees and colleges to avoid a too early determination of the type of education which the child shall ultimately pursue.

17. That a type of work be inaugurated for rural homes and schools that will combine for the present the work of the Jeanes supervisor in the United States and Africa, the home demonstration agent, and the rural public-health nurse.

18. That the practice be continued of extending courses to advanced students and workers for study in foreign countries to prepare them for positions of higher responsibility in the service.

19. That the allocation of courses at the Ecole Centrale be made to students from different parts of the island with preference to the students with rural background and agricul-tural interests.

20. That the boarding department at the Ecole Centrale be maintained for the accommodation of students from the rural districts and distant cities of the island.

21. That the policy be continued till the expiration of the treaty of placing Haitians in all positions of responsi-bility as rapidly as possible, and where necessary the associa-tion of Americans with them in an advisory capacity till the ability of such Haitians to direct the work has been satisfac-torily demonstrated.

II. Institutions—Courses

The Commission would recommend the following additions and improvements in the existing educational program of the Republic:

1. The establishment of a National University by bringing together the Schools of Medicine, Law, and Applied Science under one organization and adding a School of Liberal Arts, a School of Accounting and Business Administration, and a College for the Training of Secondary Teachers, all to be operated under one Administration.

2. The establishment of one new institution, or the adaptation of some existing institution, for the training of men teachers for elementary schools.

3. The establishment in the rural districts of home-makers' schools of primary grade for girls, with dormitory facilities.

4. The establishment of a secondary agricultural and industrial school with boarding facilities in each department of the Republic, with a view to enlarging the educational opportunities of those who live in the rural districts.

5. The enlargement of the capacity of the present normal school for girls to provide for an increase in the number of trained teachers for girls.

6. The formulation and adoption of a building program that will house the national schools and provide them with adequate equipment, this program is to extend over a definite period of years and to be sustained from a special fund set aside for this purpose.

7. The establishment of an adequate library at Port-au-Prince that shall serve the needs of the National University and public-school system as well as the general public, with assured resources sufficient to its effective maintenance and functioning.

8. The introduction into the university, when established, of two-year courses in normal training to prepare the different types of teachers required in the secondary schools.

9. The introduction into the university, when established, of advanced courses in liberal arts; natural, physical, and social sciences; and business administration to extend two

227

years beyond the present lycee courses.

10. The introduction into the present colleges and lycees for boys and girls, of normal courses designed for the training of elementary teachers.

11. The introduction into the lycees of modern courses (in social science and laboratory courses in the natural sciences) as provided in the Haitian law.

12. The operation of summer school and extension courses for teachers of the national primary schools that will raise the general level of qualifications among these teachers in the island.

13. The enrichment of primary courses with activities and studies designed to give elementary instruction in the phenomena of nature, to develop the senses in observation and construction, and to provide expression through the medium of play, singing, story telling, and dramatization.

14. The differentiation of the curricula of primary and secondary schools so as to adapt their training to a rural or an urban environment according to their location.

III. Superior Schools

The Commission recommends:

1. That the Schools of Medicine, Law, and Applied Science be consolidated into a National University, as previously indicated.

2. That the several schools be provided with a minimum staff of full-time professors.

3. That the several schools be provided with the equipment appropriate to classroom instruction, laboratory study and investigation, library facilities, and housing.

4. That fellowships be provided for members of the faculty and for advanced students that will give opportunity for study, investigation, and research in foreign countries as well as original research and investigation at home.

5. That the effort be made to increase the number of medical and dental students and nurses to meet the urgent needs of the country.

6. That the standard of requirements for admission into the Law School be raised.

7. That arrangements be made whereby students in medicine, dentistry, law, and engineering may have the benefits of the experience to be gained through contact with the practical operations of the Public Health Service, public works, the courts, and similar institutions and activities under private management.

8. That special facilities be provided in the medical school for the study of tropical diseases.

9. That the department of dentistry undertake training of dental hygienists for prophylactical health service in the schools of the Republic, such hygienists to be taken into the employ of the state.

10. That the equipment of chemical, physical, and biological laboratories in the secondary school system be completed in order to have a more adequate preparation of candidates for admission into the professional schools.

IV. A Program of Education

Reviewing the needs of Haiti for the establishment and proper maintenance of a number of different types of schools and institutions at each level—superior, secondary, and primary—the Commission recommends that the complete educational program include:

(For Superior Education)

1. A National University embracing:

    (a) The School of Medicine,
    (b) The School of Law,
    (c) The School of Applied Science,
    (d) A School of Liberal Arts,
    (e) A School of Accounting and Business Administration,
    (f) A Teachers' College for Training Secondary Teachers,
    (g) Ultimately, a School of Fine Arts.

(For Superior and Secondary Education)

2. The Agricultural and Industrial College for Boys at Damien with divisions on two levels as follows:

    (a) A superior school for training technicians, extension agents, supervisors, and teachers for schools on the secondary level in agriculture and the industrial arts.

(b) A secondary school for training farm-school and industrial-school teachers for schools on the primary level.

3. A College of Industrial Arts for Girls for training teachers of home economics, with an organization corresponding, whenever the need requires it, to that of the Agricultural and Industrial College for Boys.

(For Secondary Education)

4. (a) A normal school for training men teachers of primary schools.

(b) A normal school for training women teachers of primary schools.

(c) The Lycees already in operation in the larger cities.

(For Secondary and Primary Education)

5. (a) Industrial secondary and primary schools for boys in town and cities.

(b) Agricultural secondary and primary schools for boys in villages and rural centers, with facilities for boarding students.

(c) Industrial secondary and primary schools for girls in towns and cities.

(d) Home-makers' schools for girls in villages and rural centers, also with facilities for boarding students.

(For Primary Education)

6. (a) City primary schools with accommodations sufficient for all city children.

(b) Rural primary schools with accommodations sufficient for all rural children.

7. A general public library, with extension service.

BIBLIOGRAPHY

I. UNPUBLISHED SOURCES

A. W. Cameron Forbes. "In Retrospect." In 1950, at the age
    of eighty years, Forbes dictated to his personal sten-
    ographer, Robert C. Redmayne, a brief account of his life:
    his early years, his coaching career at Harvard, his
    entrance into public service, the Philippines administra-
    tion (which his nephew David said Forbes considered the
    monument to his life), the Brazilian Railway receivership
    during World War I, Commission to Haiti, ambassadorship
    to Japan. From time to time certain pages were destroyed
    and others substituted which Forbes considered more appro-
    priate to the narrative. The present author is aware of
    two copies in existence: one in the possession of Mr.
    Redmayne, Westwood, Massachusetts, and one in the posses-
    sion of the family firm, J. M. Forbes and Company, Boston,
    Massachusetts.

B. W. Cameron Forbes. Journals. 1904-1944. These journals
    are in the possession of the Houghton Library, Harvard
    University; Chenery Library, Boston University, and the
    Massachusetts Historical Society, Boston. Finding himself
    too busy to write many letters home to his family during
    the first year in the Philippines, Forbes started the
    Journals as a means of keeping his recollections accurate.
    He never seems to have intended them for anything but
    the use of his relatives and close friends. For the major
    part, the Journals are general accounts of his travels,
    opinions on persons and places, personal observations.

    Vol. III, 2nd Series, 1930-34, contains material re-
    lating to the Hoover Commission to Haiti in 1930: Part I,
    the narrative; Part II, Significant Letters to and from
    Forbes; Part III, Other Letters. Forbes apparently dic-
    tated the Haitian Journal after his return to the United
    States, from personal notes which he kept during the trip.
    He failed to detail by dates events as they occurred,

231

with the result that occasionally the sequence of action becomes hazy.

Forbes placed the restriction on his Journals that they were not to be used until ten years after his death (he died in 1959), but his executors granted permission to the present author to use them as of 1960.

C. W. Cameron Forbes. "Personal Copy of the Report of the President's Commission on Conditions in Haiti," Houghton Library. Harvard University. This volume is not to be confused with the printed *Report of the President's Commission for the Study and Review of Conditions in Haiti*, Publications of the Department of State, Latin-American Series, No. 2. The Personal Copy contains Forbes' Confidential Memorandum on the settlement of the internal political turmoil of Haiti; Confidential Memoranda from General John H. Russell; material relating to President of Haiti Louis Borno and the Opposition Parties; telegrams from the State Department to Forbes and from Forbes to the State Department, as well as photographs and a type-written copy of the official *Report*.

D. Heiser, Victor G. Diary. Heiser kept a diary of his personal travels throughout Haiti as a member of the staff of the Forbes Commission. The Diary is intensely valuable as a picture of the Public Health Service during the last days of the Occupation, candid commentary on various personalities concerned with the Health Service, and Haitian life in general.

E. National Archives Collection of papers gathered by the Presidential Commission for the Study and Review of Conditions in Haiti. The National Archives, Washington, D.C., Index No. 220. At the conclusion of his official report, Forbes had all papers pertaining to his task sent to Washington, D.C. These papers are an enormously valuable mine of source material not only for the particular task of the Commission but for a study of Haiti under the American Occupation.

The Six boxes contain important materials relating to the following topics: Banque Nationale; Biographies of Prominent Haitians (These were prepared for Forbes' use, for the purpose of giving him some conception of the Haitians he was likely to encounter during his mission); Clergy; the Budget, Personnel, and Correspondence of the Forbes Commission; Haitian Courts; Disbursements of the Financial Adviser-General Receiver; Dominican Republic

ín its relations with Haiti; Education; Reports of the
Financial Adviser; W. Cameron Forbes; the Garde d'Haiti;
Haitian-American Corporation; Itinerary of the Forbes
Commission; Dr. Robert Russa Moton; the Press of Haiti
from January 22, 1930, to February 18, 1930, and from
February 20, 1930, to February 28, 1930; American Press
Releases and Clippings; Public Health Service; Public
Works; Recommendations and Suggestions Submitted to the
Commission; Report of the Forbes Commission; General John
H. Russell; the Service Technique; Telegrams between
Forbes and Washington; William Allen White.

In addition, the collection contains (1) miscellaneous
copies of the *Garde News Digest* and Haitian newspapers
L'Action; L'Action Haitienne; Le Courrier Haitien; L'Essor
(Catholic); *L'Haitien; L'Heure; Jeune Haiti; Le Jeune
Haitien; Haiti Journal* (anti-Government); *Le Nouvelliste*
(anti-Government); *La Presse* (anti-Government); *Le Temps*
(anti-Government); *Le Matin* (pro-Government); *Le Moniteur*
(pro-Government; this was the official Government gazette).

(2) Hearings conducted by the Forbes Commission. (a)
Typed copies of testimony by Haitians: Pierre Eugene de
Lespinasse (historian); Antoine Rigal (lawyer, Chairman
of the Federation and President of the Union Patriotique);
Seymour Pradel (lawyer, Chairman of the National League);
Dantès Béllègarde (lawyer and historian); Ernest Chauvet
(editor and publisher); George Leger (lawyer, chosen repre-
sentative of the Opposition parties in their dealings
with the Forbes Commission); Jacques Roumain (journalist);
Pierre Hudicourt (Dean of Bar Association at Port-au-
Prince); Dr. Émmanuel Jeannot (physician); Charles Fombrun
(Councillor of State); Émile Cauvin (lawyer); Pauleus
Sannon (Senator); Frederick Reynand Burr (merchant);
Edmaund Lespinasse (lawyer); Antoine Pierre Paul (lawyer,
Labor Party), Dr. Francois D'Alencour (physician);
Émmanuel Cauvin (lawyer and Councillor of State); Dr.
Jean Price-Mars (historian, professor, sociologist,
author); Marc Seide (ex-Secretary of Customs at Port-au-
Prince); Victor Cauvin (lawyer, Secretary of Union
Patriotique, supposed to have Communist affiliations);
Etzer Velaine (lawyer); Mrs. Brun Ricot (representative
of the Haitian Association of Patriotic Women); Dr. Mather
Gilles (President of the National League of Defense);
Emmanuel Rampy (Grand Master of the Masonic Order);
Georges Sejourne (Forester); L. C. L'Herisson (Director
of the College of Toussaint L'Ouverture). (b) Typed copies
of testimony by Americans: K. C. Melhorn, Director General
of the Public Health Service; Commander G. A. Duncan,

233

USN, Engineer in Chief of Public Works; Major General
Frank E. Evans, Commandant of the Garde d'Haiti; General
John H. Russell, American High Commissioner to Haiti.

(3) Pamphlets which Forbes considered pertinent to the
Commission's task:

Rapport Annuel, Polyclinique Pean par Le Docteur Leon
Audain, Doyen, Port-au-Prince, 1901.

Congrès des Praticiens de la Ville de Port-au-Prince
par le Dr. Lebrun Bruno. Port-au-Prince, 1912.

Les Annales de Médecine Haitienne. Organe d'Expansion
de la Médecine Haitienne et de Defense des Interets
du Corps Medical fondé par les Docteurs N. St.-Louis
& F. Coicou. Mars–Avril 1927.

Les Annales de Medecine Haitienne. Organe d'Expansion
de la Médecine Haitienne et de Defense des Interets
du Corps Médical fondé par les Docteurs N. St.-Louis
& F. Coicou. Juin–Juillet 1924.

La Chambre des Députés Representait-elle la Nation?
by Luc Dorsenville. Port-au-Prince, 1930, 8 copies.

Le Sauvetage National par Le Retour a la Terre. Le
Seul Salut est dans La Terre, Par La Terre – Chapitre
II. La Phase Decisive, Dernière. Obligatoire de la
Question Agraire Haitienne by Le Docteur Francois
Dalencour. Février 1923.

La Situation Politique per Dantès Béllègarde.

La Situation Economique per Dantès Béllègarde.

Une Politique Agricole par Dantès Béllègarde.

Le Régime Douanier D'Haiti – Communication Faite a
la Troisième Conference Commerical par M. Dantès
Béllègarde, Secretaire Général de la Chambre de
Commerce d'Haiti.

Haiti and Its People by Dantès Béllègarde.

Programme Politique from Dr. Edouard-Depestr to Commission d'Enquste du president Hoover. Port-au-Prince.
1930.

La Faillite d'une Democratic from Dr. Edouard-Depestr to Commission d'Enquste du president Hoover. Port-au-Prince. 1936.

The Probing of the Haiti Scandal and an Earnest Plea for Non-partisan Investigation of the Newly Appointed Navy Court of the Present Administration.

L'Offrande de l'enfant-Jésus by Pétion Delbeau. Port-au-Prince. le 30 Decembre 1929.

Déclaration Solennelle - Pétion Delbeau. Le 24 Decembre 1929.

Tresors Litteraires - par Pétion Delbeau. Port-au-Prince, Haiti. 1929.

Haiti Économique et L'Occupation Americaine by Georges Séjourné. Port-au-Prince, Haiti.

L'Organisation Administrative en Haiti et l'Administration Americaine by Paul-Th. Romain. Port-au-Prince. 1929.

Adhérons au Parti National Progressiste by Emile Saint Clair, avocat. Port-au-Prince. 1929.

Haiti. Annual Report of the Financial Adviser-General Receiver. For the Fiscal Year October, 1927 - September, 1928.

Haiti. Annual Report of the Financial Adviser-General Receiver. For the Fiscal Year October, 1928 - September, 1929.

F.   Report covering Haiti, prepared in the Division of Latin American Affairs, January 1, 1930. Widener Library. Harvard University. This report was prepared for the use of the Commission. It contains material relating to the following topics: Haiti's historical antecedents, events leading up to the Occupation, the maintenance of order, Haitian internal politics, American official organization in Haiti, financial rehabilitation of the country, Public Technique, the working relationship between the Haitian military courts, the Haitian judiciary, the land question, Haitian emigration, American investments in Haiti, Haiti's foreign trade, the Haitian Corporation of America, the National Bank, National Railroad, and the causes and events of the recent disorders leading to the appointment of a presi-

235

dential investigatory commission.

G. Personal Interviews with David Forbes, Edward Forbes, Dr. Victor G. Heiser, Robert C. Redmayne.

H. Plummer, Brenda Gayle. Black and White in the Caribbean: Haitian-American Relations, 1902-1934. Unpublished doctoral dissertation. Ithaca, N.Y.: Cornell Univ., 1981.

II. PUBLISHED SOURCES

A. BOOKS IN ENGLISH

Alexis, Stephan. *Black Liberator: The Life of Toussaint Louverture*. New York: The MacMillan Co., 1949.

Baker, Ray Stannard and Dodd, William E. *The Public Papers of Woodrow Wilson*. 6 Vols. New York: Harper and Brothers, 1925-27.

Baker, Ray Stannard. Woodrow Wilson: Life and Letters. 8 Vols. Garden City: Doubleday, Page and Co., 1927-1939.

Balch, Emily G. (ed.) *Occupied Haiti*. New York: Writers Publishing Co., 1927.

Beard, Charles A. *The idea of National Interest*. New York: Macmillan, 1934.

Béllègarde, Dantès, *Haiti and Her Problems*. Puerto Rico: University of Puerto Rico, 1936 (Four lectures delivered under the auspices of the Ibrero-American Institute of the University, April, 1936).

Bemis, Samuel F. *A Diplomatic History of the United States*. New York: Henry Holt, 1950.

_____. *Pinckney's Treaty: America's Advantage from Europe's Distress, 1783-1800*. Revised. 2nd ed. New Haven: Yale University Press, 1960.

_____. *The Latin-American Policy of the United States*. New York: Harcourt, Brace and Co., 1943.

Buell, Raymond L. *The American Occupation of Haiti*. New York: Foreign Policy Association, 1929.

_____. *The Caribbean Situation, Cuba and Haiti.*
New York: Foreign Policy Association, 1933.

Candler, John. *Brief Notices of Haiti: with its Conditions,
Resources, and Prospects.* London: T. Ward and Co., 1842.

Carpenter, Alejo. *The Kingdom of this World.* Trans. from
the Spanish by Harriet de Onis. New York: Knopf, 1957.

Cattell, Jacques and Ross, E. E. (eds.) *Leaders in Education.* Lancaster: The Science Press, 1948.

Cave, Hugh B. *Haiti: Highroad to Adventure.* New York:
Henry Holt and Co., 1952.

Compagnie Biographique. *Blue Book of Haiti.* New York:
Kiebold Press, 1919.

Cook, Mercer. *An Introduction to Haiti; Selections and
Commentaries.* Washington, D.C.: Pan American Union, 1951.

Courlander, Harold. *The Drum and the Hoe: Life and Lore
of the Haitian People.* Berkeley: University of California
Press, 1960.

Craige, John H. *Black Bagdad.* New York: Minton, Balch
& Co., 1933.

_____. *Cannibal Cousins.* New York: Minton, Balch
& Co., 1934.

Davis, H. P. *Black Democracy: The Story of Haiti.* New
York: The Dial Press, 1928.

DeConde, Alexander. *Herbert Hoover's Latin-American Policy.*
Stanford: Stanford University Press, 1951.

Diedrich, Bernard and Al Burt. Papa Doc- *Haiti and Its
Dictator.* Harmondsworth: Penguin, 1972.

DeYoung, Maurice. *Man and Land in the Haitian Economy.*
Gainesville: University of Florida Press, 1958.

Dunham, Katherine. *Island Possessed.* New York: Doubleday,
1969.

Favrot, Leo Mortimer. *A Study of County Training Schools
for Negroes in the South.* Charlottesville, Virginia:
Trustees of the John F. Slater Fund, 1923.

237

_____. *Some Problems in the Education of the Negro in the South and How We Are Trying to Meet Them in Louisiana*. Baton Rouge: Ramirez-Jones Printing Co., 1919 (An address before the National Association for the Advancement of Colored People, Cleveland, Ohio, June 25, 1919.)

Fisher, D.C. *American Portraits*. New York: Henry Holt, 1946.

Forbes, W. Cameron. *The Philippine Islands*. 2 Vols. Boston: Houghton-Mifflin Co., 1928. Revised edition in one volume; Cambridge: Harvard University Press, 1945.

Galbraith, John Kenneth. *The Great Crash*. Boston: Houghton-Mifflin Co., Inc., 1955.

Gantenbein, James W. *The Evolution of Our Latin-American Policy: A Documentary Record*. New York: Columbia University Press, 1950.

Guerrant, Edward O. *Roosevelt's Good Neighbor Policy*. Albuquerque: University of New Mexico Press, 1950.

Gunther, John. *Inside Latin-America*. New York: Harper and Bros., 1941.

Hanke, Lewis. *Mexico and the Caribbean*. Vol. I: *Modern Latin America: Continent in Ferment*. Princeton: D. Van Nostrand Co., Inc., 1959.

Heiser, Victor G. *An American Doctor's Odyssey*. New York: W. W. Norton Co., Inc., 1936.

Herring, Hubert. *A History of Latin-America*. New York: Alfred Knopf and Co., 1955.

Herskovits, Melville J. *Life in a Haitian Valley*. New York: Alfred Knopf and Co., 1937.

Hinshaw, David. *Herbert Hoover: American Quaker*. New York: Farrar, Straus and Co., 1950.

_____. *The Man from Kansas*. New York: G. P. Putnam's Sons, 1945.

Hofstadter, Richard. *The American Political Tradition*. New York: Alfred A. Knopf, Inc., 1948.

Hoover, Herbert. *Addresses Delivered During the Visit of Herbert Hoover, President-elect of the United States, to Central and South America, November-December, 1928.* Washington, D.C.: Pan-American Union, 1929.

_____. *The Cabinet and the Presidency.* Vol. II: *The Memoirs of Herbert Hoover.* New York: Macmillan Co., 1952.

Hopkins, J.A.H. and Alexander, Melinda. *Machine Gun Diplomacy.* New York: Lewis Copeland Co., 1928.

Hughes, W.H. and Patterson, F.D. (eds.) *Robert Russa Moton of Hampton and Tuskegee.* Chapel Hill: University of North Carolina Press, 1956.

Johnson, Walter (ed.) *Selected Letters of William Allen White.* New York: Henry Holt and Co., 1947.

_____. *William Allen White's America.* New York: Henry Holt and Co., 1947.

Kelsey, Carl. *The American Intervention in Haiti and the Dominican Republic.* Philadelphia: American Academy of Political and Social Science, 1922.

Kennan, George F. *American Diplomacy, 1900-1950.* Chicago: University of Chicago Press, 1951.

Kipling, Rudyard. *Something of Myself for My Friends Known and Unknown.* London: Macmillan Co., Ltd., 1937.

Korngold, Ralph. *Citizen Toussaint.* Boston: Little, Brown and Company, 1944.

Léger, Jacques Nicholas. *Haiti: Her History and Her Detractors.* New York: Merle Publishing Co., 1907.

Leyburn, James G. *The Haitian People.* New Haven: Yale University Press, 1941.

Logan, R. W. *The Diplomatic Relations of the United States with Haiti.* Chapel Hill: University of North Carolina Press, 1941.

MacDonald, Austin F. *Latin-American Politics and Government.* Revised. 2nd ed. New York: Thomas Y. Crowell Co., 1954.

Martineau, Harriet. *The Hour and the Man*. New York: AMS Press (Reprint of original published in 1841.), 1974.

McCrocklin, James H. *Garde d'Haiti: Twenty Years of Organization and Training by the United States Marine Corps, 1915-1934*. Annapolis: United States Naval Institute, 1956.

Millspaugh, Arthur C. *Haiti Under American Control, 1915-1930*. Boston: World Peace Foundation, 1930.

Montague, Ludwell Lee. *Haiti and the United States, 1714-1938*. Durham: Duke University Press, 1940.

Montavon, William Frederick. *Haiti, Past and Present*. Washington, D.C.: The Catholic Association for International Peace, 1930.

Morgenthau, Hans J. *In Defense of the National Interest*. New York: Alfred Knopf, 1951.

Moton, Robert Russa. *Finding a Way Out: An Autobiography*. Garden City: Doubleday Doran and Co., 1929.

_____. *What the Negro Thinks*. Garden City: Doubleday Doran and Co., 1929.

Myers, William Starr. *The Foreign Policies of Herbert Hoover, 1929-1933*. New York: Charles Scribner's Sons, 1940.

_____. (ed.) *The State Papers and Other Collected Writings of Herbert Hoover*. 2 Vols. Garden City: Doubleday, Doran and Co., 1934.

Myers, William Starr and Newton, Walter H. (eds.) *The Hoover Administration: A Documented Narrative*. New York: Charles Scribner's Sons, 1936.

Nearing, Scott and Freeman, Joseph. *Dollar Diplomacy: A Study in American Imperialism*. New York: The Viking Press, 1928.

Niles, Blair. *Black Haiti*. New York: G.P. Putnam, 1926.

Notter, Harley. *The Origins of the Foreign Policy of Woodrow Wilson*. Baltimore: Johns Hopkins Press, 1937.

Pan American Union. *Haiti*. Washington, D.C.: Pan American Union Press, 1934.

Parsons, Robert P. *History of Haitian Medicine*. New York: P.B. Hoeber, Inc., 1930.

Perkins, Dexter. *The American Approach to Foreign Policy*. Cambridge: Harvard University Press, 1952.

Pratt, Julius. *History of American Foreign Policy*. New York: Prentice-Hall, Inc., 1955.

Pringle, Henry Fowler. *Theodore Roosevelt*. New York: Harcourt, Brace and Co., 1931.

Redpath, James (ed.). *A Guide to Haiti*. Westport, Ct.: Negro Universities Press (Reprint of 1861 edition), 1970.

Rippy, J. Fred. *Latin-America: A Modern History*. Ann Arbor: University of Michigan Press, 1959.

_____. *Latin-America in World Politics*. Revised. 3rd ed. New York: F.S. Crofts Co., 1938.

_____. *The Caribbean Danger Zone*. New York: G.P. Putnam's Sons, 1940.

Robbins, Lionel. *The Great Depression*. New York: Macmillan, 1935.

Rodman, Selden. *Haiti: The Black Republic*. New York: The Devin-Adair Co., 1954.

Rosenman, Samuel I (ed.) *The Public Papers and Addresses of Franklin D. Roosevelt*. 9 Vols. New York: Random House, 1938, Vol. I-IV; New York: The Macmillan Co., 1941, Vols. VI-IX.

St. John, Sir Spencer. *Haiti, or the Black Republic*. London: Smith, Elder and Co., 1884.

Seabrook, W.B. *The Magic Island*. New York: Harcourt, Brace and Co., 1929.

Steward, T.G. *The Haitian Revolution: 1791-1804*. New York: T.Y. Crowell Co., 1944.

Stoddard, T.L. *The French Revolution in San Domingo*. New York: Houghton-Mifflin Co., 1914.

Stuart, Graham H. *Latin-America and the United States*. Revised. 4th ed. New York: D. Appleton-Century Co., 1943.

Thomas, Lowell. *Old Gimlet Eye: The Adventures of Smedley D. Butler.* New York: Farrar and Rinehart, 1933.

United Nations Mission of Technical Assistance to Haiti. *Mission to Haiti.* Lake Success, New York, 1949.

Van Doren, Carl. *The Great Rehearsal: The Story of the Making and Ratifying of the Constitution of the United States.* New York: The Viking Press, 1948.

White, William Allen. *Autobiography.* New York: Macmillan Co., 1946.

Wilgus, A. Curtis (ed.) *The Caribbean Area.* Washington, D.C.: University Press, 1934.

Williams, Paul W. *The American Policy of Intervention and the Monroe Doctrine with Special Reference to the Military Occupation of Haiti and the Dominican Republic.* Cambridge: Harvard University Press, 1925.

Williams, Mary Wilhelmine. *The People and Politics of Latin-America.* Boston: Ginn and Co., 1930.

Wilson, Ruth. *Here is Haiti.* New York: Philosophical Library, 1957.

Wirkus, Faustin and Dudley, Taney. *The White King of La Gonave.* Garden City: Doubleday, Doran and Co., 1931.

Wood, Bryce. *The Making of the Good Neighbor Policy.* New York: Columbia University Press, 1961.

B. PERIODICALS IN ENGLISH

Becker, Carl L. "Afterthoughts on Constitutions," *The Yale Review.* Vol. XXVII, No. 3 (Spring, 1938).

Bekker, L.D. de. "Haiti, a Plan for Self-Government," *Nation,* Vol. 130 (Mar. 5, 1930).

_____. "The Massacre at Aux Cayes," *Nation,* Vol. 130 (Mar. 12, 1930).

Béllègarde, Dantès. "Inter-American Economic Policy," *The Annals of the American Academy of Political and Social Science.* Vol. CL (April, 1931).

Blanksten, George I. "The Aspiration for Economic Development," *The Annals of the American Academy of Political
and Social Science*, Vol. 334 (March, 1961).

Buell, Raymond L. "The Caribbean Situation: Cuba and
Haiti," *Foreign Policy Reports*, Vol. IX (June 21, 1933).

Butler, C.S. "The Medical Needs of the Republic of Haiti
at the Present Time," *United States Navy Bulletin* 24,
No. 2 (1926).

Calixte, Colonel D.P. Garde d'Haiti," *Marine Corps Gazette*
(February, 1936).

Chapman, C.E. "The Development of the Intervention in
Haiti," *Hispanic-American Historical Review*, Vol. VII
(August, 1927).

Cook, Thomas I. and Moos, Malcolm. "Hindrances to Foreign
Policy: Individualism and Legalism," *Journal of Politics*,
Vol. XV (February, 1953).

Cooper, Donald B. "The Withdrawal of the United States
from Haiti, 1928–1934," *Journal of Inter-American Studies*,
Vol. V (January, 1963).

Daniels, J. "Problem of Haiti," *Saturday Evening Post*,
Vol. 203 (July 12, 1930).

Davis, H.P. "Haiti after 1916; So Far Intervention Has
Failed," *Outlook*, Vol. 154 (March, 1930).

Douglas, Paul H. "The American Occupation of Haiti,"
Political Science Quarterly, Vol. XLII (June–September,
1927).

Evans, Colonel Frank E. "Salient Haitian Facts," *Marine
Corps Gazette* (February–May, 1931).

Fletcher, Henry P. "Quo Vadis, Haiti?" *Foreign Affairs*,
Vol. VIII (July, 1930).

Frissell, Hollis B. "The Education of the Negro,"
Proceedings of the National Education Association, Vol.
LIV (1916).

Fuller, R.N. "American Achievements in Haiti," *Current
History*, Vol. XXXII (April, 1930).

Gruening, Ernest. "Haiti Marches Toward Freedom," *Nation*, Vol. 132 (April 1, 1931).

_____. "The Issue in Haiti," *Foreign Affairs*, Vol. XI (January, 1933).

Hackett, C. W. "Haiti's New Status," *Current History*, Vol. XXXII (May, 1930).

Herring, Hubert. "Haitian Troubles Continue," *Current History*, Vol. XLII (April, 1935).

Hinshaw, A.W. "Haiti Takes a Day in Court," *World's Work*, Vol. LIX (July, 1930).

Jenks, J.H. "The Haitian Problem," in A.C. Wilgus (ed.), *The Caribbean Area*. Washington, D.C.: George Washington University Press, 1934.

Krieger, Herbert M. "The Aborigines of the Ancient Island of Hispaniola," *Annual Report of the Smithsonian Institution* (1929).

Lewis, S. "Devil-Dog Rule," *Nation*, Vol. 129 (December 18, 1929).

Lherisson, Dr. Camille. "Diseases of the Peasants of Haiti," *American Journal of Public Health*. Vol. XXV, No. 8 (August, 1935).

Logan, Rayford W. "Education in Haiti," *Journal of Negro History*, Vol. XV (October, 1930).

Melhorn, K.C. "Public Health in Haiti," *United States Naval Medical Bulletin*, Vol. XXVII, Nos. 3-4 (1929).

Miller, C.L. "Notes and News," *School and Society*, Vol. LI (June 8, 1940).

Millspaugh, Arthur C. "Our Haitian Problem," *Foreign Affairs*, Vol. VII (July, 1929).

Morgenthau, Hans J. "The Mainsprings of American Foreign Policy: The National Interest v Moral Abstractions," *American Political Science Review*, Vol. XLIV (December, 1950).

Padgett, James A. "Diplomats to Haiti and Their Diplomacy," *The Journal of Negro History*, Vol. XXV (July, 1940).

"Robert Russa Moton," *Journal of Negro History*, Vol. XXV (July, 1940).

Roosevelt, Franklin D. "Our Foreign Policy," *Foreign Affairs*, Vol. VI (July, 1928).

Silbert, K.L. "Nationalism in Latin-America," *The Annals of The American Academy of Political and Social Science*, Vol. 334 (March, 1961).

Spector, Robert M. "W. Cameron Forbes in the Philippines: A Study in Proconsular Power," *Journal, Southeast Asian History*, Vol. 7, No. 2 (Sept. 1966).

Stanley, Peter W. "William Cameron Forbes: Proconsul in the Philippines," *Pacific Historical Review*, Vol. 35, No. 3 (Aug. 1966).

Streit, Clarence. "Haiti: Intervention in Operation," *Foreign Affairs*, Vol. VI. No. 4 (July, 1928).

Thompson, Wallace. "Climatic Conditions in the Caribbean," *Current History*, Vol. XXXII (February, 1930).

Tucker, R. W. "Professor Morgenthau's Theory of Political Realism," *American Political Science Review*, Vol. XLVI (March, 1952).

Weed, Helen Hill. "Fresh Hope for Haiti," *Nation*, Vol. 130. (March 19, 1930).

_____. "Victory in Haiti," *Nation*, Vol. 130 (March 26, 1930).

Williams, M. "Healing of Haiti," *Commonwealth*, Vol. XI (March 5, 1930).

C. NEWSPAPERS AND MAGAZINES IN ENGLISH

Boston Herald. February, 1930.

Louisville *Courier-Journal*. February, 1930.

Sioux Falls *Daily Argus-Leader*. February, 1930.

Dallas Morning News. February, 1930.

Hartford Daily Courant. February, 1930.

New York *Herald Tribune.* February, 1930.

Kansas City Journal-Post. February, 1930.

Nation. 1915-1945.

Charleston *News and Courier.* February, 1930.

Newsweek. 1935-1947.

New York Times. 1910-1941.

Providence Journal. February, 1930.

San Francisco Chronicle. February, 1930.

Springfield Republican. February, 1930.

Richmond *Times-Dispatch.* February, 1930.

New Orleans *Times-Picayune.* February, 1930.

Topeka Daily Capital. February, 1930.

Wheeling Intelligencer. February, 1930.

D. BOOKS IN FRENCH

Beauvoir, Vilfort. *Le Controle financier du government des États--Unis d'Amérique sur la république d'Haiti.* Paris: Recueil Sirey, 1930.

Béllègarde, Dantès. *Haiti et ses problemes.* Montreal-Editions B. Valiquette, 1941.

_____. *Haiti et son People.* Paris: Novelles Editions Latines, 1953.

_____. *Histoire du Peuple Haitien (1492-1952).* Lausanne: Imprimerie Held, 1953.

_____. *La nation haitienne.* Paris: J. de Gigord, 1938.

_____. *La résistance haitienne; récit d'histoire contemporaine.* Montréal: Editions Beauchemin, 1937.

Benjamin, Georges J. *Contribution à l'histoire diplomatique et contemporaire.* Port-au-Prince: Imprimerie d l'Etat, 1951.

Dorsainvil, J. C. *Manuel d'historie d'Haiti*. Port-au-Prince: Procure des Frères de l'Instruction Chretienne, 1934.

Élie, Louis E. *Histoire d'Haiti*. 2 Vols. Port-au-Prince: published by the author, 1944-45.

Léger, Abel Nicholas. *Histoire diplomatique d'Haiti*. Port-au-Prince: Aug. A. Heraux, 1930.

Lepelletier de Saint-Remy, R. *Saint-Domingue: Étude et solution nouvelle de la question haitienne*. 2 Vols. Paris: A. Betrand Co., 1846.

Madiou, Thomas. *Histoire d'Haiti*. Port-au-Prince: The Courtois, Vols. I-III, 1848, Vol. IV, 1904.

Moreau de Saint-Mery, Louis Élie, *Description topographique; Physique, civile, politique et historique de la partie francaise de l'ile Saint-Domingue*. Philadelphia: 1797. New edition, 2 Vols. Société de l'histoire des colonies francaises, 1958.

Moral, Paul. *L'économie haitienne*. Publie sous les auspices de la Cour Supérieure des comptes. Port-au-Prince: Imprimerie de l'État, 1959.

Price-Mars, Dr. Jean. *Ainsi parla l'oncle*. Port-au-Prince: Imprimerie de compiegne, 1928.

_____. *La République d'Haiti et la République dominicaine, 1492-1953*. 2 Vols. Lausanne: Imprimerie Held, 1953.

_____. *La vocation de l'élite*. Port-au-Prince, 1919.

_____. *Une étape de l'évolution haitienne*. Port-au-Prince, 1929.

Vastey, Baron De. *Le Systeme Colonial Dévoile*. San Souci: Imprimerie du Roi, 1814.

Vincent, Stenio. *Efforts et résultats*. Port-au-Prince: Imprimerie de l'Etat, 1938.

E. PERIODICALS IN FRENCH

Denis, Lorimer and Duvalier, Dr. Francois. "La Civilization haitienne: notre mentalité est-elle africaine ou
gallo-latine?" *Revue de la Société d'Histoire et de Geographie d'Haiti*. Vol. VII (May, 1936).

Vaval, Duracine. "Alexandre Pétion: l'homme et sa vie,"
Revue de la Société d'Histoire et de Geographie d'Haiti,
Vol. III, No. 7 (July, 1932).

_____. "Le Roi d'Haiti Henri Christophe," *Revue
de la Société d'Histoire et de Geographie d'Haiti*, Vol.
II, No. 3 (June, 1931).

F. NEWSPAPERS IN FRENCH

Port-au-Prince *Le Matin*: 1930.

Port-au-Prince *Le Moniteur*: 1930.

G. OFFICIAL DOCUMENTS

Haiti. *Annual Report of the Technical Service of the
Department of Agriculture and Professional Education*,
1928-29, Bulletin No. 17. Port-au-Prince: Republic of
Haiti, 1930.

*Reciprocal Trade Agreement Between the United States of
America and Haiti*. Executive Agreement Series No. 78.
Washington, D.C.: United States Government Printing
Office, 1935.

Russell, General John H. *Annual Reports of the American
High Commissioner*, *1923-1929*. Washington, D.C.: United
States Government Printing Office, 1925-1929.

U. S. Bureau of Foreign and Domestic Commerce. *Haiti:
An Economic Survey*. Washington, D.C.: United States Government Printing Office, 1924.

U. S. *Congressional Record*. Vols. LXII and LXXII.

U. S. *House Document #35*. 27th Congress, 3rd Session.

U. S. President, 1929-1933 (Hoover). *Report of Commission
for the Study and Review of Conditions in Haiti*. Publications of Dept. of State, Latin-American Series, No. 2.
Washington D.C.: United States Government Printing Office,
March, 1930.

Bibliography

U. S. President, 1929–1933 (Hoover). *Report of the United States Commission on Education in Haiti.* Publications of the Dept. of State, Latin-American Series, No. 5. Washington, D.C.: United States Government Printing Office, October, 1930.

U. S. *Report of the Delegates of the United States of America to the Seventh International Conference of American States: First, Second, and Eighth Committees, Montevideo, 1933,* Department of State Conference Series, No. 19, Washington, D.C.: United States Government Printing Office, 1934.

U. S. *Senate Executive Document #113.* 32nd Congress, 1st Session.

U. S. *Senate Executive Document #25.* 34th Congress, 3rd Session.

U. S. *Senate Executive Document #37.* 36th Congress, 2nd Session.

U. S. *Senate Executive Document #17.* 41st Congress, 3rd Session.

U. S. *Senate Executive Document #64.* 49th Congress, 2nd Session.

U. S. *Senate Executive Document #69.* 50th Congress, 2nd Session.

U. S. Senate, *Inquiry into Occupation and Administration of Haiti and Santo Domingo. Hearings before a Select Committee on Haiti and Santo Domingo.* U. S. Senate, 67th Congress, 1st Sess., pursuant to Senate Res. 112. 2 Vols. Washington, D.C.: United States Government Printing Office, 1922.

U. S. Senate. *Report of the McCormick Committee,* Senate Report No. 794. Washington, D.C.: United States Government Printing Office, June 26, 1922.

H. REFERENCE BOOKS

Block, Maxine (ed.) *Current Biography.* New York: H. W. Wilson Co., 1942.

Dougan, Alice M. and Joel, Bertha (eds.) *Readers' Guide to Periodical Literature.* Vol. VIII, January, 1929 – June, 1932, p. 1092. New York: The H. W. Wilson Co., 1932.

The Hoover Commissions to Haiti

Fleming, G. James and Burckel, Christian E. (eds.) *Who's Who in Colored America.* Yonkers-on-Hudson: Christian E. Burckel and Associates, 1950.

Kunitz, Stanley J. and Haycroft, Howard (eds.) *Twentieth Century Authors.* New York: The H. W. Wilson Co., 1942.

Starr, Harris E. (ed.) *Dictionary of American Biography.* 22 Vols. New York: Charles Scribner's Sons, 1928-1958.

Weil, Thomas E., et al. *Area Handbook for Haiti.* Washington, D.C.: Superintendent of Documents, U. S. Printing Office, 1973.

Who's Who in America. 31 Vols. Chicago: A. N. Marquis Co., 1899-1961.

Who Was Who in America. 1897-1960. 3 Vols. Chicago: A. N. Marquis Co., 1942-1960.

ABOUT THE AUTHOR

Robert M. Spector, Professor of History and Law at Worcester State College, received his LL.B. (J.D.) from Boston College Law School and his Ph.D. in Anglo-American Studies from Boston University. Specializing in legal history, his articles have been published in such journals as *Social Studies, American Journal of Legal History, Journal of Negro History, Southeast Asian History, Caribbean Studies, Journal of Higher Education, Education Digest, Intellect* (formerly *School and Society)*, and the *Journal of the Illinois State Historical Society.* He is also the author of numerous book reviews. In 1976, he received the Harry E. Pratt Memorial Award for the best article on Illinois History to appear in the *Journal of the Illinois State Historical Society* for that year — "Woman Against the Law: the Struggle of Myra Bradwell for Admission to the Illinois Bar." Dr. Spector resides with his family in Framingham, Massachusetts.